ABOUT THE AUTHOR

Paul Tansey is managing partner of the economic consultancy firm Tansey, Webster and Associates, founded in 1986. A former assistant editor of *The Irish Times*, he is now adjunct Professor of Economics at the University of Limerick and a labour market expert for the European Commission in Ireland. Paul Tansey is married to Olivia O'Leary. They live in Dublin with their daughter, Emily.

IRELAND AT WORK

Economic Growth and the Labour Market, 1987–1997

Paul Tansey

Oak Tree Press
Dublin

Oak Tree Press
Merrion Building
Lower Merrion Street
Dublin 2, Ireland

© 1998 Paul Tansey

A catalogue record of this book is
available from the British Library.

ISBN 1-86076-083-X

All rights reserved. No part of this publication may be reproduced
or transmitted in any form or by any means, including
photocopying and recording, without written permission of the
publisher. Such written permission must also be obtained before
any part of this publication is stored in a retrieval system of any
nature. Requests for permission should be directed to:
Oak Tree Press, Merrion Building,
Lower Merrion Street, Dublin 2, Ireland.

Printed in Ireland by Colour Books Ltd.

CONTENTS

List of Tables .... *ix*

Acknowledgements .... *xvii*

Foreword by Professor Dermot McAleese .... *xix*

Introduction 1

Chapter 1
Ireland's Economic Take-Off 11
   1.1. Long-Run Irish Economic Trends 11
   1.2. Irish Economic Growth since 1987 16
   1.3. The Payoffs from Economic Growth 26
   1.4. Catching up on Europe 29

Chapter 2
The Irish Jobs Machine 33
   2.1. Historical Trends in Irish Employment 33
   2.2. The Great Leap Forward in Irish Employment 35

Chapter 3
Unemployment in Ireland 51
   3.1. The Causes of Irish Unemployment 51
   3.2. The Persistence of Unemployment 62
       3.2.1. Unemployment and Increases in the
              Labour Supply 64
       3.2.2. The Long-term Unemployed and Structural
              Unemployment 80
       3.2.3. Unemployment and Work Incentives 87
       3.2.4. The Measurement of Unemployment 90

Chapter 4
The Quality of the Irish Labour Force 97
4.1. Human Capital and Economic Development 97
4.2. The Effects of Human Resources Investments on
   Irish Economic Performance 106
4.3. Education, Training and Individual Incomes 109
  4.3.1. Education and Employment 109
  4.3.2. Education and Earnings 110
  4.3.3. Education and Lifetime Income 111
4.4. The Revolution in Irish Education 114
4.5. Ireland's Training Performance 121
  4.5.1. How Training Markets Work 125
  4.5.2. The Locus of the Irish Training Problem 127
4.6. EU Grants and Active Labour Market Policies 130

Chapter 5
The Determinants of Irish Income Taxes 137
5.1. The Impact of Taxation on the Labour Market 137
5.2. The Determinants of Taxation in Ireland 140
  5.2.1. The Fiscal Stance of Government 140
  5.2.2. Trends in Current Public Spending 141
  5.2.3. The Pace of Economic Activity 145
  5.2.4. National Collective Bargaining Agreements 146
5.3. The Growth of Taxation 148

Chapter 6
The Evolution of Pay and Prices 153
6.1. Real Purchasing Power 153
6.2. The Renaissance of National Pay Agreements 156
6.3. Pay Levels in Ireland: Manufacturing Industry 160
6.4. Pay Levels in Ireland: The Public Sector 163
6.5. Pay Trends in Ireland: Executive Salaries 166
6.6. Pay Trends in Ireland: National Income Data 168
6.7. Irish Employee Incomes Compared, 1987–96 170
6.8. Pay and Price Trends in Ireland
   Compared, 1987–97 172

Chapter 7
Income Taxes 175
    7.1. The Evolution of the Tax Code Since 1987 175
    7.2. Income Tax Exemption Thresholds 176
    7.3. The Evolution of Basic Personal Tax Allowances 178
    7.4. Income Tax Bands and Income Tax Rates 181
    7.5. Changes in Discretionary Tax Allowances 188
    7.6. Other Taxes on Employee Income 190
        7.6.1. Employee Pay-Related Social Insurance
             Contributions 190
        7.6.2. Health Contributions 192
        7.6.3. Employment and Training Levies 192
        7.6.4. Temporary Income Levy 193
    7.7. Employers' Pay-Related Social Insurance
        Contributions 193

Chapter 8
Incomes, Taxes and Prices since 1987 197
    8.1. Methodology 197
    8.2. Living Standards of Average Earners, 1987–97 199
    8.3. Pay, Taxes and Real Incomes of the Better-Off 203
    8.4. The Tax Treatment of the Low Paid 206
    8.5. Who Fared Best since 1987? 210

Chapter 9
The Tax Wedge and the Labour Market 215
    9.1. The Nature of the Direct Tax Wedge 215
    9.2. Calculating the Irish Tax Wedge 217
    9.3. The Tax Wedge and Average Single Employees,
        1987–97 218
    9.4. The Tax Wedge and Average One-Income Couples 219
    9.5. The Tax Wedge and Better-Off Single Employees 220
    9.6. The Tax Wedge and Better-Off One-Income Couples 222
    9.7. The Tax Wedge and Low-Income Single Workers 223
    9.8. The Tax Wedge and Low-Paid One-Income Couples 224

Chapter 10
Poverty and Unemployment Traps 227
    10.1. Explaining Poverty and Unemployment Traps 227
    10.2. Unemployment Assistance and
           Unemployment Traps 229
    10.3. Basic Income Replacement Ratios 230
    10.4. Income Replacement Ratios including "Secondary"
           Benefits 235
    10.5. Poverty Traps 239
    10.6. Employment Subsidies for the Low Paid 240

Chapter 11
Completing the Supply-Side Revolution 249
    11.1. The Reasons for Rapid Growth 249
    11.2. Education as a Catalyst for Growth 250
    11.3. Foreign Industrial Enterprises 251
    11.4. EU Infrastructural Flows 253
    11.5. Competitiveness Regained 253
    11.6. Good Housekeeping 255
    11.7. The Persistence of Unemployment 256
    11.8. Ireland's Labour Market Paradox 257
    11.9. Unemployment Traps 258
    11.10. A Modest Proposal 259

Bibliography 261

Index 269

LIST OF TABLES

1.1:	Long-Run Economic Growth in Ireland, 1961–96	14
1.2:	Real GDP Growth of Ireland's Major Trading Partners	18
1.3:	Relative European Union Inflation Rates, 1980–96	19
1.4:	Irish Pound's Exchange Rate, 1986–96	21
1.5:	Volume Changes in the Components of Irish GNP since 1987	23
1.6:	The Correction of Irish Public Finances, 1986–97	27
1.7:	Ireland — No Longer Ranked among Europe's Poor	30
1.8:	Ireland Narrows the Income Gap with Europe, 1961–97	31
2.1:	Population and Employment in Ireland, 1926–97	34
2.2:	The Great Leap Forward in Irish Employment, 1989–97	36
2.3:	Trends in Irish Employment, 1987–97 (ILO Basis)	37
2.4:	The Private Sector and Total Non-Farm Employment Growth, 1987–97 (ILO Basis)	38
2.5:	Full- and Part-Time Job Gains in Ireland, 1992–97	40
2.6:	Employment by Occupation in Ireland, 1981–95	41
2.7:	Cumulative Percentage Changes in Employment, 1990–97	42
2.8:	Employment Intensity of Economic Growth, 1960–96	44
3.1:	Trends in Irish Unemployment, 1975–97	52

3.2:	Explaining the Causes of Rising Unemployment, 1979–86	53
3.3:	Domestic Policies Raised Unemployment in the 1980s	54
3.4:	Standardised Unemployment Rates in OECD Countries, 1980–95	56
3.5:	Irish Unemployment and Unemployment Rates	58
3.6:	The Demographic Characteristics of the Unemployed	59
3.7:	Long-term Unemployment in Ireland, 1992–97	60
3.8:	Labour Force, Employment and Unemployment, 1987–97 (ILO basis)	64
3.9:	Ireland's Population of Working Age, 1986–97	67
3.10:	Emigration Swings and Immigration Roundabouts, 1985–97	68
3.11:	Deriving the Labour Force from the Population of Working Age, 1986–97	72
3.12:	Labour Force Participation Rates Compared	74
3.13:	Labour Force Participation Rates by Sex, 1973–93	75
3.14:	Ireland's Total Employment Ratio, 1992–97	77
3.15:	Employment Ratios in the European Union, 1975–95	78
3.16:	Irish Economic Outlook, 1997–2000	80
3.17:	Educational Attainment of Labour Force in 1994	82
3.18:	Ratio of Vacancies to Employment, October 1996	88
3.19:	Labour Force Survey Unemployment and Live Register Unemployment Compared	92
3.20:	Labour Force Survey Responses by a Sample of 1,496 Persons on the Live Register at April 1996	93
3.21:	Unemployment Benefit Recipients as a Percentage of Labour Force Unemployment for 18 OECD Countries in 1990 and 1995	95

List of Tables

4.1:	Sources of Ireland's Differential Growth, 1970–95	103
4.2:	Unemployment Rates one Year after Leaving School in 1994/95	109
4.3:	Estimated Returns to Education in Ireland, 1987 and 1994	111
4.4:	Internal Rates of Return to Irish Educational Investments	112
4.5:	Participation Rates in Irish Education, 1964–94	115
4.6:	Top Twelve OECD Third-Level Enrolment Rates	117
4.7:	Public Spending on Irish Education, 1961–93	118
4.8:	Young Irish People with Weak Educational Backgrounds	119
4.9:	The Incidence of Training in the European Union, 1992	122
4.10:	The Evolution of Ireland's Training Performance, 1989–93	123
4.11:	EU Structural Funds Allocated to Ireland, 1994–99	131
4.12:	Components of the Human Resources Development OP, 1994–99	132
4.13:	Participants on Active Labour Market Programmes, 1983–94	134
5.1:	The Fiscal Stance of Government, 1993–97	141
5.2:	Trends in Irish Gross Current Public Spending, 1987–97	142
5.3:	Increases in Public Spending and Prices Compared, 1988–97	143
5.4:	Public Spending's Share of GNP, 1990–96	145
5.5:	The Growth of Tax Yields by Category, 1990–97	150
5.6:	Share of Total Taxes in Gross National Product, 1990–97	151

6.1:	Trends in Consumer Prices and Manufacturing Pay, 1979–96	155
6.2:	Days Lost through Industrial Disputes, 1976–96	156
6.3:	Basic Pay Terms of National Pay Agreements	158
6.4:	Pay Trends in Irish Manufacturing since 1987	161
6.5:	Average Weekly Earnings of Clerical and Managerial Employees in Irish Manufacturing, 1987–96	162
6.6:	Average Public Sector Earnings Index	164
6.7:	Estimated Levels of Average Public Service Pay, 1987–96	165
6.8:	Executive Salaries in Ireland by Size of Company	167
6.9:	Average Annual Increases in Executive Salaries, 1987–96	167
6.10:	Trends in Annual Executive Salaries, 1987–96	168
6.11:	Trends in Non-Agricultural Pay, 1987–96	170
6.12:	Average Levels of Non-Agricultural Employee Pay, 1987–96	171
6.13:	The Evolution of Employee Incomes in Ireland, 1987–96	172
6.14:	Employee Pay and Consumer Prices Compared, 1987–97	173
7.1:	General Income Tax Exemption Thresholds, 1987–97	176
7.2:	Evolution of Basic Personal Tax Allowances, 1987–97	179
7.3:	Proportions of Average Manufacturing Earnings Exposed to Income Tax, 1987–97	180
7.4:	Income Tax Rates and Tax Bands Facing Single People	183
7.5:	Income Tax Rates and Tax Bands Facing Married Couples	184

List of Tables

7.6:	Exposure to Higher Rate of Income Tax, 1987–99	185
7.7:	Percentage of Average Manufacturing Earnings at which Liability to Income Tax at the Higher Rate Begins	187
7.8:	Employee PRSI: Contribution Rates and Ceilings, 1987–99	191
7.9:	Exemption Thresholds for Health and Training Levies	193
7.10:	Employers' PRSI Rates and Contribution Ceilings, 1987–99	194
8.1:	Pay, Taxes and Real Incomes of Average Single Earners	200
8.2:	Tax Treatment of One-Income Married Couples, 1987–97	202
8.3:	Tax Treatment of Single People on Twice Average Earnings, 1987–97	204
8.4:	Tax Treatment of One-Income Married Couples Earning Twice Average Industrial Pay, 1987–97	206
8.5:	Alleviating the Tax Burden on Low-Paid Single People	207
8.6:	Tax Treatment of One-Income Married Couples Earning Half Average Industrial Pay, 1987–97	209
8.7:	Changes in Real Purchasing Power by Household Type, 1987–97	210
8.8:	Reductions in Average Tax Rates by Household Type, 1987–97	212
9.1:	The Tax Wedge and Single Employees on Average Earnings	219
9.2:	The Tax Wedge and One-Income Couples on Average Earnings	220
9.3:	The Tax Wedge and Single People Earning Twice Average Pay	221

9.4:	The Tax Wedge and One-Income Couples Earning Twice Average Pay	223
9.5:	The Tax Wedge and Low-Income Single Workers	224
9.6:	The Tax Wedge and Low-Paid One-Income Couples	225
10.1:	Maximum Weekly Rates of Unemployment Assistance, 1987–98	230
10.2:	Basic Income Replacement Ratios for Single People on Half Average Manufacturing Earnings, 1987–97	231
10.3:	Income Replacement Ratios for Low-Paid Single People, 1996	232
10.4:	Income Replacement Ratios for Low-Paid Married Couples	233
10.5:	Income Replacement Ratios with Secondary Benefits, 1995/96	236
10.6:	Single People: Adjusted Income Replacement Ratios, 1997/98	238
10.7:	The Poverty Trap in 1995/96	240
10.8:	The Impact of FIS on the Net Income of a Married Couple with Two Children, 1997/98	242
10.9:	Impact of the Back to Work Allowance: Long-Term Unemployed Single People Returning to Work, 1997/98	244
10.10:	The Returns to Work Under the BTWA Scheme, 1997/98	245
10.11:	Net Income of Married Spouse Returning to Work under BTWA	246

For my wife Olivia O'Leary,
who always asks the hard questions.

ACKNOWLEDGEMENTS

Many people, knowingly and unknowingly, have contributed to the writing of this book. Professor Louden Ryan, my first economics teacher, has exerted a long and enduring influence on my subsequent thinking. I have benefited greatly from long-running discussions on the conduct of Irish economic policy with Colm McCarthy of DKM Economic Consultants, Dr Antoin Murphy and Dr Sean Barrett of Trinity College Dublin and Terry Corcoran of FÁS. Professor Donal Dineen and Jim Deegan, colleagues at the University of Limerick, have been extremely helpful with information and advice.

Officials at both the Central Statistics Office and the Department of Finance were prompt and painstaking above and beyond the call of duty in seeking to locate data I required.

Two people, above all, were critical to the publication of this book. Not dissuaded by his experience with this book's predecessor, Professor Dermot McAleese of Trinity College Dublin once again courageously shouldered the burden of editing the manuscript. He discharged this task with a wisdom that was equalled only by the dryness of his wit. My wife, Olivia O'Leary, commented perceptively on various drafts and ensured that most of my sentences contained a verb.

I would also like to thank the Business Research Unit, operating under the auspices of IBEC, for financial support without which this work would not have been completed.

Finally, I owe a considerable debt of gratitude to David Givens, Brian Langan and the rest of the team at Oak Tree Press. Their collective ability to turn the manuscript into a book, and to deal with extensive rewriting and updating of data in the process, was a revelation.

Any errors that remain are my own.

Paul Tansey,
Dublin, March 1998.

Foreword

By Dermot McAleese

This book is appearing at a time when the Irish economy is enjoying the longest sustained boom in its entire history and when Irish living standards have become as near as makes no difference to those in the United Kingdom and the Continent. For a nation accustomed to considering itself hard done by in the race for prosperity, this rapid accretion of material status has come as something of a shock. Many question the reality of the advance in living standards; others doubt its durability; while some focus attention on the structural defects in the Irish economy which, if not dealt with, could make growth harder to sustain and could also diminish the benefits of such growth in the broadest sense.

Among these structural defects, long-term unemployment must surely qualify as the most serious and enduring. It is not just that such unemployment remains at a high level, despite a welcome decline during the past four years, but also that its incidence is so unevenly distributed across the social spectrum. No marks for guessing that it is those with a low education level, from broken families, in low-paid occupations or residing in inner cities, who experience the highest probability, or hazard rate, of being unemployed. But knowing more about the characteristics of the unemployed does not, in itself, tell us *why* unemployment occurs. To answer this, we must probe further and address questions relating to broader aspects of the labour market and the economy, such as budgetary policy, education and training.

In this context, Paul Tansey's book is a welcome addition to the literature on the Irish labour market. Starting from 1987, when Ireland's fiscal recovery first became visible, he asks how the education system and the tax and social welfare systems have affected real incomes, work incentives and, by extension, the balance between the demand and supply of labour in the Irish market. The relevant changes affecting the outcome include: the reduction in income tax rates, the increase in personal tax allowances and tax bands, adjustments in PRSI and changes in the social welfare system. To summarise these diverse changes in a coherent and readable manner, and to bring the analysis right up to the December 1997 budget, as this book does, is an impressive achievement.

Among the many gems in this volume is an original and pioneering examination of the growth in earnings of different occupational groups. Taking account of changes in the income tax system on gross incomes, we see that public sector employees appear to have fared well relative to the average remuneration of employees in the private sector during the post-1987 reform period. Another finding is that lower-paid employees have benefited proportionately less from the tax reforms than have the better-off. This happens because the lower-paid benefit less from reductions in income tax rates. Of course, this type of analysis contains an important implicit assumption: namely that the better-off actually do pay the higher tax rates on their income. In practice, they may well not have done so. High marginal tax rates may simply have driven more income to tax shelters and the tax avoidance industry.

Employment and poverty traps are still a major problem for certain sections of the labour force. For many of the long-term unemployed with dependants, work incentives are still very weak, or non-existent. Hence the paradox, in Ireland as in many European countries, of large-scale unemployment cheek-by-jowl with labour shortages in low-paid service occupations such as pubs and catering. Efforts to address this problem, through lower taxes and better control of social welfare payments, are moving in the right direction.

The effectiveness of changing work incentives is hard to measure. One can expect the process to be slow and patchy. To speed it up, the employability of the workforce must be enhanced by upgrading skills. Training, education and human capital formation rightly receive much attention in this book. They played a key role in Ireland's economic regeneration. Having contributed over many years to the literature on this subject, including the Department of Enterprise and Employment's excellent paper on Human Resource Development (May 1997), Paul Tansey can write on this subject with some authority. He argues convincingly that the overall level of educational attainment in Ireland is improving, but there is still plenty of room for improvement if we are to attain the best international standards and get the Irish labour market closer to equilibrium.

As Ireland becomes more prosperous, thinking about the labour market has evolved. Those on the "left" have become more conscious of the importance of work incentives and of the morale-deadening effect of high marginal tax rates. It is no longer politically incorrect to ask whether certain groups in society obtain more from social welfare than they would at work. Those analysts more enthusiastic about market mechanisms, on the other hand, must remain conscious of the importance of achieving a balance in the distribution of the fruits of prosperity. Active labour market policies, targeted on the low paid and low motivated, can make a contribution to this distribution.

This book presents an objective, carefully delineated picture of the Irish labour market. In so doing, it also offers valuable insights into the growth performance and policy developments in the broader Irish economy.

Dermot McAleese,
Trinity College, Dublin,
March 1998.

INTRODUCTION

Economic growth is a means to an end, not an end in itself. High rates of economic growth are valuable only if they deliver improvements in the community's material standard of living. The factors that contribute most to material living standards are job gains and advances in real disposable incomes.

This book first seeks to chart what has happened in the Irish labour market since 1987. It is in the labour market that jobs are created and employee incomes earned.

Second, it attempts to identify the factors that account for the improved performance of the Irish labour market since the late 1980s.

Finally, it asks: what actions are necessary to secure continued employment expansion and rising living standards into the future?

The Irish economy has achieved an economic take-off since 1987. Its rate of ascent is charted in **Chapter One**. For an economy whose pursuit of "Keynesianism in one country" had brought it to the brink of bankruptcy in the early 1980s, the transformation has been remarkable. This reversal of fortune would not have been possible without a prior and decisive shift in the policy regime. From the mid-1980s, a new, broad-based economic consensus emerged. Its two principal tenets held that:

- Irish Governments cannot spend and borrow their way to prosperity;

- Competitiveness matters, not only for profits, but also for jobs.

The pay-offs from this policy shift have been substantial. Perhaps the most important, socially as well as economically, have been the cessation of net emigration and the consequent resumption of population growth during the 1990s. The population reached 3.66 million by April 1997, its highest level since the foundation of the state. Statistically, the Irish economy is as much as four-fifths larger than it was a decade ago. By 1997, when allowance is made for price differences, Gross Domestic Product (GDP) per person was higher in Ireland than in Britain and stood above the European Union average.

But economic performance should not be judged by aggregate growth statistics alone. Therein lie many snares to trap the unwary. What matters is the extent to which economic growth delivers jobs, raises living standards and enhances social protection. **Chapter Two** reviews employment trends in Ireland since the late 1980s.

The most striking feature of the Irish labour market has been the scale of employment expansion since the late 1980s, and especially since 1993. There are now a quarter of a million more people at work in Ireland than there were in 1987. This represents a jobs gain of well over one-fifth in the space of a single decade. Additions to the national workforce on this scale are unparalleled in recent Irish economic history.

Through much of the 1980s, Ireland suffered from the phenomenon of "jobless growth", where national economic growth failed to translate into extra employment. This problem has been erased during the 1990s. Economic expansion has been job-rich. Proportionately, job growth has been faster in Ireland than in the United States.

The private sector has been the engine of employment growth in the non-agricultural economy. The private sector workforce outside agriculture increased by 239,000 or 38.1 per cent, between 1989 and 1997.

The expansion in employment has not been limited to part-time jobs. The jobs boom has been concentrated in the years since 1993. Between 1992 and 1997, roughly two-thirds of the employment gains registered have been full-time jobs. Moreover, the great majority of those in part-time positions do not consider themselves under-employed.

The occupational profile of the Irish workforce indicates that Ireland is becoming a "white collar" economy. Since the early 1980s, there has been a very rapid expansion in occupations staffed by professionals, associate professionals and managers. In contrast, manual occupations, such as farming and labouring, have been in continuous decline.

Women have filled many of the new jobs created over the past decade. By 1997, there were more than half a million women employed in Ireland, accounting for almost two-fifths of the national workforce.

However, rapid job expansion has not cured the problem of unemployment. Advances in employment over the past decade have not been mirrored by proportionate falls in unemployment. **Chapter Three** examines the scale, duration and composition of Irish unemployment.

The numbers out of work have exhibited a clear and consistent downward trend only since 1993. By April 1997, Irish unemployment, as measured by the International Labour Office (ILO) definition, still stood at 159,000 people, or 10.3 per cent of the labour force.[1]

Why did unemployment remain so high? **Chapter Three** examines the forces that have diluted the impact of employment gains in reducing the level of unemployment. These reduce to one essential feature: the labour force increased significantly in size, partly in response to the strengthening of labour demand.

Three factors contributed to the growth in the labour force over the past decade. First, the "baby boomers" of the 1970s grew up, raising the underlying rate of expansion in the population of working age — those between 15 and 64 years. Second, better job opportunities kept the "baby boomers" at home during the 1990s. As a result, the underlying growth in the working-age population flowed into the domestic labour market. The heavy net emigration that characterised the second half of the 1980s ceased during the 1990s, being replaced by net immigration after 1995. The third factor swelling the size of the domestic labour force has been rising labour force participation rates amongst women, who now comprise well over one-third of the Irish labour force.

In combination, these three factors caused the labour force to expand by more than 200,000 people — or by almost one-sixth —

---

[1] On this measure, the Irish unemployment rate had declined to 9.7 per cent by February 1998 when it stood below the average European Union unemployment rate of 10.5 per cent.

between 1986 and 1997. It has been the scale of this growth in the labour force that has left unemployment so high in spite of the magnitude of employment gains.

The repeated unemployment "shocks" of the 1970s and 1980s have given rise to a particularly acute problem of long-term unemployment. The numbers out of work for a year or more reached a recent peak at 128,200 in 1994. Long-term unemployment is relatively insensitive to changes in economic conditions. However, increased provision and better targeting of state programmes on those who have been out of work for a year or more reduced long-term unemployment to 86,300 by 1997.

Notwithstanding recent declines, the scale of long-term unemployment, and the associated problem of discouraged workers, constitutes a continuing reproach to a community enjoying unprecedented abundance. Relative to their employed counterparts, the long-term unemployed are badly educated, poorly skilled and weakly motivated. They are concentrated in ghettos of deprivation, where unemployment has become an integral part of life. The scale of this problem transcends economics; the under-class it is creating poses a threat to the cohesion of society and challenges the democratic principles on which it is avowedly based.

Economic advance since 1987 has been achieved by sharpening both blades of the Marshallian demand and supply scissors. On the demand side, through the 1980s, the economy regained its cost competitiveness. The conquest of inflation, the moderation of money wage increases — assisted by the reintroduction of national collective bargaining — and realistic exchange rate policies — aided, where necessary, by Irish pound devaluations — combined to make Irish output competitive on home and foreign markets. Where a small, open, trading economy like Ireland can produce goods and services that people want to buy at prices they can afford, demand will largely take care of itself. As the payoffs from regained competitiveness percolated through the economy, domestic demand played an increasingly important role in stimulating the expansion of incomes and employment.

Concurrently, the supply-side of the economy was expanded, strengthening its physical capacity to produce the goods and services that customers want to buy. These supply-side factors included: accelerated inflows of technically advanced foreign enterprises, which modernised the economy's industrial base; much larger transfers of financial assistance from the European Union, earmarked for extending and deepening Ireland's physical and human infrastructure; the already-noted expansion of the labour force; and improvements in the quality of labour supply.

Irish education has undergone a quiet revolution over the past 30 years, in terms of structure, access and participation. The quality of Irish labour has been greatly enhanced as a result. **Chapter Four** assesses the importance of improving labour quality — human capital accumulation — to recent Irish economic development.

Participation rates in the higher reaches of the Irish education system have climbed continuously since the advent of free secondary education more than 30 years ago. A child now entering school can look forward on average to almost 15 years of education. Four out of every five children who enter second-level education complete the senior cycle. Amongst Irish 18- to 21-year-olds, participation in third-level education is above the average for both the European Union and the industrial world as a whole.

However, in the sphere of educational qualifications, it is important to differentiate between stocks and flows. Since many of the improvements in Irish education are of relatively recent vintage, the educational attainment of the Irish labour force in aggregate lags somewhat behind competitor countries. In particular, the incidence of weak literacy and numeracy amongst the working age population is unexpectedly high relative to a selection of other industrial economies.

While the country's education system earns a glowing report card, there are some areas where it could still do better. Clearly, the attainment of basic functional literacy and numeracy is a pressing requirement, not only for those still in the school system, but also for adults.

Nor is it clear that the second-level system has responded adequately to the wider ability levels, aptitudes and vocational interests that are the natural consequence of sharply increased participation rates. The unexpected popularity of Post-Leaving Certificate (PLC) courses, on which more than 18,000 students are now enrolled, provides at least an indication of the demand for vocational-type courses within the second-level system. The recent introduction of the Leaving Certificate Applied and the Leaving Certificate Vocational Programmes constitute a recognition of the need for alternatives to the traditional Leaving Certificate curriculum. It remains to be seen, however, if these new programmes will command widespread support.

While Irish education has made great strides over the past three decades, the country's training performance is more difficult to interpret. Survey data tentatively suggest that, in terms of training inputs, Ireland is a lagging, if improving, trainer. In terms of training outputs — efficiency on the job — the evidence suggests that Ireland is behind its best-practice EU competitors. Nor is this identified skills gap limited to the shopfloor; it manifests itself also in the executive suite.

The predominance of small-scale businesses in Ireland clearly constitutes a structural barrier to training at all levels. Small firms find it difficult to plan, organise and finance off-the-job training for both shopfloor staff and managers.

Nonetheless, given the quantum of extra EU structural funding pumped into the development of Irish human resources since 1989, it is surprising that the impact on Irish training performance cannot be more clearly discerned.

Economic growth during the 1990s has delivered very substantial annual increases in employment. But what of the other promise it proffers — the undertaking that growth will raise the real material living standards of the community?

In the initial years of recovery, the extra resources generated by renewed growth were channelled principally towards correcting public sector deficits. Together with strict control of public spending, this cut government deficits significantly and summarily between 1987 and 1989. **Chapter Five** shows that from 1990 onwards, day-to-day government spending started to rise rapidly once more. Thus far during the 1990s, current public spending, excluding interest payments, has risen four times as fast as retail prices. Despite this surge in public spending, the pace of economic expansion has been so strong — and tax revenues so buoyant — that the government still recorded a surplus equivalent to almost 1 per cent of Gross Domestic Product on its activities in 1997. The curtailment of public borrowing, allied with the scale of economic growth, caused the government's debt-to-GDP ratio to decline from 96.3 per cent as recently as 1993 to 66.3 per cent at the end of 1997.

The improvement in the material living standards for those at work in the decade after 1987 is then explored, using the barometer of changes in real disposable incomes. **Chapter Six** shows that average employees' money incomes — including managerial salaries — rose by two-fifths and more over the years 1987–96. Such increases in gross incomes were comfortably ahead of inflation, as the level of consumer prices rose by just over a quarter in this period. But gains in real spending power are not determined solely by the interaction of pay and prices. Governments also take a hand in shaping purchasing power through their income taxation and income transfer policies.

The evolution of the personal income tax code in the years since 1987 is examined in some detail in **Chapter Seven**. This period was characterised by a raising of tax exemption levels, increased tax allowances, wider tax bands and cuts in both the standard and top tax rates. Notwithstanding all the apparent reforms, the defining feature of the Irish income tax system still remains the rapidity with which taxpayers progress to the top rate of tax, even on relatively modest incomes. Even in 1998/99, a single person claiming basic income tax and PAYE allowances progresses to the top 46 per cent income tax rate where annual earnings exceed £13,950. Such an income is well below annual earnings in manufacturing industry.

By applying annual changes in the tax regime to the data charting the evolution of average incomes, **Chapter Eight** charts the gains in disposable incomes over the years since 1987. The data for disposable incomes are then deflated by the consumer price index to determine gains in real disposable incomes. Six representative cases are examined: single workers earning average manufacturing earnings, twice average earnings and half average earnings and married couples on similar income levels.

Two significant results are established.

First, after accounting for changes in money wages, taxes and prices, all of the groups surveyed were considerably better off in terms of real purchasing power in 1997 than a decade earlier. The gains in real spending power ranged from one-fifth to one-third over the decade. In this sense, economic growth has delivered higher material living standards as well as substantially raising the national level of employment.

Second, those who paid the heaviest income taxes in 1987 gained most from the tax reductions of the ensuing decade. In proportionate as well as absolute terms, the gains in real spending power were biggest for the better-off, smallest for the low-paid. In fact, those earning half average manufacturing pay recorded only meagre advances in their living standards between 1987 and 1992, additions to their real incomes being concentrated in the years since 1993.

The implications of changes in incomes and taxes — including PRSI contributions — for the width of "tax wedges" are explored in **Chapter Nine**. The direct tax wedge is the gap that separates the direct cost of labour to employers from the after-tax incomes of employees. The direct tax wedge thus constitutes the total labour taxes levied by government on every job. Wide tax wedges have been found to be important disincentives to employment. Tax wedges were very wide in Ireland in 1987. They narrowed considerably in the ensuing decade, most notably in their application to lower-paid workers.

Chapter Ten examines two factors which interfere with the proper functioning of the Irish labour market — "unemployment traps" and "poverty traps". Both are unfriendly to employment.

"Unemployment traps" arise where people are trapped in unemployment because attempts to move into low-paid employment would leave them worse off financially. The combined real income derived from untaxed cash benefits and "secondary" benefits such as subsidised rents, medical cards and free goods can, in certain circumstances, approach the real after-tax income provided by a low-paid job.

Strenuous efforts have been made in recent years to reduce the disincentive effects of such "unemployment traps". Income taxes on low-paid employment have been reduced and innovative schemes have been introduced which allow the unemployed to retain their benefits for a period after entering employment. Nonetheless, the perception that people are better off on the dole than in a low-paid job remains widespread.

On the other hand, "poverty traps" afflict those already at work. "Poverty traps" act to reduce real incomes as gross money wages increase. This paradoxical outcome results from rising tax bills and the progressive withdrawal of state subsidies, non-cash benefits and entitlements as gross income rises. "Poverty traps" are extensive over the gross annual income range £8,000 to £12,000. A particular problem arises because efforts to eliminate "unemployment traps" often add to the depth of future "poverty traps".

Chapter Eleven concludes that the time is now ripe to complete Ireland's supply-side revolution by extending the benefits of low taxes, concentrated to date on the corporate sector, to ordinary working people. Such cuts in effective income taxes on those earning average wages would buttress the two pillars on which Ireland's economic revival has been constructed:

- It would increase the domestic labour supply by raising the after-tax returns to work. This is particularly necessary at a time when labour scarcity is becoming evident across the economy;

- It would maintain the Irish economy's competitive edge by raising the real incomes of those at work without recourse to excessive increases in money wages.

Chapter 1

IRELAND'S ECONOMIC TAKE-OFF

1.1. Long-Run Irish Economic Trends

The past was a different country; we did things differently there. Since 1960, Irish society has been transformed. Rapid economic growth has been both the cause and the consequence of that transformation. The growth in real national income since the early 1960s has facilitated a substantial improvement in the community's material standard of living. This has been reflected not only in ascending levels of personal consumer spending, but also in better health care, more schooling and more extensive social protection. If Ireland is not yet quite as rich as its best-performing European neighbours, it is rapidly closing the gap.

The reversal of long-run population decline is perhaps the most important change engineered by economic growth since the 1960s. For Ireland, the Famine of 1845–47 was a social catas-trophe of unparalleled dimensions. It triggered a demographic decline that continued almost unbroken until 1961. Between the censuses of 1841 and 1961, the Irish population[1] fell from 6.5 million to 2.8 million. Only thereafter did it begin to recover. By the census of 1996, the population had risen to 3.6 million. In the space of 35 years, the number of people in the country had increased by 800,000, a 28.5 per cent gain on its lowest point in 1961.

Moreover, from the mid-1960s, Ireland became a predominantly urban society. Dependence on agriculture waned, both as a source of national output and as a provider of jobs. By 1997, agriculture supported just 10 per cent of total employment in Ireland.

---

[1] For the area now comprising the Republic of Ireland.

Over the long haul since 1960, the Irish economy has made remarkable progress. But sustained economic expansion did not materialise out of thin air. Faster economic growth has been a consequence of changes in the structure and operation of the Irish economy and in the policy regime that has governed it.

The most important milestone on the development road was marked by the set of decisions, taken during the late 1950s and 1960s, to open up both the society and the economy and to relinquish the introspective, protectionist world-view that had dominated the conduct of public policy since the 1930s. This set of decisions embraced three separate strands.

First, successive governments sought to recruit foreign enterprises to Ireland to modernise the country's industrial base. Determined efforts were made from the 1960s onwards to capture increasing inflows of foreign direct investment with the aid of industrial grants and tax breaks. The Industrial Grants Act of 1956 introduced the first tax concessions on export sales. Subsequent legislation extended and refined both packages of grant support and the tax treatment of corporate earnings. The existing rate of corporation tax now applying to manufacturing and internationally traded services is 10 per cent.

There are now over 1,000 overseas manufacturing and internationally traded services enterprises based in Ireland. They account for 55 per cent of manufacturing output and 70 per cent of industrial exports. In 1995, they employed 107,000 people, some 46 per cent of the 235,000-strong Irish manufacturing workforce.[2] The continuing influx of technologically advanced foreign enterprises has modernised the Irish industrial base, speeding the growth of national productivity in the process.

Second, in the early 1960s, Ireland decided to dispense with protectionism, opting instead for free trade. The Anglo-Irish Free Trade Agreement (AIFTA) was concluded in 1965. Entry to the EEC was finally secured in 1973. Ireland was amongst those countries which joined the narrow band of the Exchange Rate Mechanism (ERM) from the start in 1979. The country was an enthusiastic proponent of the Single European Market ("1992")

---

[2] Forfás (1996), pp. 132, 144–145.

programme, which set out to complete the European market by dismantling physical, technical and fiscal barriers to internal trade.

The third leg of the platform supporting modernisation was provided by a revolution in the education system. Free secondary education was introduced, the school-leaving age was raised and the capacity and range of third-level education was extended. More than three-quarters of those commencing second-level education now complete it. Two-thirds of second-level school-leavers now proceed to higher education, further education or training.

Moreover, the effects of these decisions were mutually reinforcing, introducing a new dynamic not only into Irish life, but also into Irish economic performance. The dismantling of tariff barriers created a healthier, more competitive trading environment in the domestic economy. At the same time, entry to the European Union provided non-EU foreign investors with a further incentive to locate in Ireland: unhindered access to European markets. The influx of technologically sophisticated foreign enterprises, in turn, provided job opportunities for young people graduating from schools and colleges.

The long-run performance of the Irish economy is charted in Table 1.1. It illustrates the growth in aggregate real Gross National Product since 1961, measured in constant 1990 prices throughout. It also shows the rise in real GNP per capita, along with increases in population that have been registered since 1961.

Table 1.1 indicates that, in real terms, the Irish economy grew three-and-a-half fold between 1961 and 1996, while real GNP per person has risen by almost 175 per cent. During this time-span, the national population increased by almost 29 per cent.

However, it is also apparent, from the data in Table 1.1, that the pace of economic growth over time has been uneven. Between 1961 and 1971, the economy increased in size by almost a half. In the decade to 1981, the economy expanded by a further two-fifths, despite the impact of two oil shocks, runaway inflation and a rapid deterioration of the public finance position.

In effect, in the second half of the 1970s, the future was mortgaged to pay for the present. This trick could not be played twice. Domestic mismanagement caught up with the economy in the first half of the 1980s and exacted a heavy price. In the five years

1981 to 1986, aggregate real GNP edged ahead by just 2.7 per cent. Under the weight of population expansion, real GNP per person actually fell in the first half of the 1980s.

TABLE 1.1: LONG-RUN ECONOMIC GROWTH IN IRELAND, 1961–96 (IN IR£ MILLION AT CONSTANT 1990 PRICES)

Year	Real GNP	Real GNP Per Capita	National Population ('000s)
1961	9,342	3,315	2,818
1966	10,747	3,758	2,884
1971	13,773	4,625	2,978
1976	16,188	5,015	n.c.
1981	19,347	5,619	3,443
1986	19,865	5,610	3,541
1991	24,269	6,883	3,526
1996	32,961	9,090	3,626
% Change, 1961–96	+253%	+174%	+28.7%

n.c = No census was taken in 1976.

Sources: "Revised Economic Indicators Since 1960", CSO, September 1996; Census '96, CSO, July 1997, Table 1.

But the seeds of the subsequent recovery were planted in this arid economic terrain. Enforced domestic deflation laid the foundations for future growth. Inflationary expectations were broken. Furthermore, a growing realisation by all the principal actors on the economic stage — that competitiveness shapes the prosperity of small trading nations — prompted a policy shift from the mid-1980s onwards. Big budget deficits, heavy government borrowing and rising national debt were seen increasingly as the enemies of economic promise. Good housekeeping became politically popular. Supported by a broad spectrum of social forces, there was a decisive and successful shift in the economic policy regime.

Inflation declined from the very high levels it had reached in the early 1980s. The rate of consumer price inflation fell from 20.4 per cent in 1981 to 3.8 per cent in 1986.

As the pace of price increases abated, inflationary expectations diminished. Together with the strategic decision of the trade union movement to re-enter national collective bargaining, this paved the way for the moderate three-year pay deal embodied in the Programme for National Recovery, signed in October 1987.

The Irish pound was devalued unilaterally for the first time in the summer of 1986. This 8 per cent devaluation eased external competitive pressures at a time when the domestic inflation rate was decelerating swiftly.

All of these played a part in the rapid recovery of the Irish economy from 1987 onwards. However, more important than the repairing of the economic machine was the change in the mindset of the country's political elite, inside and outside government.

The stalling of the economy in the first half of the 1980s forced politicians to confront the consequences of the economic transformation they themselves had brought about over the preceding quarter of a century. Successive governments had progressively opened up the Irish economy to foreign investment and to foreign trade. This new departure had paid handsome dividends. But the corollary of greater economic openness was greater dependence on the international economy.

This increasing dependence, allied to progressive trade liberalisation, changed the rules of the economic game for Irish governments. Enhanced investment and trade flows locked the Irish economy ever more firmly into the industrial world. Trade liberalisation determined that competitiveness would provide the key to future economic success.

Two substantive policy implications followed, but they were slow to be absorbed, even slower to be acted upon.

First, Ireland's increasing dependence on the industrial world automatically limited the scope for its pursuit of independent fiscal and monetary policies. The Irish state simply does not possess the economic muscle to roll back the forces of international deflation when trade cycles turn downwards. This stems from the nature and size of the economy. Ireland is a small, open economy, like Belgium, not a large, closed economy like the United States. In Irish circumstances, unilateral domestic reflation, financed by widening budget deficits, is not a feasible policy option. The additional demand injected into the economy through extra government spending and borrowing simply seeps out of the economy through the balance of payments.

Yet, twice in a decade (first in 1974/75 and again in 1979/81), Irish governments — of different political complexions — sought to offset external deflationary impulses by levering up public spending and raising government borrowing. The stimulus to domestic economic activity was quickly dissipated; the costs continue to weigh on the Exchequer.

Second, while the importance of competitiveness as a vital policy objective was officially recognised, it was not pursued sufficiently strenuously. The Irish economy had sustained severe cumulative losses in competitiveness from the mid-1970s onwards, induced by large public deficits, excessive inflation relative to Ireland's trading partners and an appreciating real exchange rate within the ERM. By the early 1980s, the erosion of competitiveness, coupled with the expansiveness of budgetary policy, had pushed the current balance of payments deficit towards 15 per cent of GNP.

By the mid-1980s, a new and broad consensus had emerged on two key issues. Its central tenets held that:

1. Governments cannot spend and borrow the economy back to prosperity

2. Competitiveness matters, not only for profits, but also for jobs.

These two principles recognised that, having entered the world economy, Ireland, collectively, now had to earn its living there. These principles, in various manifestations, were embedded in annual budgets, policy statements by the major political parties and the set of national collective agreements on pay concluded from 1987 onwards. They have formed the bedrock on which subsequent economic successes have been founded.

1.2. Irish Economic Growth since 1987

Having stalled in the first half of the 1980s, the Irish economy began to advance again in the second half of the decade. The origins of economic expansion from 1987 onwards can be traced to the change in the world-view of policymakers. Governments no longer sought economic salvation through increased state spending and borrowing.

On the demand side of the economy, a growing realisation percolated through the corridors of power — inside and outside government — that Ireland would have to regain competitiveness. The economy could only succeed by making and selling goods and services that others wanted to buy at prices they could afford. In short, the new consensus focused on the creation of a competitive, trading economy.

This new consensus took concrete form in the three-year Programme for National Recovery (PNR), signed by government, employers and trade unions in October 1987. Under its terms, the Government undertook to curtail public borrowing and spending, while releasing tax cuts to raise the real disposable incomes of employees. In concert, a pay deal was agreed, containing basic pay increases to 2.5 per cent annually for each of the years 1988 through 1990.

In its first budget, in March 1987, the new Government had introduced severe cuts in current public spending volumes. Together with the conclusion of a moderate pay agreement, this invested public policy with much-enhanced credibility. Against the background of subdued domestic inflation, interest rates fell.

On the supply side of the economy, the physical capital stock was augmented and modernised by continuing inflows of new foreign investment — particularly from the US. This not only accelerated the pace of domestic capital accumulation, but it directed investment to high-technology sectors and segments of industry and traded services. In parallel, the economy broadened its human capital base as participation rates in second- and third-level education continued to rise.[3]

The principal pieces required for economic reconstruction were thus in place. The economy was broadly competitive; capital and labour were productive and plentiful. When the economic tide began to rise in Europe in the late 1980s, it lifted Ireland's economic fleet.

---

[3] However, much of the potential human capital gain in the late 1980s was dissipated by very high levels of graduate emigration.

As an open economy, exports constitute a large slice of total demand for Irish goods and services. Ireland sells almost three-quarters of its total exports to other EU member-states. Britain alone still accounts for one-quarter of all Irish merchandise exports. As a result, when the economies of Ireland's principal trading partners are buoyant, and when Irish output is competitive, the demand for Irish exports increases. The strength and composition of demand growth in Europe during the late 1980s was of central importance in powering the early stages of Ireland's economic take-off. Trends in real GDP growth in Ireland's principal foreign markets since 1987 are shown in Table 1.2.

TABLE 1.2: REAL GDP GROWTH OF IRELAND'S MAJOR TRADING PARTNERS

Year	EU	Britain	Germany	Ireland
1987	2.9	4.8	1.5	4.7
1988	4.2	5.0	3.7	4.4
1989	3.5	2.2	3.6	7.0
1990	3.0	0.4	5.7	8.4
1991	1.5	−2.0	5.0	2.1
1992	1.0	−0.5	2.2	4.0
1993	−0.5	2.1	−1.1	3.1
1994	2.9	3.8	2.9	6.5
1995	2.4	2.5	1.9	10.3
1996	1.6	2.1	1.4	7.3

Source: "OECD Economic Outlook", No. 61, June 1997, Annex Table 1.

As Table 1.2 indicates, economic growth in Ireland's two principal foreign markets — Britain and Germany — was particularly robust during the late 1980s and into the early 1990s. In Britain, the Lawson consumer boom raised demand during the latter years of the 1980s. And as Britain's growth bubble burst, the reunification boom in Germany reached its apex. In short, buoyant European markets provided a revitalised Irish economy with the scope to flex its newly honed economic muscle.

European demand expansion would have been of little use if the Irish economy had not put itself on a more competitive footing. The strong revival in the British economy between 1983 and 1986 had bypassed Ireland because domestic competitiveness was debilitated.

A first indication of the extent to which the Irish economy had regained competitiveness can be seen from Table 1.3, which charts relative EU inflation rates.

TABLE 1.3: RELATIVE EUROPEAN UNION INFLATION RATES, 1980–96 (PERCENTAGE RATES AS MEASURED BY CONSUMER PRICES)

Year	EU	Ireland	Britain	Germany
1980	13.1	18.3	18.0	5.4
1981	12.0	20.4	11.9	6.3
1982	10.3	17.1	8.6	5.2
1983	8.2	10.5	4.6	3.3
1984	6.9	8.6	5.0	2.4
1985	5.9	5.5	6.1	2.1
1986	3.6	3.8	3.4	–0.1
1987	3.2	3.1	4.1	0.2
1988	3.5	2.1	4.9	1.3
1989	5.1	4.1	7.8	2.8
1990	5.5	3.3	9.5	2.7
1991	5.0	3.2	5.9	3.6
1992	4.4	3.1	3.7	5.1
1993	3.5	1.4	1.6	4.5
1994	3.0	2.3	2.5	2.7
1995	3.0	2.5	3.4	1.8
1996	2.4	1.7	2.4	1.5

Source: "OECD Economic Outlook", No. 61, June 1997, Annex Table 16.

As can be seen from Table 1.3, in the early 1980s, Irish inflation was much faster than the average inflation rate in the European Union. However, the Irish rate of price increase dipped below the EU average in 1987 and has remained there ever since.

More importantly, with inflation driven upwards by expansive demand policies in both Britain and Germany, the Irish rate of price increase slipped below the rates prevailing in its two major trading partners in the late 1980s and early 1990s. This aided Ireland in sharpening its price competitiveness in the markets where demand was growing fastest.

However, price competitiveness is not determined only by relative inflation rates but also by movements in exchange rates. Ireland suffers particular difficulties in the exchange rate sphere because the weight of its trade dictates that it must take cognisance of trends in two — often divergent — currency zones.

In the first place, Ireland has been a committed member of the narrow band of the European Monetary System's Exchange Rate Mechanism since its inception in March 1979. With Britain choosing to remain outside, joining the ERM necessitated a breaking of the long-standing one-to-one exchange rate between the Irish and British pounds. Broadly, ERM membership requires that the Irish pound tracks the currencies of the continental EU.[4]

In the second place, the importance of the British market to jobs and profits in native Irish enterprises ensures that the Irish pound's exchange rate against sterling cannot be ignored by the Irish authorities. Sterling's short sojourn in the ERM came to a close in October 1992, when the British currency was forced out of the Mechanism. Since then, sterling has floated against the currencies of the ERM, including the Irish pound.

Where sterling and the currencies of the ERM are moving in the same direction on foreign exchange markets, this presents no difficulties to Irish policy-makers. However, where sterling and the ERM currencies are moving in opposite directions, Ireland's exchange rate loyalties are divided. While Ireland is politically committed to Europe, it remains disproportionately dependent on Britain economically.

Britain accounts for one-quarter of Irish exports and supplies two-fifths of Irish imports. Its value against the Irish pound matters to the real economy. If sterling falls too far, or too precipitately, against the Irish currency, employment and earnings are lost by domestic producers. Conversely, when sterling strengthens

---

[4] The narrow bands of fluctuation were set at plus or minus 2.25 per cent around central rates in 1979. These were widened to plus or minus 15 per cent in 1993.

against the Irish pound, it threatens to raise Ireland's rate of imported inflation.

In effect, the Irish authorities have made a passable, if, on occasion, tardy, job of reconciling these conflicting exchange rate objectives. An Irish solution to an Irish problem has been fashioned. Ireland officially remains wholly committed to exchange rate stability within the ERM — including enthusiastic support for a single European currency — except where sterling volatility threatens to inflict damage on the Irish economy.

Where sterling weakness has acted to erode Irish price competitiveness, Ireland has tended to depreciate or to devalue within the ERM. Hence, the Irish pound was devalued unilaterally within the ERM by 8 per cent in 1986 and by 10 per cent in early 1993. In both cases, these devaluations were prompted by sterling's weakness. The evolution of the Irish exchange rate since 1986 is shown in Table 1.4.

TABLE 1.4: IRISH POUND'S EXCHANGE RATE, 1986–97 (IR£1 =); PERIOD AVERAGES

Year	Sterling	Deutschmark	Effective Index*
1986	0.915	2.91	66.65
1987	0.909	2.67	66.15
1988	0.857	2.67	65.08
1989	0.867	2.67	64.39
1990	0.930	2.67	68.31
1991	0.913	2.67	67.33
1992	0.969	2.66	69.48
1993	0.976	2.42	65.97
1994	0.978	2.43	66.16
1995	1.017	2.29	67.12
1996	1.026	2.41	68.47
1997	0.927	2.63	67.40

* Trade-weighted Effective Exchange Rate Index: 1971=100; this measures the average exchange rate performance of the Irish pound against the currencies of its trading partners, weighted by their trade with Ireland.

Source: "Quarterly Bulletins", Central Bank of Ireland, Table B6.

As Table 1.4 shows, the effective exchange rate of the Irish pound remained remarkably stable over the years 1986 through 1997, notwithstanding considerable volatility against individual currencies. In all, the Irish pound appreciated by just 1.1 per cent against the currencies of its trading partners. Given Ireland's lower than average inflation rate, this ensured that Irish competitiveness was not compromised in aggregate by exchange rate developments over the past decade. But during 1997, the exchange rate sands began to shift.

The strength of sterling through the first half of 1997 provided a new dimension to the continuing dilemma facing the Irish authorities in the exchange rate domain. Sterling's renewed vigour saw the value of the Irish pound fall below stg£0.90, exciting fears of imported inflation. At the same time, the trade links between the two countries saw the Irish pound dragged upwards in sterling's wake towards the top of its permitted bands within the ERM, inviting an Irish pound revaluation. Short-run Irish competitiveness improved sharply in Britain and deteriorated abruptly in continental Europe. In the second half of 1997, the Irish pound weakened against the currencies of virtually all its trading partners. The trade-weighted index had fallen to 62.0 by the end of February 1998. The cause of this effective depreciation did not lie in any deterioration in Irish economic performance, but in the strength of sterling and of the US dollar. In an effort to halt the currency's slide, the Irish pound was revalued within the ERM by 3 per cent in mid-March 1998.

The scale of Ireland's oscillations over the past decade against the currency of its principal trading partner demonstrates all too clearly the risks that attend Irish entry to the European single currency while Britain remains a non-participant.

In summary, the initial resurgence in Irish economic activity from the mid-1980s onwards was based on three foundations. First, continuous improvements on the supply-side of the economy — large inflows of foreign capital, technology and "know-how", and a growing, better-educated and more highly skilled workforce — raised the economy's potential for expansion. Second, macroeconomic management improved, enhancing the credibility of policy and the environment for doing business. Third, Irish price competitiveness exhibited a distinct improvement, due to the combined effects of subdued Irish inflation and the performance of the effective, trade-weighted exchange rate.[5]

The fruits of Ireland's economic boom over the past decade are displayed in Table 1.5. The data are presented in index number

TABLE 1.5: VOLUME CHANGES IN THE COMPONENTS OF IRISH GNP SINCE 1987 (SHOWN AS INDEX NUMBERS WITH BASES 1987 = 100)

Year	Private Consumer Spending	Current Public Spending	Exports	GDP	GNP
1987	100	100	100	100	100
1988	104	95	109	105	103
1989	111	94	120	111	108
1990	112	99	131	119	117
1991	115	102	137	121	120
1992	120	104	156	126	123
1993	123	105	171	130	127
1994	131	110	195	139	137
1995	136	114	233	153	149
1996	145	118	256	165	159
1997e	154	121	285	179	171

Note: Real GDP and GNP indices are based on an average of output and expenditure measures except for 1997, which is expenditure-based only.

e = estimated outturn.

Sources: "National Income and Expenditure 1995", CSO, July 1996, Table A; "Revised Economic Indicators Since 1960", CSO, September 1996; "1996 National Income and Expenditure — First Results", CSO, June 1997, Table 6.1; "Budget 1998: Economic Background", Department of Finance, December 1997, Tables 1, 3.

---

[5] The forces driving recent Irish economic performance are clearly surveyed in Bradley et al. (1997). The authors conclude:

> We identify five medium- to long-term factors which have each made a considerable contribution to the growth of the economy. These are the changing demographic structure, the increase in human capital, the openness of the economy, recent investment in infrastructure and the domestic macroeconomic environment (p. 64).

form, with the base year of 1987 shown as 100 in all cases. Since price changes have been filtered out, the table shows real or volume changes in the components of Irish GNP since 1987.

The trends shown in Table 1.5 are based on two sources. For the years up to and including 1996, the indices are derived from the official national income and expenditure accounts. The estimates for 1997 are taken from "Budget 1998: Economic Background", prepared by the Department of Finance and published in December 1997. They thus constitute official estimates and projections of recent Irish economic performance.

Table 1.5 charts the incline of the Irish economy's ascent since take-off was achieved in 1987. In the ten years since 1987, real Irish Gross Domestic Product (GDP) has increased by almost four-fifths while real Gross National Product (GNP) has risen by over 70 per cent. In absolute terms, annual GNP is about one-eighth lower than GDP in Ireland. Deviations between economic growth as measured by GDP and GNP are explained by outflows of factor income to the rest of the world, principally by way of repatriated corporate income.

In turn, this mirrors the vertiginous climb in export volumes. Since 1987, real exports of goods and services from Ireland have almost tripled, with Irish-based multinational enterprises providing the principal impetus to expansion.

While export growth primed the recovery process, it has not been the sole source of economic expansion over the past ten years. In fact, the contribution of net exports to economic growth is lower than might be inferred from Table 1.5, since imports also exhibited a rapid rate of increase over the period.

Economic growth has been broadly based. Domestic demand has become an increasingly important contributor to the rate of expansion in recent years. As the recovery took root, consumer confidence revived. This revival, together with the sustained increase in employment since 1990, raised the volume of personal consumer spending by more than half in the decade after 1987. Consumer spending strengthened appreciably following the resolution of the interest and exchange rate crises early in 1993.

Gross fixed investment over the decade was closely correlated to trends in interest rates and the tenor of business confidence. The investment boom of 1990–91 was punctured by the interest and exchange rate crises of 1992/93. However, as foreign exchange and money market conditions settled in the wake of the 1993 devaluation, investors recovered their collective nerve. By 1997, the level of real fixed investment was almost three-fifths higher than a decade earlier. Since 1989, domestic infrastructural investment has been supported by large inflows of European Union structural and cohesion funds.

Taken in aggregate, the economy has achieved remarkable progress over the past decade. Moreover, the traditional impediments to sustained economic growth have not materialised. In the face of sustained expansion, inflation has remained in check. The annual rate of consumer price inflation decelerated to just 1.5 per cent in 1997. While Ireland has consistently exhibited faster growth than its trading partners in the European Union, this has not triggered a descent into unmanageable balance of payments deficits. The current balance of payments remained comfortably in surplus — at an estimated 1.8 per cent of GNP — in 1997.

However, while aggregate growth has been impressive over the years since 1987, the pace of expansion has been uneven. Three separate sub-periods are identifiable.

First, between 1987 and 1990, the Irish economy rebounded strongly from the trauma of the early 1980s. Export sales benefited from the renewed strength of EU markets. In the domestic economy, gross investment raced ahead as interest rates fell and business confidence returned, a trend not unrelated to the reduction in current public spending volumes.

Real current public spending was lower in 1990 than it had been in 1987. Any deflationary impact such cuts might have engineered were swamped by the combined forces of export and investment growth. Additions to real consumer spending lagged behind the national growth rate, reflecting the slow response of employment levels to renewed economic activity and the diversion of national resources to liquidating public borrowing.

The pace of economic growth decelerated sharply in the second period, embracing the years 1991 through 1993. In part, this deceleration mirrored the collapse of the Lawson growth bubble in Britain and the ending of the reunification boom in Germany. More importantly, it reflected the interest and exchange rate crises of 1992/93 and the uncertainties that resulted.

The European economy began to stall in 1991, and by 1993 it had fallen into recession. This alone would have been sufficient to dampen Irish investment. However, the precipitate and precipitous climb in Irish interest rates through 1992 and the related collapse of sterling sent investment into a tailspin. Consumers also took fright as interest and mortgage rates leaped upwards.

The twin interest and exchange rate crises persisted until the Irish pound was devalued by 10 per cent in January 1993. Conditions in financial markets quickly returned to normal in the aftermath of the devaluation. There was virtually no knock-on effect on the domestic price level, since the devaluation effectively represented no more than a correction of a prior and unwanted appreciation in the currency's external value.

The 10 per cent devaluation of the Irish pound cleared the way for the third phase, the resumption of very rapid rates of economic expansion. Since 1993, the Irish economy has been firing on all cylinders. Significant increases in the numbers at work — 186,000 in the four years to April 1997 — have supported sharp advances in consumer demand. Investment has boomed, powered by lower interest rates. Export growth has accelerated, not least because of the revival in the fortunes of the British economy.

The national accounts for 1996 reveal that real Gross Domestic Product in Ireland increased by 7.7 per cent in 1996 following a 10.4 per cent advance in 1995. Real GNP rose by 6.9 per cent in 1996 following an increase of 8.8 per cent in 1995. Expansion has continued unabated through 1997. By the end of 1997, the Department of Finance was estimating real GDP and GNP growth rates of 8.3 per cent and 7.7 per cent for the year.

1.3. The Payoffs from Economic Growth

The speed and scale of Irish economic growth over the last decade has allowed three long-standing problems to be addressed.

First, in spite of over-zealous spending by the public authorities since 1990, the health of the public finances is much improved. The extent of the correction in the public finances since 1986 is charted in Table 1.6.

TABLE 1.6: THE CORRECTION OF IRISH PUBLIC FINANCES, 1986–97

Year	EBR as % of GNP*	PSBR as % of GNP*	Government Debt as % of GNP
1986	12.1	14.2	109.7
1987	9.4	10.8	112.4
1988**	3.1	3.7	108.3
1989	2.2	3.0	97.7
1990	1.9	2.4	92.3
1991	2.0	3.0	89.9
1992	2.7	3.4	87.9
1993	2.5	3.1	88.0
1994	2.2	2.6	83.9
1995	1.9	2.5	78.2
1996	1.2	1.5	72.3
1997	0.5	NP	66.3

* EBR = Exchequer Borrowing Requirement; PSBR = Public Sector Borrowing Requirement

** Includes 1988 tax amnesty proceeds

NP = No longer published; replaced by the "General Government Surplus/ Deficit"

Sources: Budget Book 1997, p. 115; "National Income and Expenditure 1996 — First Results", CSO, June 1997; Exchequer Returns for 1997, Department of Finance, January 1998.

As shown in Table 1.6, the Exchequer Borrowing Requirement (EBR) had been reduced from 12.1 per cent of Gross National Product in 1986 to just 1.2 per cent of GNP by 1996. In similar fashion, the Public Sector Borrowing Requirement (PSBR) — which includes the capital borrowings of state-sponsored bodies in addition to the EBR — had declined from 14.2 per cent to 1.5 per cent of GNP over the same period. Due to unprecedented inflows of tax revenues into the Exchequer, there was a further pronounced improvement in the health of the public finances during 1997. The Exchequer Returns for 1997 showed that the EBR declined to just 0.5 per cent of GNP, while a surplus of close to 1 per cent was recorded on the General Government Account.

However, it is sobering to realise that most of the public deficit correction had been achieved by 1990, in the period coinciding with tight restraint of current public spending. Since then, a loosening of control over day-to-day government spending has preempted any further significant improvement in the deficit position, despite very robust rates of national economic growth and unparalleled tax buoyancy. With the economy advancing at such speed, the government accounts should be strongly in surplus.

The burden of national indebtedness has, however, continued to ease, due to the rapid rate of GDP growth. The Maastricht criterion of government debt to Gross Domestic Product (GDP) is used to measure the weight of the debt burden. On this basis, the debt load has lightened appreciably, from almost 110 per cent of GDP in 1986 to an estimated 66 per cent in 1997, a progression interrupted only temporarily by the exchange rate crisis of 1992/93. The ratio of government debt to GDP is budgeted to decline to 61 per cent in 1998, very close to the Maastricht target.

The correction of the public finances and the reduction in the relative weight of the national debt burden have been amongst the most important dividends yielded by the economy's strong performance over the past decade. The correction of the public finances has not only lifted a weight from the economy's — and the taxpayer's — back, but it has cleared the way for sustainable growth well into the future.

Enhanced living standards have comprised the second set of benefits delivered by an expanding economy. As was shown in Table 1.5, aggregate real consumer spending increased by over half in the decade since 1987. This experience stands in stark contrast with the 1981–86 period, when the community's material living standards edged ahead by just 3 per cent.

Third, and most important of all, the Irish economy has at last started to generate jobs on a sustained basis. After cycles, first of low growth, then of jobless growth — where economic growth was not inducing gains in employment — the economy swung into a phase of rapid employment expansion in the late 1980s. Annual Labour Force Surveys show that, between 1987 and 1997, the numbers at work in Ireland increased by more than a quarter of a million. Employment expansion on this scale is unprecedented in recent Irish economic history. The sustained growth in employment after 1993 halted and reversed the rise in unemployment. By February 1998, the standardised rate of unemployment in Ireland had declined to 9.7 per cent — significantly below the average rate of unemployment within the EU.

The widespread availability of domestic employment opportunities has been a major force in reducing net emigration and spurring population growth during the 1990s. The nature and scale of this employment boom will be discussed extensively in subsequent chapters.

1.4. Catching up on Europe

The final dividend from sustained growth at home has been a sharp improvement in Ireland's relative economic position abroad. Ireland is no longer ranked amongst the poorer countries of the European Union. Fast growth at home combined with a stuttering economic performance in Europe since 1990 has allowed Ireland to close the income gap with its European neighbours.

Estimates by the European Commission indicate that, by 1996, Ireland's Gross Domestic Product[6] per capita had reached 79.2 per cent of the average for the 15 EU member states. The poorer regions within the Union are defined as those where GDP per person falls below 75 per cent of the EU average.

Moreover, using the barometer of GDP, the income gap between Ireland and the United Kingdom has been all but eliminated. GDP per person in the UK stood at 83.5 per cent of the EU average in 1996, just four percentage points ahead of the Irish ratio. In 1960, income per person in Britain was twice as high as in Ireland.

The trend in Ireland's GDP per person relative to the existing 15 EU member-states since 1960 is shown in Table 1.7.

---

[6] GDP per head of population at current market prices and current exchange rates translated into ECUs.

TABLE 1.7: IRELAND — NO LONGER RANKED AMONG EUROPE'S POOR (GDP PER CAPITA AT CURRENT PRICES AND EXCHANGE RATES 1960–96 WITH EU AVERAGE = 100; EU15 SINCE 1991)

Year	Ireland	Britain	Germany	Spain	USA
1960	60.2	128.3	120.6	35.0	264.3
1970	58.5	95.0	129.9	47.5	210.6
1972	61.5	91.8	133.8	50.3	183.9
1980	58.8	95.0	131.2	56.4	118.3
1987	64.6	88.5	132.6	55.5	134.6
1990	67.8	86.9	125.4	66.9	115.7
1991	67.7	91.8	112.9*	71.3	117.5
1992	69.4	87.0	118.1*	71.5	112.1
1993	70.7	86.7	125.7*	65.4	129.8
1994	73.4	88.1	126.9*	62.2	128.1
1995	75.5	83.2	130.6*	63.0	116.3
1996p	79.2	83.5	125.1*	65.3	120.7

* Diluted by German reunification; p = projected.

Source: "European Economy 1996", European Commission, Directorate General for Economic and Financial Affairs, 1996, Table 8, pp. 68–69.

One caveat, however, must be entered. Gross Domestic Product per person forms the basis for the comparisons shown in Table 1.7. For most European countries, GDP and GNP are virtually interchangeable. However, in Ireland's case, the scale of annual outflows of factor income — primarily in the form of repatriations of multinational corporate income — have driven a wedge between GDP and GNP. As a result, GDP — broadly, national output — is about 13 per cent higher than national income as measured by GNP. The difference between the two represents the annual amount of income generated by production in Ireland that is transferred abroad. As a result, comparisons based on GDP tend to overstate Irish per capita incomes relative to those in other EU member states.

Ireland's income per head, as measured by GDP, changed little between 1960 and 1987, relative to average income within the European Union. There were periodic fluctuations — Irish GDP per capita fell quite sharply relative to other member states in the years after EU entry in 1973 — but no discernible evidence of a narrowing of the income gap on a sustained basis.

Since 1987, however, Ireland has made significant strides in catching up on Europe, with the relative income gap closing by 15 percentage points. In effect, Irish GDP per person has moved from two-thirds of the European average in 1987 to four-fifths of that average by 1996. In consequence, the GDP gap with Britain has all but disappeared. Similarly, where GDP per person in the United States was well over four times as high as in Ireland in 1960, the gap has now closed to 50 per cent.

Such comparisons, while not odious, are distorted both by currency movements and by the differing sets of prices ruling in each country. In an effort to overcome these difficulties, GDP per capita, adjusted for differences in national prices, are shown in Table 1.8. While such purchasing parity estimates do not overcome all of the problems associated with inter-country comparisons — and do not address the particular difficulties faced by Ireland in using GDP-based statistics — they provide a better guide to relative living standards than the unadjusted series.

TABLE 1.8: IRELAND NARROWS THE INCOME GAP WITH EUROPE, 1961–97 (GDP PER CAPITA, PURCHASING POWER PARITY BASIS, WITH EU AVERAGE = 100; EU15 FOR DATA SINCE 1991)

Year	Ireland	Britain	Germany	Spain	USA
1961–70	60.5	112.5	118.4	67.4	170.9
1971–80	61.8	100.5	115.7	74.4	149.4
1981–90	66.3	99.9	116.3	71.3	143.4
1991	76.0	96.9	105.7*	79.3	136.9
1992	79.5	97.6	108.1*	77.3	136.4
1993	82.7	98.9	107.9*	77.8	141.5
1994	88.0	98.4	109.7*	75.7	142.2
1995	95.1	98.3	109.2	76.1	140.8
1996e	100.7	98.9	108.9	76.6	141.0
1997p	103.9	99.6	108.9	76.9	140.1

Note: the data for 1961–90 are annual averages

* Diluted by German reunification; e= estimated; p = projected

Source: Eurostat and Directorate-General II, Commission of the European Community, December 1996.

When the purchasing power of money is standardised, Table 1.8 shows that Ireland has caught up with Europe. By 1996, on a purchasing power parity basis, GDP per capita in Ireland had reached 100.7 per cent of the average for the 15 EU member states. Since the 1980s, Ireland's real living standards, as measured by GDP per capita adjusted for purchasing power differences, have jumped from two-thirds of the European average to equal the material standard of living enjoyed across Europe.

Moreover, in 1996, for the first time ever, per capita GDP in Ireland on a purchasing power basis, exceeded GDP per person in Britain. Even allowing for the deficiencies of GDP comparisons, this represents perhaps the most remarkable outcome produced by Ireland's ten years of sustained economic growth.

In summary, the Irish boom is not a purely statistical illusion; it possesses real substance. Over the past decade, the Irish economy has grown in size by three-quarters. Expansion on this scale has provided the resources to eliminate budget deficits, to raise real national living standards to average European levels and, for the first time in living memory, to add large numbers each year to the total at work.

More than a quarter of a million people have been added to the national workforce over the past decade, an achievement without parallel in modern Irish history. In turn, the availability of well-paid work at home has acted as a sharp brake on emigration through the 1990s. As a result, by 1997, the population had reached its highest level since Independence, at 3.661 million people.

Chapter 2

THE IRISH JOBS MACHINE

2.1. Historical Trends in Irish Employment

The most remarkable feature of the Irish economic boom during the 1990s has been the economy's hitherto undiscovered capacity for creating employment. The inability to generate jobs on a sustained basis had been the Irish economy's besetting problem since the state was founded. Total employment in Ireland was still lower in 1994 than it had been in 1926, the year in which the first Free State census was taken.

Denied decently paid work at home, millions were traditionally forced abroad in search of a livelihood. This was no novelty. The emigrants' trail was already well trodden. Commenting in the late 1860s on the pervasiveness of Irish emigration, Engels had predicted, "if this goes on for another thirty years, there will be Irishmen only in America".[1]

Independence did little to staunch the outflow of emigrants. Between 1926 and 1961, with the exception of the short period 1946–51, annual rates of net emigration from Ireland exceeded the "natural" rate of population growth, as measured by births minus deaths. In consequence, the population fell almost continuously for the first 40 years of the State's existence. The reason was clear: insufficient employment opportunities at reasonable wages caused persistent emigration, which in turn induced long-run population decline. This cycle is shown in Table 2.1.

In perusing the data in Table 2.1, it should be borne in mind that the composition of total employment in Ireland has changed utterly over time. As late as 1936, half of those at work in Ireland

---

[1] Quoted in Ó Gráda (1994). Ó Gráda estimates the outflow of people from Ireland at "about four million between 1850 and 1914" (p. 224).

were engaged in primary economic activities — agriculture, forestry, fishing and mining. Sixty years later, just over 10 per cent of those at work were employed in such activities.

TABLE 2.1: POPULATION AND EMPLOYMENT IN IRELAND, 1926–97 ('000S)

Census Date	Population	Total Employment
1926	2,972	1,220
1936	2,968	1,235
1946	2,955	1,228
1951	2,961	1,220
1961	2,818	1,053
1966	2,884	1,066
1971	2,978	1,055
1979	3,368	1,150
1981	3,443	1,135
1986	3,541	1,091
1991	3,526	1,149
1996	3,626	1,297
1997	3,661*	1,338**

Notes: * Population estimate in 1997 Labour Force Survey. ** As measured by "Principal Economic Status" (PES).

Sources: Censuses of Population 1926–1996, CSO; Labour Force Survey 1997, CSO, for employment data in 1996 and 1997; Gillmor (1985), Table 1.3.

The relationship between employment performance and population change is striking. The sharp fall in total employment during the "hungry '50s" caused a steep rise in net emigration, culminating in the population falling to its lowest ever level in 1961. In contrast, employment expansion during the 1970s caused net immigration into the country, inducing significant population gains between 1971 and 1979.

More recently, the jobs boom of the 1990s has reversed the heavy net emigration that characterised the middle and late 1980s. Instead of net emigration, there has been substantial net immigration into Ireland. Between 1992 and 1997, immigrants exceeded emigrants by over 23,000. In the year to April 1997, net immigration amounted to 15,000 people, underpinning the largest annual increase in Ireland's population since 1982.[2]

2.2. The Great Leap Forward in Irish Employment

As the economy stalled in the first half of the 1980s, employment declined sharply. Even when the level of economic activity revived from 1987 onwards, employment was initially slow to respond. However, after 1989, the numbers at work started to rise. From 1993, the pace of employment expansion became very rapid.

As Table 2.2 shows, total employment in the Irish economy increased by 250,000 between April 1989 and April 1997, from 1.088 million to 1.338 million. This represented a 23 per cent rise in the numbers at work in the space of just eight years. Additions to employment on this scale and for a sustained period are unmatched in recent Irish economic history.

Job gains were unevenly distributed across economic sectors. As illustrated in Table 2.2, the numbers at work in agriculture continued their long-run decline during the 1990s, with the farm workforce falling by over 17 per cent.

In both absolute and proportionate terms, the services sector made the biggest contribution to employment growth during the 1990s. The numbers at work in services rose by 200,000 or almost one-third between 1989 and 1997.

The advance in industrial employment has proved surprisingly swift, particularly since 1993. Over the eight-year period, total industrial employment, comprising jobs in manufacturing, construction and utilities, increased by 79,000 or over one-quarter.

Total numbers at work are estimated in Labour Force Surveys undertaken by the Central Statistics Office (CSO) each Spring on the basis of a sample of some 4 per cent of the population. The estimates shown in Table 2.2 are based on respondents' own assessments of their usual "Principal Economic Status" (PES). While this classification allows respondents a degree of discretion,

---

[2] "Population and Migration Estimates — April 1997", CSO, October 1997.

it does provide broad continuity with the employment data collected in quinquennial censuses of population.

TABLE 2.2: THE GREAT LEAP FORWARD IN IRISH EMPLOYMENT, 1989–97 (AT MID-APRIL EACH YEAR IN '000S OF PEOPLE)

Year	Total Employment in			
	Farming	Industry	Services	Total
1989	162	307	618	1,088
1990	169	321	643	1,134
1991	155	323	656	1,134
1992	154	319	672	1,145
1993	144	313	695	1,152
1994	142	333	713	1,188
1995	143	349	756	1,248
1996	138	355	804	1,297
1997	134	386	818	1,338
Change % 1989–97	–17.3	+25.7	+32.4	+23.0

Notes: Employment measured by "Principal Economic Status" in annual Labour Force Surveys; figures may not add to exact totals due to rounding.

Sources: Labour Force Survey 1997, CSO, October 1997, Table 7A; "1997 Economic Review and Outlook", Department of Finance, Summer 1997, Table 12.

The CSO's annual Labour Force Surveys also provide an alternative approach to labour force analysis based on internationally accepted criteria developed by the International Labour Office (ILO). The ILO approach classifies respondents on the basis of their actual economic activity in the week preceding the survey.

The ILO classification differentiates between the economically active and the economically inactive amongst the population aged 15 years and over. The "economically active" comprise the labour force. They include those working full- and part-time and those who are unemployed but available for work, having taken specific steps to find employment in the four weeks preceding the survey.

The "economically inactive" consist of two groups: those who are marginally attached to the labour force — including "discouraged workers" — and others who are not economically active, such as students.[3]

The ILO analysis affords both greater precision in determining employment levels and more extensive breakdowns of those at work and of the unemployed. It also provides a firm base for international comparisons.

The trend in Irish employment since 1987 — the year the boom began — is shown on an ILO basis in Table 2.3.

TABLE 2.3: TRENDS IN IRISH EMPLOYMENT, 1987–97 (IN '000S OF PEOPLE AT MID-APRIL EACH YEAR, ILO BASIS)

Year	Farming	Industry	Services	Total Employment
1987	170	302	639	1,111
1988	171	301	639	1,111
1989	168	309	634	1,111
1990	175	324	661	1,160
1991	159	325	672	1,156
1992	157	320	688	1,165
1993	150	316	718	1,183
1994	147	335	738	1,221
1995	149	352	781	1,282
1996	141	359	829	1,329
1997	142	390	848	1,380
Change % 1987–97	–16.5	+29.1	+32.7	+24.2

Note: Figures may not add to totals due to rounding.

Source: Tabulation from Labour Force Survey 1997 prepared by the Central Statistics Office, November 1997.

---

[3] Labour Force Survey 1997, CSO, October 1997, pp. 8–9.

The data in Table 2.3 show that the Irish economy increased total employment by 269,000 or almost a quarter in the ten years to April 1997. Of the total net additions to employment, services contributed 209,000 jobs, industry added 88,000 to its workforce while the numbers employed in farming fell by 28,000.

Employment growth was heavily concentrated in the second half of the decade. Between 1987 and 1992, the total numbers at work increased by just 54,000. In the following five years, employment increased by 215,000. In the year to April 1997 alone, job gains reached 51,000.

TABLE 2.4: THE PRIVATE SECTOR AND TOTAL NON-FARM EMPLOYMENT GROWTH, 1987–97 (IN '000S AT MID-APRIL EACH YEAR (ILO BASIS))

Year	(1) Non-Farm Employment	(2) State Job Schemes	(3) Public Sector Employment	Private Sector Employment = (1) – (2) – (3)
1987	941	17	304	620
1988	940	18	295	627
1989	943	13	286	644
1990	985	16	287	682
1991	997	14	288	695
1992	1,008	16	288	704
1993	1,033	17	289	727
1994	1,074	31	291	752
1995	1,133	41	294	798
1996	1,188	40	301	847
1997	1,238	41	297	900
Change % 1987–97	+31.6%	+141.2%	–2.3%	+45.2%

Sources: Tabulation from the Labour Force Survey 1997 prepared by the CSO, November 1997; Table 2.3, where total employment less employment in farming yields "non-farm employment", as shown in column 1.

Employment expansion on this scale and over this time-span represents a remarkable achievement for an economy that has traditionally found job creation so difficult. Moreover, the non-farm private sector supplied the engine for the Irish jobs machine during the 1990s. As can be seen from Table 2.4, non-farm employment growth over the past decade has been powered almost exclusively by the Irish private sector.

Table 2.4 shows that, outside agriculture, employment increased by 297,000, or almost one-third, between 1987 and 1997. Over the same period, non-farm private sector employment increased by 280,000. Thus, outside agriculture, the private sector accounted for 280,000 of the 297,000 additions to employment recorded between 1987 and 1997.

The number of jobs on state-sponsored employment schemes, most notably the Community Employment Programme (CEP), increased from 17,000 to 41,000 in the course of the decade. As will be seen later, the increased uptake on such schemes has been an important factor in reducing unemployment, especially long-term unemployment.

The level of employment in the public sector — the public services, local authorities and state-sponsored bodies — declined by 7,000 between 1987 and 1997. The decline was initiated by a tight budgetary squeeze between 1987 and 1989, which caused the numbers on the public sector payroll to drop by 18,000 in those years. Recovery thereafter was relatively slow.

After deducting the numbers on state employment schemes and in public sector employment from total non-agricultural employment, private sector non-farm employment is seen to rise from 620,000 in 1987 to 900,000 ten years later. This 45 per cent increase in private sector non-farm employment in the space of a decade indicates that, when conditions are competitive and business is profitable, private sector employers are avid recruiters.

It has been suggested that Ireland's employment boom is something of a chimera — that, in reality, it consists of little more than additional part-time jobs in low-paying unskilled occupations. As noted earlier, the bulk of the job gains recorded over the decade in question materialised over the five years after 1992. Table 2.5 allocates the job gains since 1992 between full- and part-time employment.

TABLE 2.5: FULL- AND PART-TIME JOB GAINS IN IRELAND, 1992–97 (IN '000S AT MID-APRIL EACH YEAR; ILO BASIS)

Category	1992	1993	1994	1995	1996	1997
At Work	1,165	1,183	1,221	1,282	1,329	1,380
of which:						
• Full-time	1,061	1,056	1,083	1,128	1,176	1,210
• Part-time	104	127	137	154	153	170
Analysis of Part-time Workers						
Part-time, not Under-employed	85	104	113	128	129	148
Part-time, Under-employed	19	24	25	26	24	22

Note: Figures may not add to totals due to rounding.

Source: Labour Force Survey 1997, CSO, October 1997, extracted from Table 27A.

Table 2.5 makes clear that full-time jobs have been the principal force driving total employment ahead during the strongest phase of the boom. Between 1992 and 1997, full-time jobs accounted for 149,000 of the 215,000 extra employment gained by the economy. In short, full-time jobs comprised more than two out of every three additions to employment between 1992 and 1997.

Part-time employment increased by 66,000 over this five-year span. However, the vast majority of those in part-time jobs do not want to work full-time. Of the 170,000 part-time workers enumerated in the 1997 Labour Force Survey, less than 22,000 stated that they were under-employed. In summary, part-time work meets the needs and fits the circumstances of most of those who undertake it.

The Labour Force Survey, while it contains a breakdown of employment by sector, does not contain an occupational classification of those at work. However, the national training authority, FÁS, in conjunction with the Economic and Social Research Institute, has analysed the occupational profile of the workforce.

The results, shown in Table 2.6, do not indicate any de-skilling of the workforce. On the contrary, snapshots of the workforce taken over time indicate that occupations requiring high levels of qualifications and skills have exhibited particularly rapid growth. And higher skills command higher wages.

Ireland is becoming a highly qualified "white collar" economy. Between 1981 and 1995, the number of managers, professionals and associate professionals increased by 44 per cent. By 1995, these occupational groups accounted for a quarter of all those at work in Ireland.

TABLE 2.6: EMPLOYMENT BY OCCUPATION IN IRELAND, 1981–95 ('000S, RANKED BY RATE OF INCREASE 1981–95)

Occupation	1981	1991	1995	Change % 1981–95
Catering, personal services	61	77	91	+49.2
Managers	57	71	84	+47.4
Professionals	107	131	157	+46.7
Associate professionals	49	58	66	+34.7
Sales workers	74	83	98	+32.4
Security workers	31	33	36	+16.1
Clerks, typists	158	158	170	+7.6
Proprietors, service industries	38	43	40	+5.3
Operatives	99	88	103	+4.0
Transport workers	50	45	49	–2.0
Skilled/craft workers	163	151	155	–4.9
Farmers	177	144	135	–23.7
Labourers	72	51	46	–36.1
Total At Work	1138	1134	1234	+8.4

Note: Figures may not add to exact totals due to rounding.
Source: Derived from data supplied by FÁS, November 1997.

In contrast, the number of farmers and labourers declined from 249,000 in 1981 to 181,000 in 1995. By the latter date, farmers and labourers together comprised less than 15 per cent of the Irish workforce.

The changing occupational profile of the Irish workforce reflects, in turn, continuous improvements in the educational qualifications of new labour market entrants. This rising tide of educational attainment is discussed extensively in Chapter 4.

The very substantial increases in Irish employment recorded during the 1990s are remarkable for two reasons. First, they have been achieved against a background of declining employment in Europe. Second, they constitute a significant break with past Irish experience, when the economy was characterised by "jobless growth".

TABLE 2.7: CUMULATIVE PERCENTAGE CHANGES IN EMPLOYMENT, 1990–97 (COUNTRIES RANKED BY PERFORMANCE)

Country	Employment Change % 1990–97
Luxembourg	+19.8
Ireland	**+17.3**
Netherlands	+11.5
Greece	+5.7
Austria	+2.1
Denmark	+0.5
France	–0.8
Belgium	–1.5
Spain	–2.2
Germany	–4.1
Italy	–4.6
United Kingdom	–4.7
Portugal	–5.2
Sweden	–11.8
Finland	–13.9
EU15	–2.7
United States	+9.2
Japan	+5.1

Source: "OECD Economic Outlook", No. 61, OECD, Paris, June 1997. Data extracted from Annex Table 20. Projections for 1997 are included.

The European economy lost jobs in significant numbers through most of the 1990s. Between 1990 and 1997, total employment in the European Union fell by a cumulative 2.7 per cent.

However, employment performances across the European Union were anything but uniform. Substantial rises in employment were recorded in Luxembourg, Ireland and the Netherlands, with lesser gains reported in Greece and Austria. In contrast, job losses were particularly heavy in Finland and Sweden and were also severe in Portugal, Britain, Italy and Germany. Cumulative changes in employment for 1990–97 are shown in Table 2.7.

The poverty of the European employment performance during the 1990s is illustrated by the scale of the job gains generated by both the United States and Japan over the same period. However, with the exception of Luxembourg, the Irish job creation record surpassed all others.

The sustained surge in Irish employment during the 1990s has put an end to the characterisation of Irish economic expansion as "jobless growth". A key feature of Ireland's performance during the 1990s has been the much higher job dividends delivered by economic growth. In Table 2.8, the long-run relationship between output growth and job expansion is shown for a range of industrial countries.

As can be seen from Table 2.8, the long-run rate of Irish economic growth, which averaged 3.2 per cent annually over the years 1960 through 1990, did not lag appreciably behind the corresponding EU growth rate of 3.4 per cent. However, the average annual growth in Irish employment, at just 0.26 per cent each year, trailed well behind the 0.4 per cent annual average rate of jobs growth recorded within the EU over this long span.

In consequence, the employment intensity of Irish economic expansion — the quantum of jobs delivered for every percentage point of real GNP growth — was very low. Between 1960 and 1990, the employment intensity of Irish economic growth was just 0.08. This implies that a 10 per cent increase in Irish output during this period produced, on average, an advance of just four-fifths of one per cent in Irish employment. Over this 30-year period, the job dividends yielded by Irish economic growth were one-third lower than the EU average, while the employment intensity of economic growth was twice as high in Britain as in Ireland.

TABLE 2.8: EMPLOYMENT INTENSITY OF ECONOMIC GROWTH, 1960–90 (WITH ESTIMATES FOR IRELAND 1990–96; ANNUAL AVERAGE PERCENTAGE CHANGES)

Country	Employment Expansion	Output Growth	Employment Intensity*
Ireland 1990–96	**2.1**	**5.2**	**0.40**
Sweden	0.8	2.8	0.29
Britain	0.4	2.4	0.17
Finland	0.5	3.8	0.13
France	0.4	3.7	0.10
Germany	0.3	3.1	0.09
Belgium	0.3	3.4	0.09
Ireland 1960–90	**0.26**	**3.2**	**0.08**
Greece	0.3	4.6	0.07
Spain	0.3	4.9	0.07
Italy	0.1	3.9	0.03
European Union	0.4	3.4	0.12
United States	1.9	3.2	0.59
Canada	2.4	4.2	0.57
Australia	2.2	3.9	0.56
Japan	1.1	6.3	0.17
OECD	1.1	3.6	0.31

* Employment intensity = employment growth divided by output growth. It shows the employment impact of a 1 per cent increase in output growth as measured by real GNP.

Sources: "The Association between Economic Growth and Employment Growth in Ireland", National Economic and Social Council Report No 94, Dublin, December 1992. Data extracted from Table 1, p. 13. Estimates for Ireland for the 1990–96 period are the author's own.

In mitigation, the employment effects of economic growth in Ireland were broadly similar to the experience of Spain and Greece, two other late-developing EU member-states that encountered similar structural problems in adding to employment over these years.

However, it is when the perspective is broadened that Ireland's historic deficiencies in translating economic growth into extra jobs become apparent. As Table 2.8 makes clear, the EU's long-term ability to convert output growth into additional jobs has been very poor relative to the performance of other leading industrial nations. As the National Economic and Social Council has put it:

> The most striking aspect of these global figures is the dramatic difference between the average employment intensity of growth in the EC and non-EC economies; in the EC, every 1 per cent increase in GDP during 1960–1990 was associated with a rise in employment of just 0.12 per cent; in non-EC economies such as the US, Canada and Australia, the equivalent employment rise was between 0.56 per cent and 0.59 per cent.[4]

Relative to the rest of the industrial world, the EU's central problem has not been insufficient expansion. The long-run rate of European economic growth has not differed appreciably from that of the industrial world in general. In Europe, the problem has not centred on the growth rate, but on the inability to translate growth into jobs. This suggests that rigidities in the European jobs market have prevented economic growth from being fully reflected in employment gains. This view has gained a degree of acceptance within Europe. Thus, the European Commission noted in 1996:

> The debate in recent years has increasingly cited the need for increased flexibility in European labour markets as a necessary structural condition for competitiveness and employment growth.[5]

Happily, during the 1990s, Ireland managed to break with Europe's long-run record as a poor provider of jobs. Table 2.8

---

[4] "The Association between Economic Growth and Employment Growth in Ireland", NESC, Report No. 94, December 1992, p. 4.

[5] "Employment in Europe 1996", Directorate General for Employment, Industrial Relations and Social Affairs, European Commission, 1996, p. 17.

shows that between 1990 and 1996, employment expanded at an annual rate of 2.1 per cent, powered by a growth rate that averaged 5.2 per cent annually. As a result, the employment intensity of Irish economic growth rose to 0.4. That is to say, an increase of 10 per cent in Irish real GNP induced a 4 per cent advance in Irish employment during the first half of the 1990s. In the 1990s, Ireland has become five times more efficient at translating output growth into jobs than it had been in the preceding 30 years.

Moreover, to add the startling to the remarkable, the unparalleled growth in employment during the 1990s was achieved in the face of a falling national investment ratio. "Jobless growth" has been supplanted by "investmentless growth". The Economic and Social Research Institute has pointed out that most of the period 1961–90 was characterised by strong growth in the capital stock and weak or negative growth in employment:

> This pattern was reversed in the 1990s when the growth rate in employment passed out that of the capital stock. Clearly, the capital-labour ratio in the economy has begun to fall. . . . In the 1990s [the share of investment in GNP] has fallen to its pre-1965 levels.[6]

How can this transformation in the job intensity of economic growth be explained?

In the first place, the conditions for much stronger economic growth were created by better national economic management, ranging from the containment of inflation through the elimination of public sector deficits to the negotiation of moderate pay settlements. In short, the Irish economy became much more competitive.

The economy's competitive edge was sharpened by the unilateral Irish pound devaluation in January 1993. Thereafter, the economy took off. The gains in employment have been concentrated in the post-1993 period. Hence, the scale of employment increases is explained in large measure by the height of the growth rates attained.

---

[6] "Medium-Term Review 1997–2003", No. 6, Economic and Social Research Institute, Dublin, April 1997, p. 41.

The links between employment expansion and economic growth may also have been strengthened by the changing composition of economic growth after 1993. Noting the rapid growth in domestic demand from 1994 onwards, Alan Gray has commented:

> This latter development may not have been given as much attention as it deserves as it has been a critical element in contributing to the increase in tax receipts and the expansion of employment-intensive sectors.[7]

Second, there has been a consistent, if at times almost embarrassed, reliance on the use of tax incentives to develop the economy's supply side. Low corporation tax rates have effectively allowed Ireland to purchase a modern industrial base off the shelf, and at a relatively cheap price. These rates, guaranteed far into the future, initiated an inflow of foreign direct investment. The attractions of industrial clustering made such inflows self-reinforcing over time.

In turn, continuous inflows of sophisticated modern industries from abroad greatly enhanced national productivity. As the renowned international trade theorist Paul Krugman has put it:

> To some extent, however, Ireland's favourable productivity performance is surely a result of its success in becoming the premier European host to inward foreign direct investment. (US foreign direct investment in Ireland is 50 per cent higher per capita than in the UK, 6 times as high as in France or Germany.)[8]

Productivity gains at industry level buttressed the competitive improvements won through better macroeconomic management. Krugman also points to the fact that Ireland's success owes as

---

[7] Gray (1997), p. xiv. Before 1993, Irish economic growth depended heavily on export expansion and export expansion was driven primarily by the export growth of foreign companies. The scale of this export drive may have been influenced by transfer pricing techniques. Thus a part of the weak relationship between GNP and jobs growth prior to 1993 may have been due to an overstatement of GNP growth itself. See Murphy (1998), especially pp. 5–11.

[8] Krugman (1997).

much to good luck as good management. The good luck was supplied by

> changes in the underlying geography of the world economy: as trade became less influenced by transportation costs but more critically dependent on communication, a location within Europe became necessary, but one in the centre of Europe less important. . . . Ireland got a head start over other European locations in attracting what became a surge of inward foreign direct investment; the early investments both generated a cascade through informational effects and, eventually, created external economies that further reinforced Ireland's advantages.[9]

Third, during the 1990s, and due to insistent pressure both from the electorate and the trade union movement — unlikely supply-siders — tax cutting has spread from the corporate into the personal sector. Continuous reductions in employees' average income tax rates was the price exacted for the pay restraint embodied in the series of national pay agreements concluded since 1987. The combination of moderate annual growth in money wages and greater labour market flexibility due to cuts in income and payroll taxes enhanced the attractiveness of hiring labour. The scale of the reductions, both in average income tax rates and in the width of tax wedges, is discussed extensively in subsequent chapters.

Fourth, the responsibility for improving the economy's supply-side performance has not devolved exclusively on the private sector. Government, with the support of the European Union, has contributed directly to improving the quality of the labour supply through a continuing commitment to spending on education and training.

Moreover, there is evidence to suggest that increasing participation rates in secondary and third-level education not only improves the quality of the labour force, but also its size. Over the past decade, a key feature of the Irish labour market's evolution has been the increase in female labour force participation rates.

---

[9] Krugman (1997), p. 51. For these reasons, multinational investment in Ireland may prove to be less "footloose" than many suspect.

This has been directly associated with rising levels of educational attainment amongst women.

Fifth, EU structural funds, under the Community Support Frameworks for Ireland 1989–93 and 1994–99, have assisted in developing Ireland's infrastructural base. The improved physical infrastructure has not only sharpened the competitiveness of the economy directly, but has also enhanced its attractions to investors.

When taken together, all of these factors form a coherent picture. The Irish economy is in the throes of a supply-side revolution. The productive capital stock — business and industry — has been augmented by continuous injections of foreign investment, lured to Ireland by low corporation taxes. The physical infrastructure has been upgraded with the assistance of European Union subsidies. The human capital stock has been improved through consistently high public spending on education and training. The labour market has become more flexible through direct tax cuts, introduced at the insistence of the trade unions.

The Irish experiment in supply-side economics differs from the traditional Thatcherite model of the 1980s in three distinct ways. First, it has been based on a wide public consensus rather than on ideological, class-based conflict. Second, since 1990, it has been associated with rising, rather than falling, public expenditure. Tax cuts have been made possible by pushing the economy towards its production possibility frontier rather than by cutting current public spending. Third, it has not relied exclusively on private sector responses to tax cuts for expansion. Public spending, broadly defined to include EU transfers, has been visibly important in extending and deepening both the physical infrastructural and the human capital bases of the economy. In short, it has been a supply-side revolution with a social democratic face.

Finally, two factors help to explain the conundrum of "investmentless growth". First, this phenomenon relates only to physical, and not to human, capital expansion. As will be seen in Chapter 4, investment in human capital has continued to rise at a rapid pace. Thus, in recent times, modernisation has relied less on physical investments in plant, machinery and equipment, than on investments in people.

Second, in the 1970s and early 1980s, Irish physical capital investment was inflated by high levels of public capital spending. Much of this ostensible investment was economically inefficient, contributing little to either output or job growth. It has since been severely pruned.

In summary, the Irish economy, and its employment performance, has been transformed in two fundamental ways over the past decade. First, and most importantly, the economy's supply side has been strengthened, in part through lowering taxes, in part through direct public spending on education, training and infrastructure.

This approach informed the 1998 Budget stance, which addressed both elements. On the tax-cutting side, the standard rate of income tax was reduced from 26 to 24 per cent and the top rate from 48 to 46 per cent. Capital gains tax was halved, from 40 to 20 per cent. The standard rate of corporation tax was cut from 36 to 32 per cent, with the ultimate objective of establishing a uniform 12.5 per cent corporation tax rate. At the same time, the capital budget allowed for government investment of some £250 million in a new Educational Technology Investment Fund.

Second, price competitiveness was regained, through a combination of consistently low inflation, modest wage growth, productivity advances and sensible exchange rate management.[10]

The rest follows. Once a small, open economy operating in a free trade environment can produce the goods and services that people want to buy at lower prices than its competitors, then demand will take care of itself.

---

[10] A most useful discussion of the factors underpinning Ireland's long-run growth rate is provided in Leddin and Walsh (1997).

Chapter 3

UNEMPLOYMENT IN IRELAND

3.1. The Causes of Irish Unemployment[1]

The economic successes of the past decade have not extinguished unemployment. Despite the addition of a quarter of a million people to the national workforce over the 10 years since 1987, unemployment remains deeply embedded in the Irish labour market.

The persistence of high unemployment in the midst of plenty is illustrated in Table 3.1. As recently as 1993, 230,000 people classified themselves as unemployed. The very rapid expansion of employment in the interim still left 179,000 out of work by April 1997.

The numbers out of work, as shown in Table 3.1, represent those defining their principal economic status as "unemployed" in annual Labour Force Surveys undertaken by the Central Statistics Office. In other words, the unemployment levels shown are derived not by the application of objective criteria, but by self-assessment. The unemployment rate is calculated by taking the numbers unemployed as a percentage of the labour force. The labour force consists of the employed and the unemployed.

Traditionally, Ireland suppressed its unemployment problem at home by exporting its labour surplus to the rest of the world. For this reason, historic Irish unemployment rates were low. In the population censuses taken between 1926 and 1971, the unemployment rate ranged between 7.7 per cent of the labour force in 1936 and fell as low as 4.1 per cent in 1951.[2]

---

[1] The economics of unemployment are usefully and clearly explored in McAleese (1997), Chapter 14.

[2] Gillmor (1985), p. 28.

TABLE 3.1: TRENDS IN IRISH UNEMPLOYMENT, 1975–97 (IN '000S AT MID-APRIL EACH YEAR)

Year	Numbers Unemployed	Unemployment Rate (%)
1975	85	7.3
1980	91	7.3
1985	226	17.3
1990	176	13.4
1991	209	15.6
1992	217	15.9
1993	230	16.6
1994	219	15.6
1995	192	13.3
1996	191	12.8
1997	179	11.8

Sources: Labour Force Surveys 1975–1997, CSO. Unemployment as defined by "Principal Economic Status".

Very high rates of domestic unemployment in Ireland date only from the 1970s and heavy unemployment only became a persistent feature of the Irish labour market from the 1980s onwards.

As shown in Table 3.1, unemployment rose both very sharply and very quickly during the first half of the 1980s. The numbers out of work jumped from 91,000 in 1980 to 226,000 in 1985. The level of unemployment thus increased by almost 150 per cent in the space of five years.

Once unemployment had risen to such heights, it proved remarkably intractable, even as economic activity gathered pace after 1987. A decade of unprecedented growth and a quarter of a million additional jobs have caused a relatively small decline in the level of unemployment. By April 1997, there were still 179,000 people out of work, representing 11.8 per cent of the national labour force. In short, Ireland is still suffering the effects of the unemployment shocks of the 1980s.

The scale of the rise in unemployment during the first half of the 1980s was of such magnitude that it provoked widespread investigation. The first major study, by Newell and Symons,[3] attributed most of the blame for the rise in Irish unemployment to bad luck rather than bad management. Two-thirds of the observed increase in the Irish unemployment rate between 1979 and 1986 was explained by a combination of external economic shocks and demographic developments. Domestic economic policy-makers were thus largely let off the hook.

The reasons behind the rise in Irish unemployment, as seen by Newell and Symons, are summarised in Table 3.2.

TABLE 3.2: EXPLAINING THE CAUSES OF RISING UNEMPLOYMENT, 1979–86

Cause	Contribution to Unemployment Rate
1. *External Shocks*	
• Real interest rates	2.6 percentage points
• UK demand shock	1.7 percentage points
2. *Domestic Policies*	
• Change in the tax wedge	0.7 percentage points
• Replacement ratios	1.2 percentage points
3. *Demographic Trends*	
• Population increase	1.3 percentage points
• Rise in labour force participation rates	1.7 percentage points
Total of the above	9.0 percentage points
Actual Change in the Rate of Unemployment	11.2 percentage points
Other Factors	2.2 percentage points

Source: Durkan (1997), p. 1.

In the period 1979–86, Newell and Symons attributed just 1.9 percentage points of the 11.2 percentage point increase in the

---

[3] Discussed in Durkan (1997).

Irish unemployment rate to domestic policies. Two domestic policies in particular were identified as contributing to the steep rise in unemployment. First, a widening tax wedge — the gap separating employers' pay costs from the take-home pay of employees — was estimated to have added 0.7 percentage points to the unemployment rate between 1979 and 1986. Second, rising income replacement ratios — the proportion of net income from employment replaced by unemployment benefits — were calculated to have increased the unemployment rate by a further 1.2 percentage points.

Subsequent analyses adopted a less indulgent view of domestic policy-making and its role in raising unemployment during the early 1980s. In a particularly important study, Barry and Bradley[4] looked again at the evidence and found that the thrust of domestic policies was the single biggest contributor to the rise in the Irish unemployment rate for most of the 1980s. Their results are summarised in Table 3.3.

TABLE 3.3: DOMESTIC POLICIES RAISED UNEMPLOYMENT IN THE 1980S

Cause	Effect on Irish Unemployment Rate (%)		
	1970–80	1980–87	1970–87
1. External Shocks	+1.1	+3.2	+4.3
2. Domestic Policies	–2.5	+4.5	+2.0
3. Demographic Developments	+2.9	+0.7	+3.5
All Three Factors	+1.2	+8.4	+9.7
Overall Change in Unemployment Rate	+1.5	+10.4	+11.9

Source: Barry and Bradley (1991).

As indicated in Table 3.3, Barry and Bradley held domestic policies responsible for adding 4.5 percentage points to the unemployment rate between 1980 and 1987. This constituted a substantial slice of the actual increase of 10.4 percentage points

---

[4] Barry and Bradley (1991).

observed in the unemployment rate over this period. Subsequent research by Browne and McGettigan "came down in favour of internal policy factors as the main determinants of the rise in the unemployment rate, accounting for 4.5 percentage points of the increase".[5]

Thus, the weight of evidence strongly suggests that the actions of the domestic authorities, particularly in the spheres of income taxes and income transfers, added significantly to the very steep rise in unemployment seen during the first half of the 1980s.

This was borne out by studies of trends in average tax rates and of the widths of tax wedges. Thus, Tansey found that, for single people earning average manufacturing wages, the marginal tax rates they faced rose from 39.5 per cent in 1980/81 to 56.5 per cent five years later. Over the same five-year span, the tax wedge for such workers increased from 33.4 per cent to 42.0 per cent of employers' direct payroll costs. Between 1980 and 1985, the proportion of a married person's net average earnings from work replaced by cash unemployment payments increased from 47.2 per cent to 60.7 per cent.[6]

However, even this type of analysis may tend to understate the responsibility of the domestic authorities for the increase in unemployment. Commenting on the Barry-Bradley results, the former director of the ESRI, Dr Kieran Kennedy, has pointed out that such causal analyses typically take the economy's basic operating structures as given. As a result, changes in unemployment may be attributed to external shocks when, in reality, their origins may be traced to domestic inflexibilities:

> Consequently, when conditions abroad deteriorate, one must be cautious about ascribing any consequential rise in unemployment solely to external factors: one might equally say in a more fundamental sense that the real cause is the failure of domestic economic agents to adjust internal structures in response to changes in the external environment.[7]

---

[5] Durkan (1997), p. 2.

[6] Tansey (1991), Tables 13 and 22.

[7] Kennedy (1993), p. 25.

However, the thrust of domestic economic management changed fundamentally from 1987 onwards. This change in the policy regime resuscitated the economy. Gradually, as economic conditions improved, unemployment trended downwards, if not always smoothly.

TABLE 3.4: STANDARDISED UNEMPLOYMENT RATES IN OECD COUNTRIES, 1980–95

Country	1980	1985	1990	1995
Spain	11.1	21.1	15.9	22.7
Finland	4.6	5.0	3.4	17.1
Ireland	7.3**	17.0	13.3	12.2
Italy	7.5	9.6	10.3	12.2
France	6.2	10.2	8.9	11.6
Belgium	8.8	11.3	7.2	9.5
Sweden	2.0	3.0	1.8	9.2
Britain	6.4	11.2	6.9	8.7
Germany*	2.9	7.1	4.8	8.2
Portugal	8.0**	8.5	4.6	7.1
Netherlands	6.0	10.6	7.5	6.5
EU11	6.4	10.5	8.1	11.0
US	7.0	7.1	5.6	5.5
Japan	2.0	2.6	2.1	3.1
OECD	5.8	7.8	6.1	7.5

* West Germany only until 1993

** "Commonly Used Definitions of Unemployment"

Sources: "OECD Economic Outlook" No. 61, Paris, June 1997, extracted from Annex Tables 21 and 22.

The depth of Ireland's unemployment crisis through the 1980s and the gradual reductions in the unemployment rate effected during the 1990s can be traced in Table 3.4. In this table, unemployment rates are shown on an ILO basis, facilitating comparisons of Ireland's unemployment experience with that of other countries.

The standard international definition of unemployment, as formulated by the ILO, classes the unemployed as "those of working age who, in a specified period, are without work and are both available for, and have taken specific steps to find, work". This differs from the "Principal Economic Status" definition of unemployment shown earlier in Table 3.1. However, the trends in the unemployment rates revealed in both sets of figures are similar.

Table 3.4 reveals the disconcerting extent to which EU rates of unemployment have diverged over time from the rates of unemployment both in the United States and in the industrial world generally.

In 1980, the EU rate of unemployment stood below that prevailing in the United States and just half a percentage point above the jobless rate for the industrial world. However, by 1995, the unemployment rate in Europe was twice as high as that in the United States and almost half as high again as unemployment in the whole OECD area. In the course of the last two decades, the European Union has become one of the industrial world's unemployment blackspots. The principal cause of Europe's lagging unemployment performance is its dismal record in creating jobs, as shown earlier in Table 2.7.

As indicated in Table 3.4, Ireland's unemployment rate exceeded the EU average by less than one percentage point in 1980. By 1985, however, the Irish jobless rate was six and a half percentage points above a much higher average EU unemployment rate.

Over the past decade, the Irish and EU average rates of unemployment have converged, though again, at levels that are particularly high in an international context. As shown in Table 3.5, the Irish unemployment rate had declined to 10.3 per cent by April 1997, in the process falling below the EU average of 10.8 per cent for the first time since Ireland's accession to the EU in 1973. In early 1998, Ireland's unemployment rate dipped below 10 per cent, falling to 9.7 per cent in January.

TABLE 3.5: IRISH UNEMPLOYMENT AND UNEMPLOYMENT RATES (AT MID-APRIL FOR THE YEARS 1987–97, ILO BASIS)

Year	Unemployment ('000s)	Unemployment Rate (%)
1987	226.0	16.9
1988	217.0	16.3
1989	196.8	15.0
1990	172.4	12.9
1991	198.5	14.7
1992	206.6	15.1
1993	220.1	15.7
1994	211.0	14.7
1995	177.4	12.2
1996	179.0	11.9
1997	159.0	10.3

Source: Tabulations from annual Labour Force Surveys prepared by the Central Statistics Office, November 1997.

The decline in the Irish unemployment rate since 1993 has been significant. On an ILO basis, the numbers out of work fell by more than 61,000 between 1993 and 1997. This caused the unemployment rate to drop by more than five percentage points over the four-year period.

Not all of those who are out of work are seeking full-time employment. Of the 159,000 unemployed at April 1997, 136,600 were seeking full-time work while 22,400 were looking for part-time jobs. Amongst the unemployed, the numbers seeking part-time work has remained relatively unchanged over the past four years. As a result, the reduction in unemployment has been concentrated almost totally amongst those looking for full-time work. Unemployment amongst those searching for full-time employment has declined from 196,700 in 1993 to 136,600 in 1997.[8]

---

[8] *Labour Force Survey 1997*, op. cit., Table 28A.

The principal demographic characteristics of the unemployed at April 1997 are shown in Table 3.6.

Table 3.6 reveals that almost two out of every five people unemployed at April 1997 were women, a surprisingly high figure given the conventional wisdom that unemployment is predominantly a male preserve.

TABLE 3.6: THE DEMOGRAPHIC CHARACTERISTICS OF THE UNEMPLOYED

	Number Unemployed	**% Total**
Sex:		
• Male	97,000	61.0
• Female	62,000	39.0
• Total	159,000	100.0
Marital Status:		
• Single	84,300	53.0
• Married	63,300	39.8
• Separated*	9,300	5.9
• Widowed	2,000	1.3
• Total	159,000	100.0
Age:		
• 15–24 years	47,200	29.7%
• 25–44 years	77,400	48.7%
• 45 and over	34,400	21.6%
• Total	159,000	100.0%

* Including divorced. Figures may not add to totals due to rounding.
Source: Labour Force Survey 1997, CSO, October 1997, Tables 29, 38.

Of the unemployed, over half were single, almost two out of five were married and one in fourteen were either separated, divorced or widowed.

Unemployment in Ireland is concentrated amongst those aged between 25 and 44 years — that is, of prime working age. Just under 30 per cent of the unemployed are under 25 years of age, while one in five is aged 45 years or more.

However, the most salient feature of Irish unemployment is the high proportion of people who have suffered prolonged spells without work. The long-term unemployed (LTU) are usually classified as those who have been out of work for a year or more, but who are still actively seeking employment.

Table 3.7 shows the extent of long-term unemployment amongst members of the labour force for each of the years 1992 through 1997.

Those who are "marginally attached to the labour force" are shown separately in Table 3.7. These include "discouraged workers" who are available for employment but are not actively searching for work.

TABLE 3.7: LONG-TERM UNEMPLOYMENT IN IRELAND, 1992–97 ('000S; AT MID-APRIL EACH YEAR; ILO BASIS)

Category	1992	1993	1994	1995	1996	1997
Unemployed one year or less	85.1	88.6	76.4	68.1	71.8	67.1
Unemployed one year or more	116.5	125.4	128.2	103.3	103.3	86.3
Not stated	5.0	6.1	6.4	6.0	3.9	5.7
All Unemployed	206.6	220.1	211.0	177.4	179.0	159.0
LTU as % all Unemployed	56.4	57.0	60.8	58.2	57.7	54.3
LTU as % of Labour Force	8.5	8.9	9.0	7.1	6.9	5.6
Marginally Attached to Labour Force	29.4	32.2	29.7	27.5	20.2	25.2

Source: Labour Force Survey 1997, Tables 27A, 37.

As can be seen from Table 3.7, the numbers of long-term unemployed reached a recent peak at 128,200 in 1994. At that stage, three out of five of all those out of work had been unemployed for a year or more. The long-term unemployment rate — the long-term unemployed as a proportion of the labour force — stood at 9.0 per cent, higher than the total unemployment rate then prevailing in many EU countries.

Since 1994, there has been a dramatic decline in long-term unemployment, both in absolute and proportionate terms. The numbers out of work for a year or more fell from 128,200 in 1994 to 86,300 three years later. This represented a reduction of 41,900, or almost one-third, in the numbers unemployed for prolonged periods. The long-term rate of unemployment — the long-term unemployed as a proportion of the total labour force — declined from 9.0 per cent in 1994 to just 5.6 per cent by 1997.

Three factors appear to have contributed to this substantial fall in long-term unemployment.

First, the general improvement in labour market conditions created more employment opportunities. This reduced flows into unemployment and transfer rates from short- to long-term unemployment. Given that "escape probabilities" from long-term unemployment are relatively low, the rate of inflow into long-term unemployment has, in the past, been the principal determinant of its size.

Second, greater scrutiny of unemployment benefit claims resulted in many thousands leaving the Unemployment Live Register. It is probable that many of those "signing off" found jobs.

Third, the number of places on state-sponsored employment and training schemes specifically reserved for the long-term unemployed was increased significantly. The total numbers on such schemes have increased steadily through the 1990s. By April 1997, there were 41,000 people working on state-sponsored employment schemes. In addition, the Back to Work Allowance scheme in 1998 will provide job subsidies for a further 27,000 former long-term unemployed people in the open labour market.

While the decline in long-term unemployment since 1994 has been dramatic, the extent of the remaining problem should not be underestimated. In addition to those shown as long-term unemployed in Table 3.7, there were 25,200 people "marginally attached to the labour force" at April 1997. These included "discouraged workers", who, while available for employment, were not actively searching for work because they did not feel that they could secure jobs. The sum of the long-term unemployed and those marginally attached to the labour force amounted to 111,500 at April 1997. This represents a reduction of less than a quarter on the corresponding total of 145,900 five years earlier, before the employment boom began.

Thus, while useful inroads have been made into long-term unemployment in recent years, the problem of prolonged unemployment still remains far from being resolved, particularly when the extent of the "discouraged worker" phenomenon is recognised.

3.2. The Persistence of Unemployment

The causes of the very sharp rise in unemployment experienced by Ireland in the first half of the 1980s have been extensively analysed. As we have seen, domestic policymakers must shoulder a large part of the responsibility for the lengthening dole queues during those years.

But if domestic policymakers must carry much of the burden for initiating the unemployment crisis of the 1980s, equally they are entitled to share in the credit for the 1990s employment boom.

Through the 1980s, the foundations were laid for the expansive employment performance of the 1990s. Inflation was effectively squeezed out of the Irish economy. The public finances were corrected and interest rates declined. In consequence, credibility was restored to public policy, strengthening domestic business confidence and foreign investment inflows in the process.

The attractiveness of Ireland as a location for private sector investment was further enhanced by the continuing commitment to public spending on education and training. This has raised the quality and productivity of new entrants to the labour market.

Sensible pay strategies were introduced which traded tax cuts for moderate annual increases in money wages. This resulted in declining average personal tax rates and slimmer tax wedges. The price competitiveness of Irish output was strengthened by unilateral devaluations of the Irish pound in 1986 and 1993. Cash transfers from Europe speeded the pace of investment in the country's physical and human infrastructure. These factors, which together underpinned the employment boom, were largely shaped by the domestic authorities.

In short, Ireland may have been dealt a better hand in the 1990s than in previous decades, but the cards were also played to much better effect than in the past.

Yet, in view of the scale of job creation, unemployment has persisted at very high levels. At first glance, it is difficult to reconcile the scale of employment expansion with the persistence of such high unemployment.

As seen in Table 2.3, employment in Ireland increased by 269,000 or by almost one-quarter in the ten years after 1987. At the beginning of this period, the level of unemployment stood at 226,000. The question then arises: why has unemployment not been abolished? There are four potential explanations for the modest unemployment-reducing effects of rapidly rising employment levels during the 1990s.

First, in the Irish labour market, the supply of labour is elastic relative to labour demand. When the domestic demand for labour strengthens, this induces rapid increases in the size of the labour force, both through the reversal of migration flows and by increasing labour force participation rates. Put crudely, in the Irish labour market, demand creates its own supply.

Second, as shown in Table 3.7, the long-term unemployed comprise a large component of the total numbers out of work in Ireland. Many of the long-term unemployed have relatively little education and possess few skills. They are poorly prepared for re-entry to a jobs market which is placing an increasing emphasis on certified skills and formal educational qualifications. In effect, many of the long-term unemployed are structurally unemployed. Others are "discouraged workers", lacking the will to seek work, following repeated rejections by employers.

Third, a part of Irish unemployment may be explained by the weakness of work incentives, particularly on the lower rungs of the national pay ladder. Rational, profit-maximising individuals may believe that the returns from unemployment, in cash and in kind, surpass the after-tax rewards of work, particularly where it is low-paid. Continuous increases in the real value of untaxed primary and secondary unemployment benefits may have increased the demand for unemployment.

Finally, at least some official data on unemployment may overstate the numbers actually available for work at prevailing rates of pay. Such overstatements can arise because the official data are measuring something other than involuntary unemployment. Each of these potential explanations will be examined in turn.

3.2.1. Unemployment and Increases in the Labour Supply

Increases in employment will only be mirrored by equal decreases in unemployment if the numbers in the labour force remain unchanged. But the process of job growth itself calls forth increases in the labour supply. When jobs are readily available in Ireland, more people will tend to seek work at home. It is precisely the swiftness of labour supply growth over the past decade that has checked the extent of the fall in unemployment.

Hence, on an ILO basis, total employment increased by 269,000 over the decade 1987–97. Yet, over the same period, the level of unemployment fell by only 67,000. This apparent paradox is resolved by the realisation that the numbers in the labour force rose by 202,000 over the decade. This is shown in Table 3.8.

TABLE 3.8: LABOUR FORCE, EMPLOYMENT AND UNEMPLOYMENT, 1987–97 (AT MID-APRIL EACH YEAR IN '000S; ILO BASIS)

Year	(1) Labour Force	(2) Employed	Unemployed = (1) − (2)
1987	1,337	1,111	226
1988	1,328	1,111	217
1989	1,308	1,111	197
1990	1,332	1,160	172
1991	1,354	1,156	198
1992	1,372	1,165	207
1993	1,403	1,183	220
1994	1,432	1,221	211
1995	1,459	1,282	177
1996	1,508	1,329	179
1997	1,539	1,380	159

Source: Tabulations from the Labour Force Survey 1997, prepared by the Central Statistics Office, November 1997.

As indicated in Table 3.8, unemployment measures the excess domestic supply of labour. The level of unemployment at any point represents the difference between the supply of labour — those offering themselves for employment — and the demand for labour — the numbers employers are willing to hire at prevailing rates of pay. It follows that the level of unemployment will be determined not only by changes in the demand for labour — the numbers at work — but also by changes in the size of the labour force — the numbers looking for work.

Between 1987 and 1997, the labour force — those at work and those actively seeking employment — increased from 1.337 million to 1.539 million. This rise of 202,000 in the domestic labour supply represented an increase of 15.1 per cent in the course of the decade, or about 1.5 per cent on average each year.

However, as Table 3.8 shows, the pace of labour force growth was extremely uneven. The domestic labour supply actually contracted between 1987 and 1989 and there were still fewer people in the labour force in 1990 than there had been in 1987.

Employment remained static between 1987 and 1989, yet the numbers out of work declined by almost 30,000 over these years. This fall in unemployment was wholly attributable to the reduced size of the labour force. In turn, the fall in labour force numbers reflected very heavy net emigration. With opportunities scarce in the domestic market, job seekers moved abroad in search of work.

As employment growth picked up from 1990 onwards, so too did the speed of domestic labour force expansion. And the quicker employment expanded, the faster the labour force grew. In the two years to April 1997, labour force growth averaged 40,000 people a year, a dramatic reversal of the labour force contraction witnessed in the late 1980s.

Labour force growth outpaced the rate of increase in employment between 1990 and 1993. As a result, in spite of a creditable job creation performance in the early 1990s, the speed of labour force expansion caused unemployment to rise by almost 50,000, from 172,000 in 1990 to 220,000 by 1993.

Thus, the labour market generated apparently perverse results during the late 1980s and early 1990s. Between 1987 and 1989, years when employment was at a standstill, unemployment fell. Then, as employment at last picked up between 1990 and 1993, unemployment surged ahead, due to the swiftness of labour force expansion. It is only in the post-1993 period that annual gains in employment have again exceeded the growth in the labour supply, thereby causing continuous falls in the numbers out of work.

The erratic behaviour of the labour force over the past decade is attributable to two principal factors: volatile patterns of migration and changes in labour force participation rates, particularly pronounced in the case of women.

The principal underlying engine driving changes in the size of the domestic labour force is changes in the population of working age, those between 15 and 64 years.

The domestic population of working age is, in turn, determined by three factors. First, the birth rate 15 years earlier, since this determines potential gross inflows into the domestic population of working age. Second, current trends in migration, which add to, or subtract from, the size of the working-age population. Third, the age structure of the population, which determines exit rates through death and retirement from the population aged under 65 years. The age structure of Ireland's population is shaped by past demographic and migration trends.

The evolution of the national population, the youth population and the population of working age is shown in Table 3.9, which reveals that the national population has grown slowly over the past decade. The numbers in the country actually fell in the intercensal period 1986–1991 due to heavy net emigration in the late 1980s. While population growth resumed during the 1990s, the rate of increase over the whole period amounted to just 0.3 per cent annually.

However, within the total population, there have been marked compositional shifts. Ireland's population is growing older as we become the middle-aged Europeans. The number of children aged under 15 years was 179,000 lower in 1997 than it had been in 1986. This reflects the sharp deceleration in the birth rate after 1980. The birth rate peaked at 74,388 or 21.9 births per 1,000 of population in 1980. Thereafter, the decline was both precipitate and precipitous. By 1994, the number of live births had fallen to 47,929 or just 13.4 per 1,000 of population. In the very recent past, the birth rate has edged upwards and now again exceeds

50,000 annually. However, the current birth rate remains far removed from the experience of the late 1970s.

TABLE 3.9: IRELAND'S POPULATION OF WORKING AGE, 1986–97 (AT MID-APRIL EACH YEAR IN '000S)

Year	Population			Working Age as % Total Population
	Children (0–14)	*Working Age (15–64)*	*National*	
1986*	1,025	2,132	3,541	60.2
1987	1,014	2,144	3,547	60.4
1988	994	2,144	3,531	60.7
1989	974	2,139	3,510	60.9
1990	955	2,151	3,506	61.4
1991*	941	2,182	3,526	61.9
1992	931	2,218	3,555	62.4
1993	917	2,249	3,574	62.9
1994	899	2,279	3,586	63.6
1995	878	2,312	3,601	64.2
1996*	859	2,353	3,626	64.9
1997	846	2,399	3,661	65.5
Change % 1986–97	–17.5	+12.5	+3.4	

* Census Years.
Sources: Labour Force Surveys, 1993, 1996, 1997, Table 1, CSO.

But while the numbers under 15 years have declined, there has been a steady increase in the population of working age. The population aged between 15 and 64 years rose by more than a quarter of a million or 12.5 per cent between 1986 and 1997. Extensive net emigration acted as a brake on population growth through the late 1980s. However, from 1990 onwards, the working-age population grew very rapidly. Undiluted by emigration, this expansion effectively represented the coming of age of the baby boomers born during the late 1970s.

The patchy and uneven pattern of population change amongst those of working age is largely explained by fluctuations in migration. Migration trends are heavily influenced by the economic environment. When times are tough at home, when jobs are scarce and real disposable incomes are under pressure, domestic residents migrate in greater numbers to foreign labour markets offering better job prospects and higher incomes. Conversely, when domestic economic conditions improve, not only do a higher proportion of domestic residents remain at home, but both former emigrants and foreigners are attracted into the domestic labour market.

TABLE 3.10: EMIGRATION SWINGS AND IMMIGRATION ROUNDABOUTS, 1985–97 (IN '000S, YEARS TO MID-APRIL)

Year to April	Natural Increase	Emigration/ Immigration	Actual Increase	Population (Mid-April)
1985				3,540
1986	+28	−28	+1	3,541
1987	+29	−23	+6	3,547
1988	+26	−42	−16	3,531
1989	+23	−44	−21	3,510
1990	+19	−23	−4	3,506
1991	+22	−2	+20	3,526
1992	+22	+7	+29	3,555
1993	+19	0	+19	3,574
1994	+17	−5	+12	3,586
1995	+17	−2	+15	3,601
1996	+17	+8	+25	3,626
1997	+20	+15	+35	3,661
Change 1985–97	+259	−139	+121	+121

Note: Figures may not add to exact totals due to rounding.

Sources: Table derived from data in "Economic Review and Outlook 1997", Department of Finance, Summer 1997, Table 13; and "Population and Migration Estimates April 1997", CSO, October 1997, Tables 1 and 2.

Given relatively free movement of labour within Europe, and the virtual joint labour market which Ireland forms with Britain, migration is a major swing factor determining short-run changes in the rates of domestic population and labour force growth. The extent of its impact can be gauged from Table 3.10.

The "natural" increase in the population from year to year simply represents the excess of births over deaths. Between the mid-1980s and the mid-1990s, as shown in Table 3.10, the annual "natural" additions to the population became smaller, mirroring the decline in the birth rate.

Migration flows proved extremely volatile. Reflecting the weakness of the domestic labour market, both in terms of job opportunities and real disposable incomes, and the strength of labour demand in Britain, there was a major exodus from Ireland in the second half of the 1980s. Net emigration from Ireland between 1985 and 1990 amounted to 160,000 people, equivalent to 4.5 per cent of the 1985 population.

With heavy and persistent net emigration superimposed on a decelerating rate of "natural" population growth, the actual number of residents in the country fell by 15,000 between the censuses of 1986 and 1991.

About two-thirds of the gross outflow of emigrants from Ireland each year are aged between 15 and 24 years.[9] Thus, the exodus of the late 1980s not only caused the population to fall, but it stalled the growth in the population of working age. As seen in Table 3.9, the population of working age in Ireland was only 7,000 higher in 1989 than it had been in 1986.

The departure of young job seekers from the country during the late 1980s depressed domestic unemployment. Yet again in the late 1980s, emigration performed its traditional task. It acted as an economic and social safety valve, relieving pressure in the domestic labour market. In the absence of the heavy emigrant outflows in the late 1980s, the domestic unemployment crisis would have been substantially worse.

---

[9] The gross outflow of emigrants from Ireland numbered 196,600 between April 1991 and April 1996. Of these, 132,500 or 67.4 per cent were aged between 15 and 24 years. See "Population and Migration Estimates April 1997", CSO, October 1997, Table 3.

As labour market conditions improved in the first half of the 1990s, net emigration almost evaporated. In the five years to April 1995, total cumulative net emigration amounted to just 2,000 people.

With jobs increasingly plentiful in the domestic labour market as the 1990s progressed, most of the baby boomers born in the 1970s stayed at home rather than venturing abroad. This was reflected in very substantial growth amongst the population of working age. As shown in Table 3.9, the population aged between 15 and 64, which had increased by only 19,000 between 1986 and 1990, surged ahead by 161,000 in the succeeding five years.

After 1995, emigration was eclipsed by immigration. Over the two years 1995-97, net inflows into the country numbered 23,000 people. With substantial net immigration of 15,000 turbo-charging the rate of "natural" increase, the total population in the year to April 1997 recorded its largest annual rise since 1982.

In summary, heavy net emigration by jobseekers during the late 1980s and early 1990s, concentrated amongst the younger cohorts of working age, caused the domestic labour force to contract. As a result, unemployment fell in the period up to 1991, even though employment itself remained relatively static.

As domestic conditions improved through the 1990s, net emigration ceased, being replaced after 1995 by fairly substantial net immigration. As a result, the potential increase in the population of working age, dictated by the high birth rates of the 1970s, was channelled into the domestic labour market, where it swelled the labour supply. Very rapid growth in the labour force, powered in part by the expansion of the working-age population, caused unemployment to rise up to 1993, in spite of an improving job creation performance. Only when employment growth accelerated after 1993 did the numbers unemployed begin to fall.

Thus, the turnaround in migration trends, from heavy net emigration in the late 1980s to appreciable net immigration by the late 1990s, constitutes the first reason why unemployment has persisted at high levels, even in the face of unprecedented employment growth. The virtual elimination of net emigration in the first half of the 1990s channelled the underlying substantial growth in the population of working age into the domestic labour force, rather than diverting it abroad.

In other words, those born during the baby boom of the 1970s came of age in the 1990s. As they entered the working-age population, they chose to remain in Ireland in greater numbers. They decided to stay because the domestic labour market had become more attractive relative to foreign alternatives. Jobs at home were becoming plentiful and real incomes were rising. This swift expansion of the domestic working-age population caused the home labour force to increase at a rapid pace.

The domestic supply of labour increased sharply in response to rising labour demand. Put more formally, because of swings in migration, the domestic labour supply has proved highly elastic in response to changes in labour demand. Thus, many of the new jobs on offer were taken, not by the unemployed, but by new labour market entrants.

The underlying growth in the domestic population of working age, buttressed by the ending of net emigration, has been one of the two principal factors driving the rapid growth of the labour force through the 1990s.

The second factor has been a continuous increase in labour force participation rates, particularly amongst Irish women.

Not everyone of working age wants to join the labour force. Some may be engaged in home duties, others studying, yet others may have taken early retirement. In addition, many may not be able to participate in the labour force due to illness or disability.

Thus, only a proportion of the population aged between 15 and 64 years are active participants in the labour force. The labour force participation rate measures the proportion of the working-age population that is either in employment or is unemployed but actively seeking work. Table 3.11 shows, on a Principal Economic Status (PES) basis, how the labour force is derived from the population of working age for selected years since 1986.

It indicates that just over half the population aged 15 years and over are members of the labour force, a proportion that is low by international standards.

TABLE 3.11: DERIVING THE LABOUR FORCE FROM THE POPULATION OF WORKING AGE, 1986–97 (IN '000S AT MID-APRIL EACH YEAR)

Category	1986	1992	1996	1997
Population aged 15 and over	2,516	2,624	2,767	2,815
of which:				
• students	248	310	353	358
• on home duties	685	654	583	597
• retired	200	213	252	246
• ill/disabled	64	69	65	66
• other	11	16	25	30
Population over 15 outside labour force	1,208	1,262	1,278	1,298
Labour Force	1,308	1,362	1,488	1,517
Labour Force Participation Rate (%)	52.0	51.9	53.8	53.9

Note: Measured by "Principal Economic Status" (PES).
Sources: Labour Force Surveys 1988, 1993, 1997, CSO.

Between 1986 and 1997, the population aged 15 and over increased much faster than the national population. Whereas the total population advanced by only 120,000 over this period, the number of residents over 14 years rose by almost 300,000. This represented an increase of about one per cent a year between 1986 and 1997.

Amongst the population aged 15 and over, the numbers remaining outside the labour force increased by just 90,000. Thus, most of the growth in the working-age population percolated through to the labour market. In summary, two out of every three net entrants to the working-age population between 1986 and 1997 also joined the domestic labour force.

Changes in the numbers remaining outside the labour force mirror a number of countervailing developments. First, reflecting rising rates of participation in second- and third-level education, students staying on in school and college after the age of 15 increased by 110,000 to reach 358,000 by April 1997.

Second, the number of retired people also increased, rising by 46,000 to 246,000 in the eleven years to April 1997. This reflects both the ageing of the population and the trend towards earlier retirements.

These increases in the numbers remaining outside the labour market were counterbalanced by a decline in those engaged in home duties. A reduction of 88,000 in the numbers working in the home reflected increasing participation in the labour force amongst women. Those engaged on home duties are overwhelmingly women. Of the 597,200 people working in the home at April 1997, just 9,200 were men.

With the population aged 15 and over increasing by 299,000 between 1986 and 1997, and with the numbers of non-labour force participants in these age cohorts rising by just 90,000, the labour force increased by 209,000 between 1986 and 1997. As we have seen, the evolution of the labour force over the years since 1986 was extremely uneven. Nonetheless, over the period as a whole the labour force on a PES basis expanded by 16 per cent or just under 1.5 per cent per year.

The labour force thus expanded appreciably faster than the population aged over 14. This is explained by an increase in labour force participation rates. In effect, not only did the domestic working-age population increase, but also, a higher proportion of that population joined the labour market. As Table 3.11 shows, the proportion of the population aged 15 and over who were members of the labour force increased from 52.0 per cent in 1986 to 53.9 per cent by 1997.

These figures actually understate Irish labour force participation rates, since they embrace all of the population aged 15 and over rather than the working-age population aged 15 to 64 years.

In order to facilitate international comparisons, labour force participants are shown as a proportion of working-age populations for a range of countries in Table 3.12. Within the European Union, labour force participation rates are much higher in the northern Scandinavian countries than in the southern Mediterranean nations.

Ireland's labour force participation rate in 1995 was the fifth lowest in the European Union. With just 63.3 per cent of the working-age population signed up to the labour force, Ireland ranked ahead of only Spain, Italy, Greece and Luxembourg. The Irish labour force participation rate trailed the European Union average by over four percentage points and the UK participation rate by ten and a half percentage points.

Again, European labour force participation rates lag behind the average for the industrial world. Thus, participation in the labour force amongst the working-age population is ten percentage points higher in the United States and Japan than in the EU.

TABLE 3.12: LABOUR FORCE PARTICIPATION RATES COMPARED (LABOUR FORCE AS A PROPORTION OF THE POPULATION AGED BETWEEN 15 AND 64 YEARS; RANKED BY 1995 PERFORMANCE)

Country/Area	1983	1993	1995
Denmark	80.9	82.6	78.7
Sweden	81.3	77.6	77.0
Austria	69.3	73.7	75.4
Finland	77.4	73.9	73.9
United Kingdom	72.4	74.7	73.8
Germany	67.5	71.7	71.0
Portugal	71.4	71.2	70.8
Netherlands	59.0	67.5	68.8
France	66.4	66.7	67.3
Belgium	62.8	63.7	65.0
Ireland	62.7	62.4	63.3
Luxembourg	63.3	62.5	60.4
Greece	59.9	58.9	60.0
Italy	60.1	58.9	59.6
Spain	56.7	58.9	59.3
European Union	65.7	67.4	67.5
United States	73.2	76.8	77.8
Japan	73.0	76.1	76.5
Total OECD	69.5	70.9	71.4

Source: "OECD Employment Outlook 1996", OECD, July 1996, data extracted from Statistical Annex Table J.

Ireland's relatively low overall labour force participation rate is due principally to the low incidence of women who work. As a 1997 OECD study of the Irish economy noted:

> The low (labour force) participation rate in Ireland is primarily a result of the relatively small proportion of women who work. Despite increasing from 34 per cent in 1973 to 48 per cent in 1995, the female participation rate remains far below the OECD average.[10]

The low proportion of Irish women in the labour force relative to the average European experience should not be allowed to obscure the remarkable advances made by women in the Irish labour market over the past two decades. The compositional shifts that have resulted have utterly transformed the profile of the Irish labour market.

TABLE 3.13: LABOUR FORCE PARTICIPATION RATES BY SEX, 1973–93 (LABOUR FORCE PARTICIPANTS AS % WORKING-AGE POPULATION)

Country/Area	Men			Women		
	1973	1983	1993	1973	1983	1993
Ireland	92.3	87.1	78.6	34.1	37.8	46.1
Britain	93.0	87.5	84.0	53.2	57.2	65.3
EU15	88.5	82.0	78.3	44.5	49.5	56.5
USA	86.2	84.7	85.3	51.1	61.9	69.0
OECD	88.2	84.4	83.2	48.3	55.2	58.6

Source: "OECD Employment Outlook 1996", Annex Table K.

As shown in Table 3.13, the proportion of women of working age participating in the Irish labour force edged ahead from 34.1 per cent in 1973 to 37.8 per cent in 1983. Thereafter, Irish women moved into the labour market in ever-greater numbers. By 1993, 46.1 per cent of working-age women were either in employment or actively seeking work.

---

[10] "OECD Economic Surveys 1997 — Ireland", OECD, 1997, p. 69.

The results of the 1997 Labour Force Survey indicate that, of the 1.194 million women of working age, 594,000 were members of the labour force. Thus, almost half — 49.7 per cent — of all working-age Irish women were participating in the labour market by April 1997, with participation rates very much higher amongst those under 45. More than half a million women in Ireland now work outside the home, the women's workforce being estimated at 532,500 in 1997.[11]

The recent sharp increases in women's labour force participation rates have been facilitated by declining fertility rates and have been strongly associated with rising levels of educational attainment by women.

In sharp contrast, labour force participation by Irish men has been falling steadily since 1973, in line with the general European experience. The proportion of working-age men either in employment or actively looking for work has declined from 92.3 per cent in 1973 to 78.6 per cent in 1993. By 1997, labour force participation amongst working-age males had fallen further, to 75.6 per cent.

Twenty-five years ago, more than nine out of ten working-age males were engaged in the labour force while just one out of every three women participated in the labour market. These weightings have changed radically in the intervening years. By 1997, one in every two women of working age had joined the labour force, but only three out of every four working-age males were participating in the labour market.

The combined effects of rising labour force participation rates amongst women and declining rates amongst men have increased women's share of total employment. In 1971, women held only 26 per cent of all Irish jobs. By 1996, this proportion had increased to 38 per cent, and it rose further to 39 per cent in 1997. In short, two out of every five jobs in Ireland are now filled by women.

Historically, Ireland's relatively low labour force participation rate, together with its relatively high rate of unemployment, explained its low total employment ratio. Thus, in spite of the employment boom during the 1990s, less than three out of every five

---

[11] Labour force participation rates for 1997 have been calculated from Tables 1 and 28 of the 1997 Labour Force Survey.

Irish people aged between 15 and 64 were at work in 1997. This is shown in Table 3.14.

TABLE 3.14: IRELAND'S TOTAL EMPLOYMENT RATIO, 1992–97 (IN '000S; PROPORTION OF THOSE AGED BETWEEN 15 AND 64 AT WORK)

Category	1992	1995	1996	1997
Population 15–64 years	2,218	2,312	2,353	2,399
Labour Force 15–64 years	1,372	1,459	1,508	1,539
At Work	1,165	1,282	1,329	1,380
Labour Force Participation Rate*	61.9%	63.1%	64.1%	64.2%
Employment Ratio**	52.5%	55.4%	56.5%	57.5%

* Labour force as percentage of the working-age population;

** Total at work as percentage of working-age population.

Source: Labour Force Survey 1997, ILO basis, CSO, October 1997, Tables 1, 27A; Labour force and total at work measured on an ILO basis.

The employment ratio measures the proportion of the working-age population that is actually employed. Ireland's total employment ratio improved by five percentage points from 52.5 per cent in 1992 to 57.5 per cent in 1997. Nonetheless, it still lags behind the average for the European Union.

As Table 3.15 shows, in 1995, the proportion of the working-age population at work in Ireland, at 55.5 per cent, trailed behind the EU average by some five percentage points. More strikingly, the proportion of the working-age population at work in Ireland in 1995 was almost 15 percentage points below the employment ratio then obtaining in the United Kingdom.

In summary, jobs have been added to the Irish workforce at unprecedented rates during the 1990s. In turn, the sheer scale of the expansion in labour demand has induced an acceleration in labour supply growth. The swift pace of expansion in the labour force has been dictated by the ending of net emigration and its replacement by net immigration and by rising labour force participation rates, particularly amongst Irish women.

TABLE 3.15: EMPLOYMENT RATIOS IN THE EUROPEAN UNION, 1975–95 (TOTAL AT WORK AS % OF POPULATION AGED 15 TO 64 YEARS)

Country/Area	1975	1985	1995
Austria	66.7	67.3	70.8
Belgium	58.6	53.1	56.6
Denmark	73.6	76.0	75.6
Finland	71.6	74.6	61.7
France	69.0	62.0	60.6
Germany	65.2	63.1	63.6
Greece	57.5	57.3	56.4
Ireland	**59.4**	**51.9**	**55.5**
Italy	55.1	53.1	51.2
Luxembourg	67.4	64.4	77.2
Netherlands	61.3	57.5	64.0
Portugal	66.4	63.5	65.4
Spain	57.9	44.2	46.4
Sweden	78.7	81.2	72.1
UK	70.7	66.3	70.0
EU15	64.2	59.8	60.4

Source: "Employment Indicators in the European Union", pp. 147–162 in *Employment in Europe 1996*, European Commission, 1996.

In consequence, most of the employment gains registered during the 1990s have been absorbed by additions to the labour supply. As a result, the decline in unemployment has lagged far behind the increase in employment.

While the fall in unemployment has not come close to matching the increase in employment, the numbers out of work have declined significantly since 1993. These were years of tigerish output growth and antelope-like leaps in employment.

Through the 1990s, Ireland reaped rich employment rewards from the advances in national output. The era of "jobless growth" had been consigned to the past. But while the links between output expansion and employment growth had been strengthened immeasurably, what of the relationship between output growth and reductions in unemployment?

Okun's Law postulates a relationship between national output growth and reductions in unemployment.[12] In the United States, Okun's Law suggests that every three per cent increase in real GNP leads to a one percentage point fall in the rate of unemployment. More recently, the US version of Okun's law has been refined, indicating that each one per cent increase in the GNP growth rate above three per cent causes a 0.4 percentage point decline in the rate of unemployment.

The applicability of Okun's Law to Irish labour market conditions has been tested by Professor Brendan Walsh. Despite the disparities in the scale and nature of the US and Irish economies, Professor Walsh found that Okun's Law stood up remarkably well in Ireland for the period 1974–1996:

> The estimates . . . suggest that the growth rate of potential GNP is in the region of 4 per cent. Every percentage point of growth in excess of 4 per cent leads to a drop of about 0.6 per cent in the rate of unemployment. Annual growth in GNP in the region of 7 per cent, as was recorded over the period 1993–1996, implies an annual reduction in the unemployment rate of over 1.8 percentage points a year. Four more years of this growth . . . would bring the overall rate of unemployment down to about 5 per cent. . . . Under the changed conditions of the late 1990s, the labour market would surely have begun to overheat long before this.[13]

Macroeconomic projections for the Irish economy's performance to the year 2000 indicate that both economic growth and employment expansion will remain robust through the millennium. These projections are shown in Table 3.16.

Applying Walsh's estimates of the unemployment-reducing capacity of strong economic growth to the Department of Finance's GNP projections yields an unemployment rate just above 5 per cent by the year 2000.

---

[12] Leddin and Walsh (1990), p. 171.

[13] Walsh (1997), p. 10.

TABLE 3.16: IRISH ECONOMIC OUTLOOK, 1997–2000 (% VOLUME CHANGES ON PREVIOUS YEAR)

Category	1997	1998	1999	2000
Real GNP	7.7	7.0	5.7	4.9
Employment ('000s)	+52	+48	+41	+33
Unemployment Rate (%)	10.3*	8.1f	6.3f	5.3f

* Unemployment rate at April 1997 (ILO basis). The unemployment forecasts (f) are lagged nine months on the output performance and are the author's own.

Source: Budget 1998, December 3, 1997.

But why should the labour market begin to "overheat" well in advance of the unemployment rate completing its descent to 5 per cent? The existence of significant levels of "structural" unemployment in the Irish economy provides the first part of the explanation.

3.2.2. The Long-Term Unemployed and Structural Unemployment

Labour is not a homogenous, interchangeable factor of production. Labour shortages in one segment of the economy cannot immediately be relieved by surpluses in other sectors. A shortage of computer software specialists will not be alleviated by a surplus of agricultural labourers. Square pegs will not fit into round holes.

Structural unemployment arises in the labour market where the jobs offered by employers do not coincide with the skills possessed by the unemployed. There is thus a mismatch between the supply of and demand for labour. In the medium term, education and training policies can be utilised to achieve a better fit between the supply of and the demand for labour. However, in the short-term, such mismatches are virtually impossible to correct.

An important policy conclusion follows. Increases in the demand for computer software specialists will have no short-run impact on the level of unemployment amongst farm labourers. It will, however, drive up the wages of software specialists as employers compete against each other for this scarce resource. Generalising the result, increases in the demand for labour, no matter how strong, will have little or no effect on the level of structural unemployment in the short-run.

The tighter targeting of state employment schemes on the long-term unemployed, coupled with extensive job subsidies for the long-term unemployed in open labour markets, have reduced long-term unemployment significantly in recent years. Nonetheless, very large numbers of people have remained out of work for prolonged periods.

As shown in Table 3.7, more than half of those classified as unemployed on an ILO basis in April 1997 — 86,300 people — had been out of work for a year or more. So defined, the long-term unemployed constituted 5.6 per cent of the 1997 labour force. In addition, a further 25,200 people were "marginally attached to the labour force" at April 1997. These "discouraged workers" were available for employment, but not actively seeking work. Thus, in 1997, 111,500 people had been either out of work for more than a year or were unemployed and so discouraged by their previous failed attempts to find employment that they were no longer conducting active job searches.

The structural unemployment dimension can be seen by comparing the evolving demand for labour against the supply-side characteristics of the long-term unemployed.

The Irish workforce is becoming more educated, more skilled and more qualified over time. Increasingly, it is becoming a "white collar" workforce. As shown in Table 2.6, managers, professionals and associate professionals accounted for only 18.7 per cent of the Irish workforce in 1981. By 1995, their share of a much bigger employment total had risen to 24.9 per cent. Conversely, over the same period, farmers and labourers saw their combined share of total employment shrink from 21.9 per cent to just 14.7 per cent.

Yet as the profile of the employed workforce becomes more skilled, the defining characteristic of those who are long-term unemployed is their weak educational backgrounds. This is illustrated graphically in Table 3.17.

The employed are significantly better educated than the unemployed and much better educated than the long-term unemployed.

TABLE 3.17: EDUCATIONAL ATTAINMENT OF LABOUR FORCE IN 1994

Status	Highest Level of Formal Education Attained (%)				
	None	Junior Cert.	Leaving Cert.	Third Level	Total
At Work	18	25	33	25	100
Unemployed	28	36	26	10	100
of which:					
• Short-term	20	36	30	14	100
• Long-term	37	37	21	5	100

Note: Figures may not add to exact totals due to rounding.
Source: Labour Force Survey 1994, CSO.

As Table 3.17 shows, almost three-fifths of those in employment possess at least a Leaving Certificate. Amongst the long-term unemployed, more than one-third have no educational qualifications while three-quarters have not progressed past the Junior Certificate. Only one in twenty amongst the long-term unemployed has received a third-level education.

Nor is it solely a matter of educational qualifications serving as a "screening" device for employers. Amongst the poorly educated, literacy is, at best, basic. Within the working-age population, more than three-fifths of those who had left school without having completed the Junior Cycle of secondary education were ranked at the lowest level of literacy in 1995.[14]

Moreover, those at the lowest level of literacy rarely participate in adult education and training programmes. The International Adult Literacy Survey found in 1995 that in Ireland:

> Adults who had completed the Leaving Certificate programme were about four times more likely to be involved in adult education than people who had left school without

---

[14] *International Adult Literacy Survey: Results for Ireland*, Education Research Centre, St. Patrick's College Dublin, published by the Department of Education, September 1997, p. x.

having completed the junior cycle in a post-primary school.[15]

In the year preceding the 1995 literacy survey, only one-tenth of those ranked at the lowest literacy level participated in any form of education or training.

Thus, in terms of education, the long-term unemployed are particularly ill-prepared for the type of employment opportunities opening up in a dynamic economy. Education is becoming ever more important as a gateway to employment, and the long-term unemployed rarely possess the key. The growing importance of education as a determinant of subsequent labour market success has been noted in a recent ESRI study of poverty in Ireland:

> The distinguishing characteristic of those bearing most of the burden of unemployment was a low level of educational attainment: few (of the unemployed surveyed) had a second-level qualification, and over half did not have a Primary Certificate.

And:

> The risk of poverty in turn is about five times as high for someone with no qualifications as it is for someone with a Leaving Certificate. Education has become increasingly important over time in determining life chances, and the consequences of failing to acquire any educational qualification for successful participation in the labour market have become much more pronounced.[16]

This widening gap between the increasingly sophisticated demands of employment and the weak capacities of the long-term unemployed to meet these demands account, in large part, for the structural dimension in Irish unemployment. In such circumstances, increases in demand for many types of labour cannot be satisfied despite the continuing existence of a large labour surplus.

---

[15] *International Adult Literacy Survey*, p. xi.

[16] Nolan et al. (1994), pp. xi, xiii.

The long-term unemployed are thus finding themselves shut out of the labour market on two structural counts. In the first place, they do not possess the education, skills or qualifications to take up many of the new jobs created by an expanding economy. In the second place, many of the jobs traditionally filled by unskilled labour have been abolished by technological advances and organisational changes.

However, the problem of long-term unemployment requires a deeper explanation than structural and occupational shifts in the economy. At its essence, it is a social problem, caused by the progressive detachment of a segment of the community from the mainstream of national life.

The unemployment shocks of the 1970s and 1980s led to a very substantial increase in the numbers unemployed. The downturn in employment was not cyclical. When conditions improved, not all of those who had lost their jobs regained employment. Instead, over time, many drifted into long-term unemployment.

The rise in long-term unemployment in Ireland up to 1994 is explained primarily by increased inflows into the pool of long-term unemployed. Probabilities of escape from long-term unemployment are low, declining significantly with the duration of unemployment. As a recent OECD study of the Irish economy noted:

> the duration of unemployment has a strong effect on the probability of finding employment. While two-thirds of those unemployed for less than 12 months find a job within one year, a person out of work for more than two years has only a one-in-four chance of securing employment.[17]

Hysteresis theory shows that the links between the long-term unemployed and the labour market become progressively more tenuous over time for an array of social and economic reasons.[18]

---

[17] "OECD Economic Surveys 1997 — Ireland", p. 64. In spite of much more vigorous use of labour market measures targeted specifically at the long-term unemployed, probabilities of escape from long-term unemployment have remained disconcertingly low since 1994. See Honohan (ed.) (1997), p. 120.

[18] Lee (1991).

The National Economic and Social Forum in 1994 examined five such factors, to which long-term unemployment is usually ascribed internationally, and evaluated their importance in Irish conditions.[19] These were:

1. *Policy Factors:* These include the availability and duration of unemployment compensation and the extent to which labour market policies are "passive" (that is, income-supporting) rather than "active" (that is, employment driven). The NESF considered that the thrust of Irish policy was not so different from the general European experience that it could explain the divergence in long-term unemployment rates.

2. *The Changing Nature of Work:* While this has clearly made it more difficult for the long-term unemployed to re-enter the workforce, the NESF did not find that technological unemployment was more extensive in Ireland than elsewhere in Europe.

3. *Skill and Education Levels:* As has already been seen, the educational qualifications of those at work are significantly higher than those of the long-term unemployed.

4. *Barriers Facing the Long-term Unemployed:* These include a reluctance on the part of employers to recruit from amongst the long-term unemployed, the isolation of the long-term unemployed from market information about vacancies and training opportunities and, as the NESF noted,

> ... the interaction between the tax and social welfare systems, which may operate to "trap" people in long-term unemployment, especially those with larger families. . . . The concern here is that issues such as the fear of loss of secondary benefits and taxation treatment may create a disincentive for long-term unemployed people and/or their spouses to take up employment.[20]

---

[19] "Ending Long-term Unemployment", National Economic and Social Forum, Report No. 4, June 1994, Section II.

[20] NESF Report No. 4, 1994, p. 23.

5. *Persistence Factors:* The longer people are unemployed, the more likely they are to remain unemployed. The NESF found that for males aged 45 to 54 who have been out of work for two years, the probability of them remaining unemployed one year later is 90 per cent. The persistence of unemployment may be influenced, on the one hand, by the depreciation of skills and work habits and, on the other, by discouragement and diminished motivation in searching for employment.

Many of these factors are mutually reinforcing over time, creating a subculture of social and economic exclusion. This process has been well described by Frank Barry and Aoife Hannan in a paper to the Dublin Economics Workshop:

> ... we are concerned with a more profound form of hysteresis, and one that has attracted less attention from economists; by this we mean the likelihood that today's early school-leavers contain disproportionate numbers of the children of those who are currently long-term unemployed, and that these will become the long-term unemployed of the future. ... To state our argument bluntly: "if you are poorly qualified, you tend to be poor, and, if poor, your children tend to receive poor qualifications".[21]

This view is corroborated by the National Economic and Social Forum's report, "Early School-leavers and Youth Unemployment":

> 55 per cent of early [school] leavers come from families where fathers are unemployed, compared to less than 20 per cent in the total cohort. Most of the unemployed, of course, are working class so that the combined percentage of early leavers who are either [from] working class or unemployed [backgrounds] comes to ... 88 per cent.[22]

The existence of such sealed enclaves of poverty and deprivation in the midst of unparalleled prosperity is offensive. It is also economically inefficient, as it represents an absolute waste of un-

---

[21] Barry and Hannan (1997), p. 2.

[22] "Early School Leavers and Youth Unemployment", National Economic and Social Forum, Forum Report No. 11, January 1997, p. 28.

tapped human resources in an economy that is showing signs of labour scarcity. Necessarily, this waste of human resources through social and economic exclusion will cause the national labour market to overheat, even where labour appears nominally abundant.

3.2.3. Unemployment and Work Incentives

Not all of the new jobs coming on stream in the economy demand sophisticated skills or the possession of advanced qualifications. A host of new employment opportunities are appearing in unskilled and semi-skilled occupations. Yet, in spite of the scale of unemployment, many of these vacancies are being left unfilled.

In October 1996, FÁS, the national training authority, in conjunction with Irish Marketing Surveys, reviewed the level of vacancies in 1,000 Irish firms employing 306,000 people. Some 36 per cent of those enterprises surveyed reported that they had some unfilled vacancies at the survey date. Of those who reported vacancies, 90 per cent classified them as "difficult to fill".[23]

Moreover, the vacancies were not concentrated only in rapidly expanding high technology sectors, but were widely dispersed across the economy. In terms of the ratio of current vacancies to existing employment levels, labour shortages were more pronounced in services than in manufacturing industry.

As shown in Table 3.18, the overall vacancies-to-employment ratio at October 1996 was 2 per cent. Vacancies were highest in transport and communications, at 4.6 per cent of existing employment, and in business services (3.2 per cent).

Nor were shortages concentrated exclusively in high-skill occupations. In those sectors where vacancies were particularly difficult to fill, the survey identified labour shortages in the following occupations: cleaners, general operatives, machine operatives, packers and assemblers, drivers, truck and forklift drivers, programmers, team leaders, technicians, computer controllers, surveyors, technical staff, software and finance professionals and general engineers.

---

[23] "Survey of Current Vacancies in Selected Sectors of the Irish Economy" FÁS/IMS, August 1997, pp. 2–3.

TABLE 3.18: RATIO OF VACANCIES TO EMPLOYMENT, OCTOBER 1996

Sector/Segment	Vacancy/Employment Ratio (%)
Engineering	2.2
Food, drink, tobacco	2.5
Printing/paper	1.9
Textiles/clothing/footwear	0.9
Chemicals	1.5
All manufacturing	2.0
Business services	3.2
Wholesaling	2.3
Finance/insurance	1.1
Transport/communications	4.6
Construction	1.6
Garages/filling stations	2.3
All services	2.1
Total for all sectors covered	2.0

Source: "Survey of Current Vacancies in Selected Sectors of the Irish Economy, October 1996", FÁS/IMS, August 1997.

Thus, even towards the end of 1996, the Irish labour market was characterised not simply by specific labour shortages in high-skill occupations, but by the beginnings of a general scarcity of labour.

Given the scale of subsequent employment growth — 51,000 were added to the numbers at work in the year to April 1997 and the demand for labour remained buoyant thereafter — it is likely that the number of vacancies has increased and that existing vacancies have become more difficult to fill in the period subsequent to the FÁS/IMS survey. More recent indications suggest that the vacancy rate climbed towards 5 per cent in late 1997.

Many of the vacancies that were difficult to fill were suitable for unskilled or semi-skilled labour. Thus, such vacancies cannot be attributed to mismatches between the supply and demand for labour. This suggests that such jobs were left vacant because there was little economic incentive for the unemployed to take them up.

The existence of perceived "unemployment traps", where those out of work believe that they would be financially worse off on returning to employment, help to explain why many vacancies for relatively unskilled labour remain unfilled. The strengths and weaknesses of work incentives will be investigated in considerable detail in later chapters.

Thus far, three potential reasons have been advanced to explain why the very rapid growth in employment during the 1990s has produced a relatively small reduction in unemployment.

First, the labour supply has expanded swiftly in response to the growth in the demand for labour. In the absence of further rapid growth in net immigration, the pace of labour force expansion will decelerate in the early years of the next century. This deceleration will be driven by demographic factors; the fall in the birth rate after 1980 will cause a steep decline in the numbers of domestic new entrants to the labour force in the decade from 2000 onwards.

Second, unemployment has remained relatively high because a large proportion of those out of work do not possess the education or skills required to win jobs in an increasingly "white collar" economy. The alleviation of such structural unemployment requires education and training interventions targeted particularly at early school-leavers and the long-term unemployed.

Third, a further slice of unemployment may result from work incentives that are too weak, particularly on the lower rungs of the pay ladder. A combination of wage subsidies, direct tax cuts and the retention of social welfare benefits following a return to employment offer the best prospects of strengthening work incentives. Tax cuts alone will not suffice; their value to the long-term unemployed returning to low-paid work is minimal at this stage.

If Ireland is to resolve its labour market paradox, whereby increasing labour scarcity is coexisting contentedly with continuing high unemployment, two related steps need to be taken:

1. State education and training efforts, targeted on those who have slipped through the system, must be reinforced. In particular, strenuous efforts are required to improve basic literacy

and numeracy amongst those in the working-age population who left school early;

2. Work incentives must be strengthened, particularly for those entering low-paid employment. However, it is not sufficient only to improve the after-tax returns to working in low-paid employment. It is also necessary to make it patently and transparently clear that work pays.

The final potential explanation for the height of unemployment lies in the statistical domain. To date in this text, unemployment has been measured exclusively using annual Labour Force Survey estimates. But there is another set of statistics that is widely used and popularly presented as an indicator of unemployment: Live Register Unemployment. The final segment of this chapter assesses whether Live Register Unemployment is an accurate guide to the numbers out of work in Ireland.

3.2.4. The Measurement of Unemployment

Analytically, the unemployed consist only of those who cannot find employment after an active job search. In other words, they are involuntarily unemployed — out of work against their will. Since they are seeking work at existing rates of pay, the involuntarily unemployed are a part of the labour force. Those who are voluntarily unemployed — unwilling to accept jobs at existing wage rates or unavailable for work — are not regarded as part of the labour force.

While the analytical definition of unemployment is relatively straightforward, measuring unemployment with any degree of accuracy is very difficult. Two principal measures of unemployment are used in Ireland:

1. Unemployment as measured by annual Labour Force Surveys conducted by the Central Statistics Office. These surveys were introduced in 1975 and are based on a sample of some 4 per cent of all households in the state. Their principal strength derives from the fact that respondents themselves define their "Principal Economic Status". As a result, the estimates for unemployment they provide are based on respondents' own views of their position in the labour market. The annual LFS also

contains a more objective assessment of labour market status, obtained by asking respondents about their labour market activity in the week preceding the survey. This ILO method also provides data which allows comparisons to be drawn with other countries.

The weaknesses of the Labour Force Survey approach are twofold. First, the unemployment estimates they generate are based on samples. As with all such exercises, they are subject to sampling error. Second, to date, the surveys have been undertaken only once a year. As a result, they have provided relatively few observations of the level of unemployment and have been unable to account for seasonal variations in either employment or unemployment. This shortcoming is being rectified during 1998 through the publication of Labour Force Surveys on a quarterly rather than an annual basis.

2. Live Register Unemployment is the second, and older, measure of the numbers out of work in Ireland. In essence, Live Register Unemployment is an enumeration of those in receipt of state unemployment benefits in cash or in kind. As a result, it measures those "signing on" the Live Register rather than constituting an estimate of those who are unemployed, actively seeking, and available for, employment. Live Register Unemployment possesses two strengths. First, its coverage is high, since it is an enumeration of all those collecting unemployment benefits in cash and those signing on in order to retain eligibility for secondary benefits. Second, data is collected regularly and published monthly throughout the year. However, the strengths of the Live Register as a measure of unemployment are overshadowed by its weaknesses. The principal weakness of the Live Register as an indicator of unemployment lies in the fact that it is measuring something else — the number of claimants.

As the *Statistical Bulletin* for March 1996 put it:

> The Labour Force Survey is the definitive annual measure of employment and unemployment. . . . The primary use of the Live Register series, in terms of measuring unemploy-

ment, is as a short-term trend indicator. The Live Register is essentially a count of claimants falling within the scope of certain Department of Social Welfare schemes. . . . Changes in the administrative rules governing these schemes will have an impact on the Live Register.[24]

Over the years, the gap between unemployment as measured by Labour Force Surveys and by Live Register Unemployment has grown progressively wider. This is shown in Table 3.19.

TABLE 3.19: LABOUR FORCE SURVEY UNEMPLOYMENT AND LIVE REGISTER UNEMPLOYMENT COMPARED

Year	Labour Force Survey Unemployment ('000s)	Live Register Unemployment ('000s)	Variance* (%)
1987	232	247	6.5
1988	218	241	10.6
1989	201	232	15.4
1990	176	225	27.8
1991	209	254	21.5
1992	217	283	30.4
1993	230	294	27.8
1994	219	282	28.8
1995	192	278	44.8
1996	191	279	46.1

* Calculated as (LRU – LFS U)/LFS U

Sources: Labour Force Surveys, 1990–1997, CSO; Live Register Unemployment, CSO. Results have been rounded.

As can be seen from Table 3.19, unemployment on a Live Register basis exceeded the Labour Force Survey measure of unemployment by 15,000 in 1987. By 1996, this gap had widened to 88,000.

In 1996, the Central Statistics Office conducted an investigation, seeking to ascertain the reasons for the widening gap between both measures of unemployment. A sample of 2,672 people on the Live Register at April 1996 was selected and was asked to

---

[24] "Live Register Coverage and Analysis", *Statistical Bulletin*, Volume LXXI, No. 1, March 1996, p. 156.

complete the Labour Force Survey. The sample was weighted towards the short-term unemployed. Some 2,414 usable responses were collected. However, of these, 679 were not listed as usual residents at the addresses they had given and were therefore excluded. A further 161 were found to have left the Live Register while 78 fell into categories not included in the Live Register count, including those on systematic short-time working. This provided a sample of 1,496 as a basis for further analysis. The results are shown in Table 3.20.

TABLE 3.20: LABOUR FORCE SURVEY RESPONSES BY A SAMPLE OF 1,496 PERSONS ON THE LIVE REGISTER AT APRIL 1996

Category*	Sample Persons	Results (%)	Weighted Persons	Results (%)
Employed full-time	220	14.7	167	11.4
Employed part-time	162	10.8	146	10.0
Unemployed	664	44.4	724	49.5
Marginally attached to the labour force	64	4.3	66	4.5
Not economically active/others	386	25.8	359	24.6
Totals	1,496	100.0	1,462**	100.0

* International Labour Office Economic Activity Status.

** Sample reweighted to reflect Live Register composition and adjusted for a small level of outflows (34).

Source: "Unemployment Statistics: Study of the Differences between the Labour Force Survey (LFS) Estimates of Unemployment and the Live Register", CSO, September 1996, derived from Tables 1 and 2.

The raw sample results make illuminating reading. Over a quarter of the Live Register respondents were in full- or part-time employment, a quarter were not economically active and well under half described themselves as unemployed.

As noted earlier, the raw sample was biased towards the short-term unemployed. The sample was then re-weighted to reflect the profile of all those on the Live Register. On this more telling basis, 11.4 per cent of those on the Live Register revealed they were in full-time employment and about three-quarters of these indicated that their employment was permanent. A further 10 per cent said that they were working part-time and the majority of these respondents indicated that they were not under-employed. Almost 25 per cent of the adjusted sample respondents were not economically active and three-quarters of these were neither looking for, nor wanted, work.

Most tellingly of all, the re-weighted sample shows, using internationally accepted definitions, that less than half of the Live Register respondents classified themselves as unemployed.

The study found that "many persons who are not statistically classified as unemployed in the Labour Force Survey are included in the monthly Live Register total". The CSO therefore concluded that "the most consistent measures of unemployment are those derived from the Labour Force Survey".

Ireland is not the only country where the numbers registered for state unemployment benefits exceed the level of unemployment reported in labour force surveys. Benefit recipients also exceeded the numbers out of work on a labour force survey basis in Belgium, New Zealand, the Netherlands, Sweden, Finland and Australia. However, the OECD found that "the gap was significantly higher in Ireland than in other OECD countries".[25]

Unemployment benefit recipients as a percentage of Labour Force Survey unemployment are shown for 18 OECD countries in Table 3.21. As can be seen, those in receipt of unemployment benefits in Ireland in 1995 amounted to 149 per cent of the numbers out of work as measured by that year's Labour Force Survey. The Irish ratio was the highest of the 18 OECD countries surveyed and was over half as high again as the unweighted OECD average for those countries.

Two conclusions can be drawn from the CSO's exercise. First, the numbers out of work are overstated by Live Register Unemployment. For this reason, the numbers out of work are not as high as many believe. Second, even though Live Register Unemployment is an inaccurate guide to the numbers seeking work, a very large number of Irish people remain unemployed. On a La-

---

[25] "OECD Economic Surveys 1997 — Ireland", OECD, 1997, p. 68.

bour Force Survey (PES) basis, total unemployment still stood at 179,000 at April 1997.

TABLE 3.21: UNEMPLOYMENT BENEFIT RECIPIENTS* AS A PERCENTAGE OF LABOUR FORCE UNEMPLOYMENT FOR 18 OECD COUNTRIES IN 1990 AND 1995

Country	1995	1990
Ireland	149	124
Belgium	138	126
New Zealand	127	112
Netherlands	125	124
Sweden	109	102
Finland	108	101
Australia	101	82
Denmark	100	100
Norway	94	81
United Kingdom	94	73
Austria	90	89
Germany	87	67
France	76	87
Switzerland	71	99
Spain	40	54
Japan	39	36
United States	36	33
Greece	36	30
Unweighted average	89	85

* Includes those on unemployment benefit and assistance and on guaranteed incomes.

Source: "OECD Economic Surveys 1997 — Ireland", OECD, 1997, Table 25.

Chapter 4

THE QUALITY OF THE IRISH LABOUR FORCE

4.1. Human Capital and Economic Development

Education and training are vital forces in creating and sustaining international competitive advantage. As Michael Porter concluded in his sweeping international survey of competitive advantage:

> there is little doubt from our research that education and training are decisive in national competitive advantage. The nations that invest most heavily in education had advantages in many industries that could be traced in part to human resources. What is even more telling is that in every nation, those industries that were most competitive were often those where specialised investment in education and training had been unusually great.[1]

This chapter examines the myriad ways in which education and training influence the pace of economic progress. It then surveys recent Irish education and training policies and performance.

Every economy is governed by a production function. A production function is the mechanism by which inputs of the factors of production — land, labour, capital — are converted into outputs.

Economic growth measures the increases in outputs of goods and services recorded by an economy. In any economy, extra output can be achieved by increasing the amount of inputs, by raising the quality of those inputs or by combining factor inputs more efficiently. In the real world, economic growth is usually the result of some mix of all three.

---

[1] Porter (1990), p. 628.

Economic growth is not determined by economic variables alone. The process of economic development is extremely complex. In addition to economic variables, the pace of progress is necessarily shaped by an array of political, social, institutional and legal factors. No economy can operate independently of the values and the system of which it is a part. This important caveat is implicit in any discussions of the growth process.

Early post-war neo-classical growth models focused particularly on the importance of investment in physical capital — buildings and machinery, plant and equipment — as the motive force in the economic growth process.

In brutally simplified form, these models saw increased investment in physical capital as the surest route to faster economic growth. They recommended increased national savings to finance quicker physical capital formation. Once the extra investments were efficient, faster growth would follow. Technical change was not an integral part of most such models. It was treated either as zero or as exogenously determined. Labour did not merit much of a showing either. It was usually treated as a homogenous and undifferentiated input into the productive process.

In summary, these early post-war neo-classical growth models accorded primacy of place to physical capital formation in raising the rate of economic growth.

However, from the 1960s onwards, greater attention was directed to human capital as a driving force in the growth process.

Learning and knowledge are highly prized in all societies. Their cultivation is the hallmark of civilisation itself. While knowledge is highly valued in its own right, it also possesses an economic dimension. Knowledge, applied in the economic domain, is the wellspring of innovation, of technical advance and, ultimately, of enhanced productivity.

Human capital is the stock of economically relevant knowledge, skills and learning embodied in a population. Investments in education, training and knowledge add to the national stock of human capital. As with physical capital, investments in human capital are undertaken in the expectation of a positive financial rate of return.

Private investments in schooling (including earnings foregone while studying) are made with a view to securing higher subsequent earnings. Employers invest in training where higher profits are in prospect. While the primary rationale for state investment in education and training lies outside the economic arena, the higher levels of employment and earnings generated by such investments raise the future stream of tax revenues flowing into the Exchequer.

The greater prominence accorded to human capital from the 1960s stemmed from two sources. First, research clearly showed that education paid in personal terms. The longer the span of education an individual enjoyed, the higher were subsequent earnings. Moreover, what held for the individual held also for society in general. Thus, the OECD wrote in 1995:

> Human capital — the value of incomes that stem from education, training and other investments in human development — is an important element enabling countries to move from a low to a high level of income.[2]

Recognition of human capital's contribution to the growth rate provided an economic rationale for the sustained expansion of publicly funded education throughout the industrial world, which dated from the 1960s onwards. Ireland was not immune to these trends, introducing limited grants for third-level students and free secondary education during the decade.

Second, "growth accounting" models sought to trace the forces driving economic growth by relating outputs to previously identified inputs of the factors of production. These models produced unexpected results. Typically, less than half of long-run growth in the leading industrial countries could be assigned to identified factors of production. In other words, identifiable increases in factor inputs could be held responsible for only half the growth in output. There was a ghost in the economic machine.

The residual, unexplained part of economic growth was assigned to "total factor productivity". Some saw this merely as a measure of ignorance, of what could not be explained or quanti-

---

[2] "OECD Economic Surveys 1995 — Ireland", OECD, June 1995, p. 56.

fied. Others, more numerous, attributed it to the fruits of technological advances based on increases in learning and knowledge.

For the latter, technical change then became a positive, and endogenously determined, contributor to the growth process. But technology does not advance in a vacuum. Technical change is decisively influenced by the current state of knowledge and by the skills and capacities of the workforce.

There are "push" and "pull" relationships between training, education and economic growth. On the one hand, technical advances can be seen as the results both of increased investment in physical capital per worker and of learning from experience as embodied in successively more productive vintages of capital equipment. Further, the current state of applied knowledge determines the capacity for economic innovation, whether in microbiology or marketing. But the current state of knowledge itself derives from the extensiveness of education and research. Thus, the fruits of training and education are pushing forward the frontiers of technical change and, hence, the potential for growth.

At the same time, technological advances increase the complexity of the techniques of production. In turn, more sophisticated products and processes require more highly skilled and trained workers to operate them. Thus, technical changes "pull" upwards the skills and knowledge required of the workforce.

Productivity-yielding advances are not, however, limited to the domain of science and technology. Additions to knowledge in management, organisation, finance and social psychology can each generate greater efficiencies in production.

Thus, investments in education and training that add to the stock of human capital make a twofold contribution to the process of economic growth.

First, improvements in the quality of labour, usually proxied by secondary school enrolment rates or by participation rates in third-level education, raise the productivity of labour directly. The better-trained and better-educated can undertake more complex tasks and complete them more efficiently than those with less education and training.

Moreover, the higher the quality of labour, the more flexible and adaptive it is likely to be. Hence, a high quality labour force facilitates the introduction of new product and process technologies. Enhancing the quality of labour will thus stimulate investments in the physical capital stock. The national education and training system can thus act as a fulcrum for levering the economy from a low skill, low productivity equilibrium to a high skill, high productivity plane.

As Layard, Mayhew and Owen put it in discussing Britain's training deficit:

> Differences in training matter. In a series of brilliant case studies, S.J. Prais and his colleagues have shown clearly how higher skill levels on the continent make possible quite different systems of work, involving much greater productivity. They make it possible to get a proper economic return from investing in more sophisticated capital equipment.[3]

Second, and much more difficult to ascertain, is the indirect impact which a deeper national reservoir of knowledge has on spurring national efficiency, creativity and innovation.

Much recent research stresses the positive "spillovers" or external effects of investments in human capital. Highly trained or educated individuals are likely to raise their marginal productivity when working with those possessing similarly elevated skills.[4]

These positive spillovers suggest that investments in education and training can generate increasing returns on physical capital and quicken the pace of economic growth.

The Nobel prizewinner Kenneth Arrow, who has written extensively on technical change, has recently restated the critical importance of knowledge in the process of economic development:

> Many, though not all, scholars would explain most of economic growth over time, or differences among economic performance among countries at a given moment of time, as attributable to variations in technological knowledge, knowledge of how to produce goods.[5]

---

[3] Layard, Mayhew and Owen (1994), p. 12.

[4] Hitchens and Bernie in NESC Report No. 95 (1993), especially pp. 48–49.

[5] Arrow (1997), p. 6.

Over the past decade, empirical studies have identified three common factors as explaining most of the long-run differences in productivity and economic growth rates between countries. These three factors are: high rates of physical capital formation; extensive investments in human capital; and convergence effects, the tendency for lagging countries to catch up on industrial leaders.[6]

Thus, the OECD's 1995 report on the Irish economy noted:

> Overall, there seems to be a strong correlation within the OECD area between the growth of human capital and the rate of growth of both labour and total factor productivity. If the growth of human capital is incorporated into a standard production function, this correlation is apparent, and is indeed strengthened when allowance is made for the process whereby the technology of the leading country is gradually diffused across those that are catching up, so confirming the general importance of education to economic growth.[7]

In its 1995 study, the OECD found that the growth in the Irish human capital stock — as proxied by the increase in the ratio of secondary school enrolments to the working age population — had contributed 0.8 percentage points to the annual rate of economic growth in Ireland over the period 1960 through 1985.[8]

Over the 25 years 1970–95, Ireland's average growth in per capita incomes has exceeded the average for 19 OECD countries by almost 1.2 percentage points per year. Table 4.1 seeks to explain this positive growth differential in a growth accounting context.

---

[6] See Englander and Gurney (1994).

[7] "OECD Economic Surveys 1995 — Ireland", p. 58.

[8] The OECD goes on to note that, between 1960 and 1985, growth in Irish total factor productivity (TFP), was particularly high "with the contribution of TFP to the growth performance reaching more than 70 per cent, significantly above the OECD average". An alternative explanation suggests that much of the apparent output growth in Ireland reflects the effects of MNC transfer pricing. See Murphy (1998).

TABLE 4.1: SOURCES OF IRELAND'S DIFFERENTIAL GROWTH, 1970–95 (PERCENTAGE POINTS, ANNUAL AVERAGES)

	1970–85	1985–95	1970–95
Actual differential over OECD average growth rate	0.39	2.34	1.17
explained by:			
Labour market performance	–0.54	0.31	–0.20
Convergence factors	1.83	0.61	1.34
Physical capital accumulation	–0.05	–0.10	–0.07
Human capital accumulation	–0.04	0.36	0.12
Investment in R&D	–0.20	–0.16	–0.18
Government size	–0.07	0.72	0.25
Error	–0.54	0.61	–0.08

Source: Adapted from de la Fuente and Vives (1997), Table 1, p. 122.

Column 3 in Table 4.1 shows that over the quarter-century to 1995, the growth in Irish per capita incomes outpaced the OECD average by 1.17 percentage points per year. Convergence effects — the tendency for lagging countries to catch up with industrial leaders due to technology diffusion and decreasing returns to scale — predominate in explaining Ireland's comparative advantage in generating economic growth. The only other positive contributors to the growth differential were found to be investment in human resources and the impact of reduced government size on national productivity.

Since this period coincides with Ireland's entry to the European Union and the consequent opening up of the economy, there may be a tendency to explain Ireland's above-average expansion as the natural growth spurt of a late developer.

But this is not the whole story. De la Fuente and Vives ran their model for a composite Spain/Portugal, also latecomers to development. Throughout the 25 years, they found that

> The pattern is qualitatively similar in the case of Spain and Portugal, but with some differences which help to account for the 0.84 per cent (annual average) differential in Ireland's favour. In particular, relatively high rates of invest-

ment in education and R&D and a lower rate of growth in the share of government expenditures contributed around a third of a point each to this differential.[9]

Column 1 of Table 4.1 shows that Ireland's growth rate in the period 1970 through 1985 outperformed the OECD average by almost 0.4 percentage points a year — a solid, if unspectacular performance.

However, in the ensuing decade, 1985–95, Ireland sprinted away from its competitors. Over this period, shown as column 2 in Table 4.1, the annual average growth rate was 2.34 percentage points ahead of the OECD average and 1.37 percentage points a year faster than income growth in Spain and Portugal.

In the ten years to 1995, de la Fuente and Vives estimate that convergence factors weakened, accounting for just over a quarter of Ireland's growth lead over other industrial countries. Enhanced investments in human capital were responsible for almost one-sixth of Ireland's positive growth differential. Increased labour inputs — as reflected in rising employment levels — contributed over one-eighth to Ireland's super-normal growth. However, fiscal discipline, as captured by the "government size" variable, was found to be the largest single source of Ireland's growth advantage over the rest of the industrial world.

This model is instructive in three respects. First, it shows that, while convergence or "catch up" factors explain much of Ireland's growth lead, they do not explain it all. The Irish growth rate has signally outperformed the rates of expansion recorded by Spain and Portugal, two other EU member-states that are latecomers to development. Moreover, the influence of convergence factors has waned since the mid-1980s as the growth differential widened.

Second, the direct contribution of human capital formation — investments in education and training — to accelerating the Irish growth rate are made manifest. Over the decade 1985–95, investments in human capital were the third largest identified contributor to Ireland's positive growth differential over the rest of the industrialised world.

---

[9] de la Fuente and Vives (1997), p. 122.

Third, fiscal discipline, perhaps through its effects on reinforcing the credibility of economic policy or of strengthening investor confidence, has been particularly important in underpinning sustained sharp growth. As de la Fuente and Vives remark:

> ... our results are consistent with the view that fiscal adjustment was directly responsible for a sizeable increase in the growth rate.[10]

While the model explicitly recognises the direct contribution of human capital in powering Ireland's growth rate, its indirect contribution has also been of signal importance. There is nothing automatic about convergence or the speed with which it takes place. Arrow notes perceptively:

> Knowledge developed elsewhere is not made useful to Ireland automatically; it takes effort and understanding. It is necessary to have what development economists call "absorptive capacity". Among other factors is the presence of scientists and technologists who are up-to-date with new developments elsewhere. ... As has been shown in a number of studies, foreign trade and especially foreign investment facilitate considerably the acquisition of new ideas from abroad. It is in the acquisition of knowledge from abroad that foreign trade and investment assume their greatest economic significance.[11]

Decreasing returns and technological diffusion are the principal economic forces driving convergence. In Ireland's case, catching up with Europe has been greatly aided by the strength and continuity of private foreign investment inflows. But Ireland carved out its niche in the global market for mobile investment by offering a location that was highly profitable, where labour was plentiful, educated and technologically adept.

---

[10] de la Fuente and Vives (1997), p. 125.

[11] K.J. Arrow (1997), p. 6.

4.2. The Effects of Human Resources Investments on Irish Economic Performance

Investments in education and training — by individuals, by businesses and by the state — raise the quality of labour. Improvements in labour quality promote output growth and employment expansion by raising national productivity. In turn, gains in national productivity relative to trade rivals improve the international competitiveness of Irish output. In addition, available high-quality labour acts as a magnet, attracting modern foreign industries to Ireland. The process by which human capital investments strengthen economic performance can be sketched out in the following sequence:

1. Investments in education and training raise the productivity of labour directly. More skilled workers will produce greater levels of output per unit of labour input. Further, a skilled workforce will utilise a given stock of physical capital — plant and machinery — more efficiently, with less machine downtime. Trained managers will make better-informed decisions, enhancing enterprise profitability. In these ways, increases in labour quality resulting from investments in education and training will raise total operating efficiency above the initial gains in labour productivity.

2. Productivity and efficiency gains act to reduce unit costs of production. Where such reductions in unit costs are not offset by productivity-related pay increases, the competitiveness of Irish output on foreign and domestic markets is improved.[12] Such competitive gains allow Irish firms to secure larger and more profitable shares of international markets. The expansion of output thus generated is employment-enhancing.

3. Additional relevant education and training not only increases the stock of knowledge and skills vested in the national workforce, but also its flexibility and adaptability. These characteristics facilitate the introduction of new product and proc-

---

[12] Paul Krugman has noted: "Between 1979 and 1995, labour productivity in Ireland's business sector rose 3.3 per cent per year — more than twice as fast as the G7 average. Meanwhile, real wages, though rising, lagged . . ." (Krugman, 1997, p. 42).

ess technologies in industry. Hence, raising the skills of the workforce is likely to induce additional investments in widening and deepening the physical capital stock, thereby reinforcing initial productivity gains. In modern economies, investments in physical capital and labour are not substitutes, but complements.

4. In a wider international context, the availability of a large pool of highly qualified labour acts as a magnet in attracting new mobile foreign investment to Ireland. The ready supply of skilled labour ranks with the 10 per cent corporation tax rate as the principal incentives attracting foreign direct investment to Ireland.[13] Such multinational investments in industry and traded services have yielded Ireland a rich harvest of jobs. Direct employment in such multinational enterprises now numbers over 100,000. Moreover, the associated physical capital and knowledge investments have transformed the nature of the Irish industrial economy.

5. Additional inputs of education and training act to prevent specific skills shortages and to minimise structural unemployment. In the absence of sufficient relevant education and training, sustained, rapid economic growth can quickly exhaust the labour supply, even in the face of substantial unemployment. Necessarily, the emergence of labour scarcity forces the economy on to a lower growth path.

Relatively high unemployment constitutes no automatic defence against labour scarcity. Labour is not homogenous, but highly differentiated. Mismatches between the supply and demand for labour and the weakness of work incentives in the lower reaches of the labour market can leave the economy experiencing shortages and surpluses of labour simultaneously.

---

[13] IDA Ireland indicates that US corporations are relatively more attracted by the highly qualified labour supply, while Europeans are attracted by low corporation tax rates.

The 1998 Budget explicitly recognised the scale of the threat posed to continuing economic growth by the tightening of labour markets:

> ... this favourable outlook [for 1998] is not without risk. The most immediate arises from emerging shortages of both skilled and unskilled labour. If not dealt with, these shortages have the potential to bring the current strong growth phase to a premature end. Tackling the changing needs of the labour market will be one of the most important features of Government policy over the next few years.[14]

6. Investments in training, by raising productivity, lead to improvements in business profitability. While measuring the incidence of workplace training is notoriously difficult, a recent ESRI study noted:

   > most research suggests that training improves productivity as well as leading to higher earnings for trained employees.[15]

7. Education and training, targeted at those most at risk, can stem initial inflows into unemployment. Over time, this will also reduce flows from short-term to long-term unemployment. In the final analysis, the most effective way of reducing long-term unemployment is the prevention of short-term unemployment. Curbing inflows into unemployment, particularly amongst early school-leavers, will not only reduce subsequent levels of long-term unemployment, but will increase the labour supply, thereby easing labour shortages.

In these disparate ways, investments in education and training raise national productivity, both directly and indirectly, encourage a widening and deepening of the physical capital stock, remove structural barriers to economic growth and employment expansion and act to alleviate unemployment. Together, they all com-

---

[14] "Budget 1998: Economic Background", Department of Finance, December 1997, paragraph 2.6, p. 5.

[15] O'Connell and Lyons (1995), p. 6.

bine to sharpen the competitiveness of Irish output and to enhance the prospects for further additions to employment.

4.3. Education, Training and Individual Incomes

The positive national economic impact of investments in education and training represent the aggregation of income gains captured by individuals, enterprise and government. Just as improvements in national productivity raise national income, productivity advances at individual and enterprise levels raise personal incomes and corporate profits.

Individuals benefit in three distinct ways from investments in their education and training.

4.3.1. Education and Employment

Education and training enhance an individual's initial chances of success in the labour market. The educated and trained find jobs relatively easily. The higher the level of education attained, the lower the probability of remaining involuntarily unemployed for prolonged periods. Conversely, the incidence of unemployment amongst the poorly educated is exceptionally high.

A survey of those who left school in 1994/95 found that 12.7 per cent were unemployed a year later. However, the probability of unemployment was directly related to the level of qualifications attained, as shown in Table 4.2.

TABLE 4.2: UNEMPLOYMENT RATES ONE YEAR AFTER LEAVING SCHOOL IN 1994/95

Qualification	Unemployment Rate One Year Later
No Qualification	69.2%
Junior Certificate	28.5%
Junior Certificate + VPT	31.8%
Leaving Certificate	15.3%
Leaving Certificate + PLC	12.6%

Notes: VPT = Vocational Preparation and Training year; PLC = Post-Leaving Certificate course (1–2 years).

Source: "The Economic Status of School-leavers 1994–1996", Economic and Social Research Institute, December 1997.

Thus, despite the buoyancy of labour demand, more than two out of every three who left school without any qualifications in 1994/1995 were out of work in 1996.

In 1996, a year after leaving school, those with no qualifications were five times more likely to be unemployed than those with a Leaving Certificate. The unemployment rate for those with a Junior Certificate was roughly twice as high as for those holding a Leaving Certificate.

Moreover, as indicated in Chapter 3, educational qualifications are becoming increasingly important as passports to employment. As a result, the gap separating the labour market experience of those with qualifications from those with none is growing much wider. In 1980, the unemployment rate amongst those with no qualifications was 14 percentage points higher than for those who possessed a Leaving Certificate. By 1996, the gap in their relative unemployment rates had widened to 53 percentage points.

4.3.2. Education and Earnings

Educational qualifications not only provide a gateway to employment, but a ticket to higher earnings. There is a strong positive association between levels of educational attainment and levels of pay. In broad terms, higher qualifications translate directly into higher personal incomes.

Estimates of the returns to education in Ireland for four educational categories in 1987 and 1994 are shown in Table 4.3. These show the average percentage increase in wages that can be commanded on each step of the educational ladder over those who have no educational qualifications. Thus, in 1994, holders of university degrees could expect to earn between 98 per cent and 101 per cent more than those who possessed no qualifications.

The estimates in Table 4.3 reveal two important features. First, personal incomes rise in step with the level of education attained and the pay differentials conferred by additional increments of education are significant.

TABLE 4.3: ESTIMATED RETURNS TO EDUCATION IN IRELAND, 1987 AND 1994 (FOR A SAMPLE OF ALL EMPLOYEES, NON AGE-SPECIFIC)

Educational Attainment	Range of Returns to Education	
	1987	*1994*
Group/Inter/Junior Certificate	0.11–0.17	0.17–0.22
Leaving Certificate	0.34–0.37	0.34–0.41
Third-Level Diploma/Certificate	0.56–0.59	0.51–0.54
University Degree	0.85–0.88	0.98–1.01

Note: For each educational category, the range covers three sets of specifications.
Source: Honohan (1997), Adapted from Table 4.2.3, p. 245.

Second, over time, the returns to most types of education have increased in Ireland. Between 1987 and 1994, the returns to a Junior Certificate and to a university degree increased, while the Leaving Certificate yielded constant returns. Only in the case of third-level diplomas and certificates did the returns fall between 1987 and 1994.

The increasing returns to most types of education is a somewhat surprising outcome, given the very sharp increases in education participation rates and the consequent rise in the supply of educated labour. The estimates suggest that the increasing demand for educated and skilled labour since the late 1980s has outpaced the rapidly rising supply of educated young people.

4.3.3. Education and Lifetime Income

Poor educational qualifications and low skills restrict career opportunities. Low-skilled workers can find that their earnings peak relatively early in their working lives. The more highly educated tend to see their earnings rise over a longer stretch of their careers. The absence of qualifications blocks promotion and progression.

Estimates of the enhancement of lifetime personal incomes provided through investments in education were also calculated by the ESRI. Lifetime income streams were estimated for average individuals who (i) leave school at 15 with no qualifications;

(ii) leave school at 16 with a Junior Certificate; (iii) leave at 18 with a Leaving Certificate; (iv) complete a third-level diploma or certificate and commence work at 20; (v) successfully complete a university degree and enter the workforce at 22. In all cases, it is assumed that individuals work full-time until they retire at 65. The impact of income taxes is excluded from the analysis.

On the basis of the estimated lifetime income streams, internal rates of return were calculated for each additional step up the educational ladder. Income foregone was treated as the value of investment in education. The yield on this educational investment is the higher lifetime income stream generated relative to lifetime incomes on lower levels of education. The results of this exercise are shown in Table 4.4.

Table 4.4 shows that each step up the educational ladder yields a significantly positive rate of return in terms of higher lifetime earnings. The highest rates of return are thus generated by university degrees.

However, while the premium earned by a university degree relative to a Leaving Certificate edged ahead slightly between 1987 and 1994, this did not hold for all educational qualifications.

The rate of return generated by third-level non-degree qualifications relative to the Leaving Certificate declined very sharply, as did the premium commanded by the Leaving Certificate over the Junior Certificate.

TABLE 4.4: INTERNAL RATES OF RETURN TO IRISH EDUCATIONAL INVESTMENTS

Educational Investment Levels	Range Of Private IRRs	
	1987	1994
Junior Cert v No Qualifications	0.136–0.163	0.171–0.263
Leaving Cert v Junior Cert	0.106–0.125	0.053–0.086
Third-level Diploma v Leaving Cert	0.103–0.128	0.038–0.063
University Degree v Leaving Cert	0.162–0.183	0.177–0.188

Source: ESRI, 1997, Paper 31, adapted from Table 4.2.5.

Above all, the most notable outcome is the very high and rapidly increasing rate of return accruing to those who passed the Junior Certificate compared with those who have no educational qualifications. As the ESRI notes:

> Returns to Intermediate Certificates and similar level qualifications have increased relative to having no qualifications. . . . This is important as it points to an increased earnings disadvantage for the lowest-skilled and hence a greater marginalisation of this group.[16]

All of this demonstrates quite convincingly that education pays. Relative to the poorly qualified, the highly educated face much lower probabilities of unemployment, earn higher pay and enjoy the prospect of considerably larger lifetime incomes.

Moreover, the financial returns on most types of education in Ireland have increased rather than diminished during the past decade, despite the sustained increase in education participation rates. This indicates that the demand for highly educated labour is rising particularly rapidly in the face of much-enhanced supply.

Those earning personal incomes are not the only beneficiaries of investments in education and training. Enterprises hiring more educated and trained labour will, as noted earlier, improve their productivity and efficiency, thereby reducing unit costs and sharpening their competitiveness.[17]

In the absence of a "brain drain", government also earns a return from its investments in education and training. To the extent that productivity gains induce extra employment, the government's tax base is widened. Similarly, since earnings rise in step with educational qualifications, a highly progressive income tax code such as Ireland's will ensure that the Exchequer will cream off a large slice of the personal returns on educational invest-

---

[16] Honohan (1997), p. 249. The paper assumes a 7.5 per cent rate of return to the economy in the long term from investments in education and a rate of return of about 6 per cent on investments in training (p. 43).

[17] The ESRI notes that, with respect to human resources investments under the current CSF, "the benefits of increased productivity will reduce firms' costs even if they are shared equally with employees, as past experience would suggest is likely" (Honohan, 1997, p. 43).

ments. It will be recalled that the internal rates of return on educational investments, illustrated in Table 4.4, were shown gross of income taxes.

Thus, to the extent that the educated and trained remain in the domestic economy, individuals, enterprises and government itself will all capture a part of the return on investments in human resources.

However, this should not be construed as an invitation to provide open-ended cheques for all education and training programmes. In developed economies, amongst which Ireland is now numbered, the OECD has noted that productivity advances in the future are likely to emanate not simply from increased education provision, but from improved quality:

> While basic scholastic skills are obviously a necessary condition to implement technology, the incremental value of additional schooling in countries where average length of schooling is already high is less obvious, and probably greatly depends on the type and quality of education.[18]

4.4. The Revolution in Irish Education

An educational revolution has transformed the nature of Irish society in general, and the quality of the Irish labour force in particular, over the past 30 years. The agents of this revolution have been rising rates of participation in the educational system, and an extension of the range of educational opportunities.

Between 1964 and 1994, total enrolments in the Irish education system increased by over 50 per cent, from 642,000 to 979,000. While there was relatively little change in the numbers attending primary schools over the period, student numbers in second-level schools almost tripled while, at third level, there was a near-sixfold increase. Even allowing for population growth, this increase in the absolute level of educational enrolments has triggered a sharp rise in participation rates, particularly in the post-compulsory education segments. This is illustrated in Table 4.5.

---

[18] Englander and Gurney (1994), p. 89.

TABLE 4.5: PARTICIPATION RATES IN IRISH EDUCATION, 1964–94
(THOSE IN FULL-TIME EDUCATION AS % OF THAT AGE COHORT)

Age (years)	Participation Rate 1964 (%)	Participation Rate 1994 (%)
4–5	58.0	75.0e
6–12	98.9	100.0
13	94.6	100.0
14	66.4	100.0
15	51.5	95.8
16	36.8	93.6
17	24.8	83.3
18	14.5	63.7
19	8.8	46.0
20	6.6*	33.7
21	6.6*	21.6

e: Estimated at 75 per cent since 54.1 per cent of all four year-olds and almost all five year-olds attend school.

* "20 and over" as per cent of the 20–24 age cohort for 1964.

Sources: "Investment in Education", Government of Ireland, 1966, Table 1.4; Department of Education Statistical Report 1993/94, Dublin, 1995, Table 1.4.

As shown in Table 4.5, the improvement in participation rates has been concentrated in post-compulsory education. The compulsory school-leaving age was raised from 14 to 15 years in 1972. By 1993/94, over four-fifths of Irish 17-year-olds were still engaged in education; 30 years earlier, less than a quarter of 17-year-olds were still at school. The scale of the transformation in educational participation in Ireland is neatly encapsulated by the ESRI:

> For those born 65 years ago who are now at retirement age, approximately two-thirds left school with only primary education and less than 10 per cent had the benefit of third-level education. . . . For those born in the late 1960s, that is, those who were aged 25 to 30 in 1994, early school leavers were down to only 10 per cent of the cohort, with around 60 per cent having at least a Leaving Certificate and around a quarter having some form of third-level education. . . . At present, between 40 per cent and 50 per cent of those leaving the educational system have experienced third-level education and

over 80 per cent of the (relevant) population have reached Leaving Certificate standard.[19]

Since marked improvements in Irish education participation rates date only from the late 1960s, many of those currently at work missed out on the revolution in Irish education. As a result, the educational qualifications of the Irish workforce as a whole still trail behind average education levels in the developed industrial world.

However, in the realm of educational qualifications, it is important to distinguish between stocks and flows. The educational attainments of the total labour force reflect educational provision as long as 50 years ago. At 1994 participation rates — and participation rates are still rising — a child entering the Irish education system at the age of four-and-a-half could expect to complete 14.9 years of education. On the basis of current inflows and participation rates, Irish education provision at least equals, if it does not exceed, average years of schooling completed in the EU and OECD.[20]

This finding corresponds with the conclusion of the ESRI's *Medium-Term Review*. It notes:

> This further rise in participation in the 1990s is quite striking and it has raised Irish participation in education up to the levels reached in some of the more developed economies and above those currently experienced in the UK.[21]

Among those aged between 18 and 21, Irish enrolment rates in third-level education in 1994 were higher than the averages for the European Union and the OECD. This is shown in Table 4.6.

---

[19] Fahey and Fitz Gerald (1997), p. 9.

[20] Tansey and McCarthy (1996).

[21] Fahey and Fitz Gerald (1997), pp. 9–10.

TABLE 4.6: TOP TWELVE OECD THIRD-LEVEL ENROLMENT RATES, 1994 (PARTICIPANTS AGED 18–21 AS % OF AGE COHORT*)

Country	University	Other Third-Level	Total
Canada	26.2	14.0	40.3
Belgium	18.5	18.9	37.4
Greece	28.9	7.8	36.7
United States	21.3	13.6	34.9
France	23.3	9.9	33.2
New Zealand	23.8	7.1	30.9
Korea	19.8	11.0	30.8
Ireland	**18.3**	**12.2**	**30.5**
Australia	20.5	8.7	29.3
Spain	24.9	0.6	25.4
United Kingdom	18.7	4.8	23.6
Netherlands	22.1	n/a	22.1
EU Average	17.2	5.1	22.3
OECD Average	15.9	5.6	21.5

* Participation rates for this age cohort are influenced by the length of the secondary cycle and by military service requirements.

Source: "Education at a Glance", OECD, Paris, 1996.

Irish education is increasingly financed from public funds. This development, coupled with the continuous rise in participation rates, has caused a steep increase in public expenditure on education, in both absolute and proportionate terms.

Since the early 1960s, public spending on education has doubled its share of national income. Government spending on education increased from 3.1 per cent of GNP in 1961 to 6.5 per cent in 1993. This rise in the share of national income allocated to education has taken place against a background where real Gross Domestic Product itself has increased more than threefold. Hence, over the past three decades, spending on Irish education has been taking larger slices of a much bigger cake. These trends are illustrated in Table 4.7.

TABLE 4.7: PUBLIC SPENDING ON IRISH EDUCATION, 1961–93
(£ MILLION, AT CURRENT PRICES)

Category	1961	1991	1992	1993
Current spending on goods and services	19	851	991	1,098
Transfer payments	1	566	617	681
Capital spending	2	37	35	41
Public spending on education	22	1,454	1,643	1,820
As % of GNP	3.1%	5.7%	6.2%	6.5%
Real GDP index (1990 = 100)	33.5	101.6	105.6	108.8

Sources: "Investment in Education", 1966, Tables 5.21 (a) and 5.21 (b); National Income and Expenditure, 1994, CSO, July 1995, data extracted from Tables A, 5 and 28.

Increased funding provision for education, mirrored in rising education participation rates, has made a clear, critical contribution both to the process of economic development and to the expansion of employment in Ireland in recent decades.

Over the long haul, public spending on education has been largely insulated from budgetary cutbacks. This commitment to raising participation rates will ensure a continuing flow of highly educated young people into the labour market in the years ahead.

Nonetheless, certain weaknesses in the education system still remain, many of which have been identified in published official reports. The principal deficiencies can be summarised thus:

1. The Government's 1995 White Paper on Education admitted that: "a significant minority of students do not acquire satisfactory levels of literacy or numeracy while at primary school".[22] A major 1991 international study found that the literacy of Irish nine-year-olds was just above average, ranking them twelfth of 27 countries surveyed. In relative terms, the literacy performance of Irish 14-year-olds was rather worse, leaving them in twentieth place of 31 countries surveyed.[23]

---

[22] "Charting Our Education Future", White Paper on Education, Stationery Office, Dublin, 1995, p. 20.

[23] Findings reported in *The Sunday Tribune*, 31 August 1997, p. 8.

2. The White Paper also noted that: "surveys have shown that the overall science achievement of 13-year-old students in Ireland is low compared to a number of other OECD countries".[24]

3. Since the abolition of the Primary Certificate in 1967, there has been no nationally administered testing of the proficiency of primary school students in reading, writing and basic computational skills. Most pupils do not now sit a nationwide state examination until the Junior Certificate, taken at about the age of 15.

4. In spite of very considerable improvements, the number of students failing to complete second-level education remains relatively high. Table 4.8 shows that in 1992, 26 per cent of Irish young people had no qualifications beyond junior second-level, while 8 per cent possessed no educational qualifications at all.

More recently, of the estimated 66,500 young people who left the school system in 1996, some 25 per cent departed without a Leaving Certificate.

TABLE 4.8: YOUNG IRISH PEOPLE WITH WEAK EDUCATIONAL BACKGROUNDS (AS % OF AGE GROUP FOR 1992)

Category	% of Age Group
Without any formal qualification	8
With no qualification beyond compulsory education	18
Total	26

Source: "Early School Leavers and Youth Unemployment", Economic and Social Forum, Report No. 11, January 1997, data extracted from Table 2.4, p. 20.

5. Vocational education at second level is weak. Official recognition of the deficiencies in vocational education has not significantly diluted the hold of the dominant generalist educational philosophy. The result has been an attempt to have it both ways:

> The Government accepts the need for a new, increased emphasis on vocational subjects and practical or usable skills in

---

[24] White Paper on Education, p. 22.

the school curriculum. Increased emphasis will be placed on learning languages. This will not imply less emphasis on the broader cultural, social and spiritual objectives of education.[25]

Less emphasis is given to vocational education at second level in Ireland than in best practice EU competitors. Comparing the Irish, Dutch and Danish education systems, the National Economic and Social Council found in 1993:

> the major differences in provision emerge at the end of compulsory education. The very distinctive feature of Irish education is that, despite a background of sharp distinction between vocational and academic schools, provision for academic and vocational education is now made in the same schools. While Irish schools differ in their emphasis and subject choice, they are all basically teaching the same curriculum towards the same end goal.[26]

The cost of each of these deficiencies in the education system, if they are allowed to persist, will be measured in blunted competitiveness and, ultimately, additional unemployment. In a labour market where unskilled and semi-skilled jobs are fast disappearing, the illiterate and the innumerate will find it increasingly difficult to secure employment. In a world where decent jobs are rationed by educational attainment and qualifications, early school-leavers and school dropouts will be at the back of the queue. Moreover, initial failure to find a job is the first step on the road to long-term unemployment.

The education system at second level has been slow to adjust, not only in the face of technological and occupational changes, but also in response to alterations in the profile of its own student intake. The threefold increase in the second-level school numbers over the past 30 years has changed the composition of the student population in terms of aptitudes and abilities, interests and ambitions. It is not clear that the supply-side of second-level education

---

[25] Government Response to the Moriarty Task Force on the Implementation of the Culliton Report, April 1993, p. 6.

[26] "Training Policies for Economic and Social Development", NESC Paper No. 95, October 1993, p. 210.

has responded sufficiently to these compositional shifts by offering courses that appeal to the wider array of students.

Indeed, the relatively high rate of non-completion at second-level, combined with the robust demand for Post Leaving Certificate courses (PLCs), most of which are vocational in character, point to an unsatisfied demand for vocational education within the school system.[27]

On the broader economic front, the weaknesses in the sciences, in languages and in vocational education relative to best practice amongst Ireland's principal trading partners have clear implications for future competitiveness.

Genuine efforts have been made to remedy these shortcomings, most notably in the restructuring of the senior cycle of second-level education in 1995 and in the recommendations of the 1995 White Paper on Education. Restructuring has seen the revision of the syllabus for the established Leaving Certificate, the introduction of the Leaving Certificate Applied and the development of a Leaving Certificate Vocational Programme. As yet, it is too early to say if these initiatives will be successful in raising second-level completion rates towards 90 per cent.

4.5. Ireland's Training Performance

Within the context of the European Union, Ireland is a lagging, if improving, trainer. Data from Labour Force Surveys conducted across the European Union in 1992 indicate that the total incidence of all forms of training in Ireland is somewhat below the European average. This can be seen from Table 4.9.

In the four weeks before the surveys were conducted, 7.1 per cent of the Irish labour force undertook some education or training compared to 9.3 per cent in the EU as a whole.

The amount of training provided within Irish firms, at 4.4 per cent, was considerably higher than the EU average of 2.3 per cent. This bears out the contention that much of Irish training is provided "on-the-job". Such "learning by doing" is usually regarded as inferior to formal training.

---

[27] In 1996/97, 18,700 students were enrolled on Post-Leaving Certificate (PLC) courses.

TABLE 4.9: THE INCIDENCE OF TRAINING IN THE EUROPEAN UNION, 1992 (% OF LABOUR FORCE RECEIVING TRAINING IN THE FOUR WEEKS PRECEDING SURVEYS)

Country	Total	In-Firm Only	Dual	In-Education Only
Belgium	2.8	1.2	0.3	1.2
Denmark	23.6	9.5	3.1	11.0
Germany	10.1	1.2	4.0	4.9
Greece	1.4	0.5	0.0	0.9
Spain	3.7	0.8	0.0	2.9
France	4.3	1.0	0.7	2.6
Ireland	**7.1**	**4.4**	**0.9**	**1.8**
Italy	2.7	1.2	0.1	1.4
Luxembourg	4.4	2.2	1.2	1.0
Netherlands	24.3	5.8	1.9	16.6
Portugal	5.3	0.6	0.1	4.7
United Kingdom	18.3	5.6	2.7	10.1
EU12	9.3	2.3	1.8	5.2

Source: 1992 EU Labour Force Surveys, quoted in "OECD Economic Surveys 1995 — Ireland", OECD, June 1995.

Even where in-company training is combined with courses jointly provided with the education system, the Irish training effort still exceeds the EU average. As the OECD notes:

> The only area where the survey showed Ireland to be markedly below the EU average was in training undertaken as part of general education or in institutes of higher education.[28]

While this may, in part, reflect respondents' perceptions about the nature of courses followed, it also again demonstrates the much stronger vocational education effort in competitor countries such as Denmark, the Netherlands and, particularly, the UK.

---

[28] "OECD Economic Surveys 1995 — Ireland", OECD, June 1995, pp. 85–86.

Comparing survey data on training for 1989 and 1993, Fox tentatively concluded that training performance in Ireland had improved somewhat. The comparative data on which he based his findings is summarised in Table 4.10.

TABLE 4.10: THE EVOLUTION OF IRELAND'S TRAINING PERFORMANCE, 1989–93

Category	1989 Survey (%)	1993 Survey (%)
Employees receiving some training	42	43 and 37*
Employees receiving off-the-job training	21	43
Training expenditures as % of payroll	0.9	1.5

* In 1993, 43 per cent of employees attended formal training courses while 37 per cent received on-the-job training. As some employees could have benefited from both, the figures cannot be added.

Sources: MRBI/FÁS Survey 1989; FÁS/EU Survey 1993; Fox (1996).

However, Fox noted:

> While the present survey seems to show higher levels of training than in 1989, it would be unwise to draw too strong comparisons between the 1989 survey and the present one as the definitions and methodology were significantly different.[29]

Yet, O'Connell and Lyons discerned little difference in the amounts of training provided in 1988 and 1993. This they found

> ... disturbing in the light both of the greater emphasis on the importance of investment in human resources in recent years and of the increased investment in human resources development financed by European Union structural funds under the 1989–1993 Community Support Framework.[30]

The weaknesses in national training are not confined to the shop-floor. The Galvin Report of 1988 found that only one-third of Irish managers had attended a training course of any type in the pre-

---

[29] Fox (1996), p. 46.

[30] O'Connell and Lyons (1995), p. 22.

ceding year. Galvin concluded that the commitment to management training in Ireland was unacceptably low and that:

> Irish expenditure on management training is significantly lower than that of our more successful international competitors.[31]

Measuring the training effort by inputs — expenditure on training as a percentage of payroll, days' training completed each year by employees — is useful, but inconclusive in itself. Training is a functionalist discipline that must be judged by its outputs rather than its inputs. The outputs are the skills levels attained by Irish labour relative to competitors.

Hitchens and Bernie conducted an important study seeking to explain productivity differences between "good practice" plants in Ireland, Denmark and the Netherlands. Commenting on the results in 1993, the National Economic and Social Council noted:

> Competitive performance is adversely affected by poor quality human capital. Skills differences are noticeable at all levels: shopfloor worker, supervisor, manager. The findings from the matched plant studies are in line with the conclusions of the Industrial Policy Review Group: there is a skills gap between Ireland and best practice firms in competitor countries.

NESC continued:

> Our shopfloor workers tend to have less formal training than their counterparts who are usually apprentice-trained. . . . The important question is whether or not the different skill levels arising from different training practices affect performance. The matched plant studies suggest that they do: poorer quality skills, less attention to detail, inadequate supervision and quality control procedures, lower skilled management with poorer marketing and fi-

---

[31] "Managers for Ireland: Report and Recommendations of the Advisory Committee on Management Training", 1988.

nancial skills have all affected the quality and the marketability of the Irish product.[32]

Thus, while the incidence of training in Ireland may be improving, Ireland still lags behind the "best practice" training performance within the European Union. More importantly, the skills embodied in Irish workers, at shopfloor, supervisory and management levels, are lower than those possessed by their counterparts in EU "best practice" competitors.

Attempts to remedy existing skills deficiencies require:

1. A basic understanding of how training markets work

2. An identification of the locus of the training problem in Ireland.

4.5.1. How Training Markets Work

Effective training increases employee productivity and, hence, employee wages. Most substantial employee training of any duration is general in character. It increases the trained individual's productivity, and therefore wages, across a range of enterprises and even industries. Since the gains from general training are reflected in enhanced individual productivity and wages, the returns from training are captured principally by those who have received that training.

Where training is general, there is little incentive for employers to finance its provision. In addition to incurring the direct and indirect costs of training, employers will be forced to raise wages subsequently to reflect the increased employee productivity caused by training. Otherwise, once trained, employees will simply seek jobs in other firms which are prepared to pay wages that mirror their enhanced productivity.

In short, the provision of general training generates strong external effects. In these circumstances, it is rational for individual employers not to train but instead to seek to take a "free ride" on the training provided by others by "poaching" trained workers from competitors. This enables employers to avoid training costs

---

[32] "Education and Training Policies for Economic and Social Development", NESC Report No. 95, 1993, pp. 206–207.

while still recruiting the trained workers they require. However, where all firms behave in this manner, this can lead to a general under-provision of training.

Alternatively, since employers cannot capture the returns on general training, they may seek to shift the incidence of training costs on to trainees by paying them wages below the value of their marginal product. As trainees know that ultimately they will trap the benefits of the training provided in higher lifetime incomes, they may acquiesce in funding their own training costs through accepting low pay. Traditional apprenticeships in the crafts and professions bear witness to the willingness of trainees to finance the costs of their own training.

However, outside such traditional apprenticeship systems, where training must be purchased in markets, transferring the costs of training to trainees is much more difficult. Trainees may be unable or unwilling to pay for their training because of imperfections in capital markets. Without collateral, banks may be unwilling to provide trainees with loans to cover the costs of their training. Similarly, trainees may be unwilling to borrow because of the risk of unemployment once they have completed their training and their subsequent inability to finance their debts. In similar fashion, they may be unwilling to finance the cost of their own training because they underestimate the rate of return on training over their working lives.[33] Such inaccurate assessments are likely to be reinforced by high tax regimes.

Hence, economic analysis suggests that employers will not be prepared to finance the provision of general training but will, instead, seek to poach rather than to train the skilled workers they need.[34] Trainees may be unable or unwilling to finance the cost of their training because of imperfections in capital markets, the riskiness of training investments and faulty expectations. For these reasons, pure market solutions are likely to result in an under-provision of general training. Such under-provision may not be of material importance where the economy is extensively

---

[33] See Richard Layard, "The Welfare Economics of Training" in Layard, Mayhew and Owen (1994), pp. 31–49.

[34] Employers will, however, finance all specific training, since they capture all the returns on such investments. See Becker (1964).

underemployed. However, it assumes critical importance where the economy is approaching effective full employment.

In consequence, there is a strong economic case for the collective provision of general skills training, both by the state and by industry groups themselves. That case rests on the following foundations:

1. Collective provision is necessary because, on the supply side, general training exhibits many of the hallmarks of a collective good.

2. On the demand side, the market is subject to failure because of imperfections in capital markets, the inherent riskiness of personal investments in training and faulty expectations about potential rates of return.

3. Where strong labour demand coexists with extensive structural unemployment, the social returns on effective investments in general skills training can be high. Pressures on wages are eased and shortages relieved by increased labour market competition. Capacity utilisation in the economy improves and output increases. In summary, there is a real improvement in the structural characteristics of the labour market's, and the economy's, supply side.

However, it must be emphasised that these benefits only flow from the collective provision of general training that is economic, efficient and effective. These criteria are likely to be met where collective provision is delivered by industry at a general or sectoral level, since the motivation is clearly commercial. They are less likely to be met by government-sponsored training schemes, which are remote from the labour market and the world of work.

4.5.2. The Locus of the Irish Training Problem
The inherent difficulties in ensuring the adequate provision of training are exacerbated in the Irish case by particular problems of firm structure and size.

In a nutshell, larger firms are better trainers than smaller firms, and enterprises in modern industries — foreign and domestic — provide more training than those engaged in more traditional businesses. Relative to other EU members, the average size of firms in Ireland is small; Irish small firms are *very* small. The Government Task Force on Small Business, reporting in 1994, found that 97 per cent of all Irish businesses employ less than 50 people, while 85 per cent of Irish firms employ less than ten people.

Small firms and micro-businesses are the primary source of employment growth both in Ireland and the EU. Yet, they encounter severe structural impediments in the provision of training. The diseconomies of small scale in providing training include:

1. With few employees, small businesses find it particularly difficult to schedule the release of staff for off-the-job training.

2. Management resources are scarce, and managers cannot be spared from day-to-day operations to attend formal management training courses.

3. Financial resources are insufficient to fund adequate training programmes and external training courses are seen as expensive.

4. Time horizons are short and strategic planning is weak. There is insufficient awareness of the impact of training on future enterprise productivity.

Many Irish-based enterprises, domestic and foreign-owned, are good trainers. Because they compete on international markets, training in large modern industries and in financial services is particularly strong. The training problem in Ireland is thus concentrated amongst smaller enterprises, many of which operate in traditional industry segments.

As FÁS, the national training authority, put it in 1994:

> SMEs have been consistently identified as the least able to develop strategic training plans and the least able to fund them. There is, therefore, a need for the state to prioritise support for SMEs — providing it is done in a manner most

likely to lead to the individual companies being able to meet their own training needs in the longer term.[35]

The 1997 Government White Paper on Human Resource Development attempted to address many of the identified deficiencies. It set out, as its central strategic objective:

> to secure an upgrading in the quality of our human resources to the level of best practice in competitor countries — and to ensure that these best-practice standards are maintained over the long-run.[36]

The broad thrust of the White Paper is directed towards increasing both the quantum and the quality of training by correcting market imperfections and compensating for market failure in the sphere of enterprise training. The White Paper defined three specific objectives for enterprise training policy:

- *Objective 1*: Promoting an increase in the level, the relevance and the quality of training undertaken by enterprise to achieve best international practice.
- *Objective 2*: Assisting small enterprise to overcome the skill barriers to business development.
- *Objective 3*: Improving the level of management training and development.[37]

In pursuit of the first objective, the White Paper proposed the establishment of a publicly supported training network programme for groups of firms with similar training and skills needs. This represents an initial attempt to address the "free rider" problem that characterises enterprise training markets, and the consequent tendency for such markets to under-provide training.

The specific assistance proffered for training in small enterprise, even if insufficient in terms of the scale of the problem, con-

---

[35] "A Strategy for Training the Employed", FÁS, Dublin, 1994, p. 12.

[36] "Human Resource Development", Department of Enterprise and Employment, May 1997, pp. 13–14.

[37] "Human Resource Development", op. cit., p. 16.

stitutes at least an acknowledgement of the particular structural difficulties that inhibit training provision in smaller firms. But have Ireland's training problems not been greatly alleviated by vast inflows of EU cash in recent years? This question is addressed in the next section.

4.6. EU Grants and Active Labour Market Policies

Over the past decade, Ireland's human resources revolution has been financed, in significant measure, from abroad. The first EU Community Support Framework for Ireland, covering the years 1989–93, injected large sums of European money into Irish education, training and active labour market programmes. Its successor, spanning the years 1994–99, has proved even more supportive.

Over the period 1994–99, structural-type funds will deliver some £6.1 billion to Ireland in the form of cash grants from the European Union, equivalent to some 2.5 per cent of Irish GNP each year. At a projected £4,655 million, the Community Support Framework for Ireland comprises the largest component of the structural fund inflows. Amongst its 11 operational programmes, human resources development is the largest, with an allocation of £1,435 million. This is shown in Table 4.11.

The original rationale for EU structural aid was to upgrade the Irish economy's infrastructural base, thereby improving its capacity for survival in a single market dominated by more sophisticated trading partners. In essence, such efforts were directed at strengthening the supply side of the Irish economy.

Ireland's infrastructural base comprises not only its stock of physical assets such as telecommunications, roads and airports, but also its human capital. Thus, within the Community Support Framework for Ireland:

> The central aim of the Operational Programme for Human Resources Development is to maximise the potential of Ireland's most significant resources, namely its people.[38]

---

[38] "Operational Programme for Human Resources Development 1994–99", Stationery Office, 1995, p. 1.

TABLE 4.11: EU STRUCTURAL FUNDS ALLOCATED TO IRELAND, 1994–99

Operational Programme	1994–99, £m	% Total CSF
Human Resources Development	1,435	30.8
Industrial Development	853	18.3
Agriculture, Forestry and Rural Development	782	16.8
Transport	737	15.8
Tourism	377	8.1
Local Urban and Rural Development	214	4.6
Economic Infrastructure	89	1.9
Fisheries	64	1.4
Environmental Services	63	1.4
Hospital Infrastructure	32	0.7
CSF Technical Assistance	8	0.2
Community Support Framework	4,655	100.0
Cohesion Funds	1,012	–
Community Initiatives/EEA Funds	396	–
Total Structural Funds 1994–99	6,065	–

Note: Figures may not add to totals due to rounding.

Source: Honohan (1997), extracted from Tables 1.1.1 and 1.1.2, based on data provided by the Department of Finance, January 1997.

The component sub-programmes of the Operational Programme (OP) for human resources development 1994–99 are shown in Table 4.12. This captures about four-fifths of the EU grants available for education and training over the period, with the remainder flowing through the operational programmes for industrial development, tourism and local urban and rural development.

As can be seen from Table 4.12, EU grant assistance for initial education and training is set to absorb £678 million, or almost half the total programme resources. The reintegration of the socially excluded attracts the second-largest slice of grant support.

TABLE 4.12: COMPONENTS OF THE HUMAN RESOURCES DEVELOPMENT OP, 1994–99 (ESTIMATED EU GRANT AID AT END-1996 IN IR£ MILLION)

Sub-Programmes	EU Grant Aid	% Total OP
1. Initial education and training	678	47.2
2. Continuing training for the unemployed	162	11.3
3. Reintegration of the socially excluded	336	23.4
4. Adaptation to Industrial Change	55	3.8
5. Improving the Quality of Training Provision	188	13.1
Other	16	1.2
Human Resources Development	1,435	100.0

Source: Honohan (1997), Table 1.1.3.

Adaptation to industrial change, embracing those already at work, has been allocated just £55 million or less than 4 per cent of total EU funding on human resources development. In the light of the major threats posed to indigenous Irish industry by the completion of the single market and the advent of the single currency, this appears to be a decidedly parsimonious allocation.

In analytical terms, the operational programme for human resources development has set itself two central objectives.[39]

The first objective centres on widening and deepening the economy's human capital base in order to hasten future economic development and to avert skills shortages. This objective broadly embraces the first, fourth and fifth sub-programmes.

---

[39] The OP explicitly defines the following objectives:

- To boost human capital by enhancing education and skill levels.
- To enhance the employment prospects of the unemployed, particularly the long-term unemployed, and persons excluded from the labour market.

"OP for Human Resources Development 1994–99", Stationery Office, Dublin, 1995, p. 2.

The first sub-programme, relating to initial education and training, aims to "increase the education and skill levels of new entrants to the labour force and therefore improve their labour market opportunities, while also responding to the skills needs of the economy".[40]

The fourth sub-programme seeks to facilitate adaptation to industrial change and changes in production systems for those already at work. The fifth sub-programme is geared to improving the quality of training provision, including adding to the capacity of systems that will deliver education and training well into the future.

The second objective is to improve the job prospects of the unemployed and other marginalised groups on the periphery of the labour market. Sub-programmes two and three address this objective.

Sub-programme two provides continuing training and re-skilling opportunities for the unemployed and other marginalised groups with a view to improving their labour market prospects and performance.

Sub-programme three focuses on reintegrating the socially excluded into the labour market. The instruments utilised include initial guidance, placement and counselling supported by a range of active labour market measures, including Community Employment.

The turbo-charging of EU structural fund aid for Ireland from 1989 onwards has greatly increased participant numbers on active labour market programmes in Ireland. This can be seen from Table 4.13. However, as noted in Section 4.5, the evidence that enhanced structural funds have significantly improved the national training effort is, at best, mixed.

The number of participants on active labour market programmes almost doubled between 1983 and 1994, increasing from 45,958 to 90,339 over the period.

---

[40] "OP for Human Resources Development 1994–99", op. cit., p. 4.

TABLE 4.13: PARTICIPANTS ON ACTIVE LABOUR MARKET PROGRAMMES, 1983–94

Category	Participant Numbers		
	1983	*1990*	*1994*
I Supply-Side Measures			
General* Training	15,206	22,980	15,860
Specific Skills Training	14,752	14,706	17,961
II Demand-Side Measures			
Employment subsidies	11,000	4,792	21,020
Direct Employment Schemes	5,000	14,598	35,498
(of which: Community Employment)**	(2,600)	(12,279)	(32,670)
Total: All Programmes	45,958	57,076	90,339

Notes: * Foundation; ** Formerly, the Social Employment Scheme
Source: O'Connell and McGinnity (1997), Appendix, Table A 2.1.

The extensive scale of state-backed active labour market policies in Ireland can be gauged from the fact that, by 1994, participant numbers were equivalent to 6.5 per cent of the total Irish labour force and 43 per cent of the numbers unemployed in that year.[41]

However, this virtual doubling of programme participants disguises the fact that there was relatively little increase in training activity. Participants in general training programmes barely advanced at all between 1983 and 1994. The numbers undertaking specific skills training rose by just over one-fifth. In all, total trainees on active labour market programmes were just 12.9 per cent higher in 1994 than in 1983.

Against this, demand-side programmes exhibited phenomenal growth. Between 1983 and 1994, there was a sevenfold increase in the numbers participating in direct employment schemes. This was due principally to the expansion of the Community Employment Programme, where participants increased from 2,600 in 1983 to 32,670 in 1994. The training component in Community

---

[41] O'Connell and McGinnity (1997), p. 26.

Employment is minimal. Furthermore, there was a near-doubling of those benefiting from employment subsidies.

Put another way, demand-side measures — direct job creation and employment subsidies — were strongly favoured over supply-side initiatives — enhanced training provision — in the decade after 1983.

In addition, there was a shift away from active measures with strong links to the jobs market, such as specific skills programmes and the subsidisation of open employment, and towards programmes with a weak labour market orientation.

This has led O'Connell and McGinnity to conclude:

> Most of the expansion in provision is accounted for by the growth of demand-side measures, and the balance in provision has shifted away from training and towards work subsidies and direct employment schemes. Over time, the balance between market oriented programmes — skills training and employment subsidies — versus programmes with weak market linkages — general training and direct employment schemes — has also shifted towards the latter, largely due to the dramatic growth in Community Employment.[42]

The shift towards direct employment measures in the decade after 1983 can be comprehended as a response to the scale of the unemployment shock of the early 1980s, the persistence of unemployment and the weakness of national labour demand that continued through to the end of the decade. The switch away from market-oriented programmes is less understandable.

In the previous section, it was seen that the impact of enhanced inflows of EU structural funds after 1989 on Irish training performance was disappointingly limited.

The low priority afforded to training, and particularly to market-relevant training, in the hierarchy of active labour market measures may help to explain why the expansion of training was so muted in spite of the availability of much more cash from Europe for human resources development.

---

[42] O'Connell and McGinnity (1997), p. 32.

While the circumstances of the 1980s may have justified increased provision of direct employment on state schemes, times have changed. The labour market of the late 1990s is characterised by rapidly rising employment levels, diminished unemployment and emerging labour scarcity.

These features point to the need to expand the supply-side of the labour market through a greater emphasis on training, and, more specifically, on training for open market employment.

At the same time, within the panoply of active labour market measures, O'Connell and McGinnity have tested and clearly demonstrated the superiority of programmes with strong links to the labour market:

> We argued that programmes characterised by strong linkages to the labour market — training programmes that are designed to meet the demands of employers and wage subsidies for real jobs in the marketplace — are more likely to improve the job prospects of participants than those characterised by weak market linkages. . . . Our expectations were confirmed both with respect to employment prospects and earnings from employment: participants in market oriented programmes were more likely to find work in both the short- and long-term, they spent a larger proportion of their post-programme time in employment and their earnings were significantly higher than participants in programmes with weak market linkages.[43]

---

[43] O'Connell and McGinnity (1997), pp. 139–140.

Chapter 5

THE DETERMINANTS OF IRISH INCOME TAXES

5.1. The Impact of Taxation on the Labour Market

Extensive efficient investments in education and training increase the community's stock of human capital. In conjunction with additions to the physical capital stock, increased labour inputs of improving quality provide the impetus to the process of economic growth and, ultimately, to the alleviation of unemployment.

However, raising the skills base of the economy is a necessary, though not a sufficient, condition for advancing economic well-being. The full economic potential of more education and better training will not be realised unless the enhanced labour resources are fully and creatively employed in the domestic economy. In other words, those individuals newly invested with skills and qualifications as a result of additional expenditures on human resources development must be encouraged to exercise their enhanced abilities to the full in Ireland. They will do so only where Ireland adequately remunerates the skills they have acquired.

Fundamentally, people work to earn purchasing power. Individuals will not seek jobs unless the real wages on offer compensate them for the inherent unpleasantness or "disutility" of work. It is for this reason that the supply of labour increases as the real wage rate rises. Thus, amongst those of working age, participation in the domestic labour force is conditioned by the availability of suitable jobs at real wage rates that are deemed acceptable. Where these conditions are not met, individuals will refuse to participate in the domestic labour market or will emigrate to more remunerative jobs in foreign labour markets.

In assessing whether pay levels are sufficient to justify participation in the domestic labour market, workers are concerned with more than just the money wages on offer. Income earners are interested less in the gross money total on their payslip, more in how far the cash they receive will stretch in terms of purchasing goods and services.

But wage bargains are struck in terms of money, not real purchasing power. Two factors intervene to dilute the purchasing power of gross money wages: inflation and income taxes. Inflation devalues the purchasing power of every pound in the pay packet. Where prices are rising faster than money wages, real wages are being forced downwards.

When prices are rising very rapidly, employees may suffer from short-term "money illusion", being seduced initially by large concurrent increases in their money wages. However, such illusions tend to be dissipated quickly. Hence, when inflation accelerated in the 1970s and early 1980s, trade unions quickly sought the insertion of "indexation" clauses in pay agreements, tying pay rises to price increases.

Inflation in Ireland has been mild throughout the last decade. As a result, the confiscatory effect of rising prices on money wages has been relatively muted. In turn, this has provided one of the foundations for the moderate pace of increases in money wages negotiated in a succession of national pay deals since 1987.

Income taxes act in a similar fashion to inflation in reducing the real purchasing power of a given money wage. The income taxes deducted from money wages reduce the real spending power conferred by a given money wage.

In summary, both inflation and direct taxes on income cut real wages in the first instance. Where inflation is high and the income tax code is rigid, the two can combine in a particularly vicious manner to deplete the real purchasing power of employees' earnings.

Such attacks on the real living standards of employees will inevitably provoke resistance. In its most public form, that resistance can take the form of demands for compensating increases in money wages, efforts to link pay to prices and sustained pressure on the political process to deliver tax cuts.

However, high taxes can engender more insidious distortions of labour market performance. In particular, high average tax rates can dilute the value of investments in education and training in the following ways:

- Where highly qualified young labour market entrants face very steep tax rates on entry to the domestic labour market, they may choose to emigrate to more financially rewarding jobs abroad. These circumstances characterised the late 1980s in Ireland, when both total and graduate emigration reached very high levels. In this instance, the economy not only suffered the export of the capital it expended in creating skilled and highly trained people, but the State lost the future stream of tax revenue it would have collected from those who emigrated had they remained in employment at home.

- A steeply progressive tax code at low levels of income may act to suppress the acquisition of skills by those already at work. Many employees may not deem it financially worthwhile to incur substantial education or training costs — measured in time as well as money — when high marginal income tax rates will relieve them of a large slice of any additional income they may subsequently earn.

- High marginal tax rates also weaken the financial incentives to accept promotions and to work overtime.

- High average tax rates on low incomes, combined with open-ended, tax-free social welfare benefits in cash and kind, can make it appear financially unattractive for the unemployed to accept job offers at low wages. As the Department of Enterprise and Employment has pointed out:

    > An essential element of future labour market development will be our capacity ... to secure wage, tax and welfare structures which do not crowd out viable productive activity and condemn a large section of our people to unemployment.[1]

---

[1] Department of Enterprise and Employment (1996), p. 74.

In short, high income tax rates, particularly where they fall heavily on low to average gross incomes, can inhibit the community from reaping the full rewards of the extensive investments it has made in education and training.

The central point is that neither accelerated levels of investment in human capital nor lower average tax rates can, by themselves, provide adequate and lasting solutions to Ireland's labour market problems. Raising productivity and reducing unemployment require simultaneous action on both fronts. More effective and relevant investments in people must be augmented by lower average tax charges on their incomes.

5.2. The Determinants of Taxation in Ireland

Electoral considerations apart, there are four principal factors that have determined the level and distribution of taxation in Ireland over the past decade. They are:

5.2.1. The Fiscal Stance of Government

Successive Irish governments during the 1990s have been committed to containing budget deficits, reducing the scale of government borrowing and curbing additions to national indebtedness.

The pursuit of fiscal correction has been driven by two forces. First, governments have found that, in a small open economy, Keynesian-style demand management is self-defeating, both politically and economically.[2] Large-scale deficit budgeting reduced, rather than increased, government flexibility in managing the economy. Second, and more recently, governments have sought to ensure that Ireland meets the Maastricht criteria which determine eligibility for participation in European Monetary Union (EMU). Of the five Maastricht criteria, two are particularly relevant to fiscal policy:

---

[2] The Programme for Economic and Social Progress (1991, p. 43) noted: "Within the overall umbrella of economic stability, fiscal activism can play a very limited role in enhancing the performance of the economy. The role of policy, therefore, is to provide economic stability which ensures that the economy realises its full potential for increased output and employment."

1. The General Government Deficit (GGD) should not exceed 3 per cent of Gross Domestic Product.

2. The ratio of government debt to GDP should not exceed 60 per cent. Where the debt/GDP ratio does exceed 60 per cent, progress in reducing it to the targeted level must be shown to be satisfactory.

In broad terms, Irish governments have met the Maastricht criteria in recent years, with room to spare. As Table 5.1 shows, the General Government Account swung into a surplus in 1997. The Government Debt to GDP ratio fell to 66.3 per cent in 1997, a 30 percentage point decline on its level just four years earlier.

TABLE 5.1: THE FISCAL STANCE OF GOVERNMENT, 1993–97

Year	Exchequer Borrowing/GNP (%)	GGB* as % of GDP	Government Debt as % of GDP
1993	−2.4	−2.4	96.3
1994	−2.1	−1.7	89.1
1995	−1.8	−2.1	82.2
1996	−1.2	−0.4	72.7
1997	−0.5	+0.9	66.3

* General Government Balance: − = deficit; + = surplus.

Sources: 1997 Budget Book; "1998 Budget: Statistics and Tables"; "Budget 1998: Economic Background"; Exchequer Returns 1997, Department of Finance, January 1998.

The combined effects of voluntary and externally imposed restraints on budget deficits and public borrowing carry a simple message for tax policy. Given tight restrictions on the scale of government borrowing, increases in public spending can be financed only by an increased flow of tax revenue into the Exchequer. The larger the rise planned for public spending, the bigger the revenues required from taxation.

5.2.2. Trends in Current Public Spending

With government deficits and borrowing tightly constrained, the level and rate of increase in current public spending will determine the amount of taxation that must be raised. For the government, as for all others, spending must be financed either by current income or by borrowing. Where recourse to increased borrowing is ruled out, then additions to spending can be funded only by additions to income. Taxation is by far the largest source of current income available to government. It is also the easiest to extract.

The volume of Irish current public spending was pruned back severely during the years from 1987 to 1989. From 1990 onwards, however, day-to-day government spending again began to increase at a rapid pace. The trend in gross current public spending since 1987 is shown in Table 5.2.

TABLE 5.2: TRENDS IN IRISH GROSS CURRENT PUBLIC SPENDING, 1987–98 (IN £ MILLION AT CURRENT PRICES; RISES ON PREVIOUS YEAR)

Year	Public Spending	Rise (%)	Spending after Interest	Rise (%)
1987	9,587	—	7,652	—
1988	9,684	+1.0	7,722	+0.9
1989	9,762	+0.8	7,806	+1.1
1990	10,406	+6.6	8,299	+6.3
1991	11,307	+8.7	9,160	+10.4
1992	12,151	+7.5	10,009	+9.3
1993	13,017	+7.1	10,858	+8.5
1994	13,713	+5.3	11,709	+7.8
1995	14,625	+6.7	12,469	+6.5
1996	15,367	+5.1	13,268	+6.4
1997e	16,824	+9.5	14,399	+8.5
1998f	17,499	+4.0	15,189	+5.5

e = estimate; f = 1998 Budget forecast.

Sources: Data extracted from "Trend in Current Government Expenditure by Functional Classification", Budget Books 1990–1997; "Budget 1998: Statistics and Tables", Table 3, December 1997, Department of Finance.

The speed at which public spending has been advancing in recent years can be gauged by comparing year-on-year increases in public spending against the annual rate of increase in consumer prices. This comparison is effected in Table 5.3.

TABLE 5.3: INCREASES IN PUBLIC SPENDING AND PRICES COMPARED, 1988–97

Year	Gross Public Spending (%)	Spending after Interest (%)	Inflation Rate (CPI) (%)
1988	+1.0	+0.9	+2.1
1989	+0.8	+1.1	+4.1
1990	+6.6	+6.3	+3.3
1991	+8.7	+10.4	+3.2
1992	+7.5	+9.3	+3.1
1993	+7.1	+8.5	+1.5
1994	+5.3	+7.8	+2.4
1995	+6.7	+6.5	+2.5
1996	+5.1	+6.4	+1.6
1997e	+9.5	+8.5	+1.5
1987–97	+75.5	+88.2	+28.4
1989–97	+72.3	+84.5	+20.8

Sources: Table 5.2; "Consumer Price Index", *Statistical Bulletin*, Vol., LXXII, No. 3, September 1997, CSO.

Table 5.3 shows that, in the decade ending 1997, the general level of Irish consumer prices rose by 28.4 per cent, an exemplary performance. Against this, total gross current public spending increased by 75.5 per cent, more than two-and-a-half times as fast as retail prices. In 1997 alone, gross public spending advanced by an extraordinary 9.5 per cent, over six times as fast as price increases in the nation's shops.

Gross current public spending includes the annual interest bills paid by government on its outstanding debts. Interest costs in cash terms have changed little over the past decade since the growth of the debt stock has been contained and interest rates have — barring exchange rate accidents — remained low. When the annual interest bills borne by government are excluded, non-interest current expenditure has increased by 88.2 per cent over the past decade. Hence, discretionary current public spending, that part of day-to-day spending within the direct control of government, has risen more than three times as fast as retail prices over the decade.

Over the years 1989–1997, the government's day-to-day spending increased by 72.3 per cent and gross spending after interest rose by 84.5 per cent, in the face of a one-fifth advance in domestic consumer prices. Thus far during the 1990s, current public spending excluding interest payments has been rising four times as fast as retail prices.

Both volume and price effects contributed to the acceleration in public spending growth after 1989. On the volume side, new spending programmes were introduced, the scope of existing programmes was widened and public service recruitment was stepped up. On the prices side, the major impetus to public expenditure growth was delivered by rising rates of pay for existing public service workers. In part, this reflected the "carry over" of public service special pay increases from the late 1980s to the years after 1990.

Given continuing adherence to tight borrowing targets by successive governments, large annual increases in public spending can only be financed by increases of a broadly similar magnitude in the national tax take.

However, it should be noted that, despite the scale of the annual additions to gross current public spending since 1990, gross government spending's share of Gross National Product was somewhat lower in 1997 than at the beginning of the decade. Moreover, the trend has been downwards since 1993. This is explained by the fact that, while public spending has been rising rapidly, the growth in money GNP has been even faster in recent years. This is shown in Table 5.4.

As Table 5.4 indicates, between 1990 and 1993, gross current public spending increased its share of GNP by two-and-a-half percentage points while net current spending advanced its stake in GNP by almost two percentage points. However, the sustained boom released by the 1993 devaluation added almost £12 billion to money GNP between 1993 and 1997. As a result, even with swift advances in annual public spending levels, their shares of GNP were lower in 1997 than in 1993.

TABLE 5.4: PUBLIC SPENDING'S SHARE OF GNP, 1990–97

Year	GNP (IR£ million)	Gross Spending as % of GNP	Net Spending as % of GNP*
1990	24,269	42.9	34.8
1991	25,427	44.5	35.7
1992	26,771	45.4	36.7
1993	28,698	45.4	36.7
1994	31,269	43.9	35.7
1995	34,129	42.9	35.3
1996	36,983	41.6	34.3
1997e	40,525	41.5	35.5

* Gross current spending less PRSI receipts less supply services appropriations-in-aid = net current spending. e = estimate.

Sources: "Trend in Current Government Expenditure by Functional Classification", Budget Books, 1994–1997; "1996 National Income and Expenditure First Results", CSO, June 1997, Table 5; "Budget 1998: Statistics and Tables", December 1997, Tables 1, 3.

Hence, rapid rates of economic expansion effectively disguise large absolute year-on-year increases in public spending. When the economy is moving ahead smartly, the ratio of public spending to GNP will decline, even when public spending itself is climbing sharply.

5.2.3. The Pace of Economic Activity

Just as quickening economic growth assists in disguising the extent of public spending increases, so it also helps government in raising additional income from taxation. A strongly performing economy will both broaden the tax base and generate revenue buoyancy. Where economic activity and domestic spending are rising swiftly, the flow of tax receipts into the Exchequer will increase at unchanged, or even declining, tax rates.

The main sources of tax revenue in Ireland are taxes on spending and taxes on personal and corporate incomes. In consequence, taxation revenues will be buoyant where consumer spending is rising, employment is increasing and corporate profitability is improving.

Since 1987, and especially since the currency crisis of 1992/93, the Irish economy has exhibited spectacularly fast rates of economic expansion. As shown in Table 1.5 in Chapter 1, in the decade after 1987, real GDP advanced by almost four-fifths while real GNP registered a rise of more than 70 per cent. Over these years, the volume of consumer spending in Ireland advanced by well over 50 per cent. All of these manifestations of economic success have acted to accelerate the inflow of tax revenues into the Exchequer.

The extra tax receipts generated by rapid economic expansion can be utilised in three principal ways. First, the proceeds can be allocated to reducing budget deficits and government borrowing. Second, the additional tax receipts can be channelled to finance higher levels of current government spending. Finally, increased tax inflows into the Exchequer can be used to fund reductions in tax rates.

Most commonly, the proceeds of tax buoyancy are divided between all three. Between 1987 and 1989, higher tax yields, in concert with tight public spending controls, were used to cut government budget deficits. Since 1990, in the Irish case, the tax dividends yielded by strong and sustained economic growth have been used principally to finance progressively higher levels of current public spending. However, there have been sufficient spare resources to fund fairly steep reductions in the rates of both direct and indirect taxation.

5.2.4. National Collective Bargaining Agreements

After a gap of more than five years, centralised collective pay bargaining agreements resumed in 1987 with the signing by the social partners of the Programme for National Recovery. The series of national agreements commencing in 1987 have been broader and more comprehensive than were their predecessors. Three innovations, in particular, have differentiated the current cycle of national agreements:

1. Governments have traded explicit tax cuts for moderate pay settlements. In this way, national collective bargaining has not only determined trends in basic pay increases but has influ-

enced the effective rates and incidence of personal taxes on income.

Under the umbrella of national agreements, governments have, on occasion, been quite explicit in quantifying the tax reductions they were prepared to implement in order to secure pay restraint. The Programme for National Recovery, spanning the years 1988 through 1990, undertook to introduce £225 million in tax reductions. In fact, the cumulative cost of the tax cuts implemented under the PNR was later calculated at £800 million. Under its successor, the Programme for Economic and Social Progress (PESP), the government proposed a tax reduction package costing up to £400 million for the years 1991–93, subject to certain conditions.

The Programme for Competitiveness and Work, which came into effect in 1994, was more circumspect in quantifying the cost of future tax changes. The fourth in the current series of national agreements, Partnership 2000, will be backed by "tax reductions of £1 billion on a full-year cost basis representing real reductions (on average) of over 0.5 per cent of GDP per year" during its 39-month life.[3]

2. Pay and taxation policies have been integrated into a broader macroeconomic context. The role of pay restraint in furthering the expansion of employment through improved competitiveness was clearly stated in the Programme for National Recovery. The impact of income tax reductions in slowing the rate of pay growth, thereby aiding competitiveness, was recognised in the PESP. The principal features of the agreements concluded since 1987 are reviewed in more detail in Chapter 6, Section 2.

3. The involvement of the social partners has not been limited to influencing pay increases and tax rates. Their participation has also directly levered upwards the amount of public spending. Thus, in the 1998 Budget, the Minister for Finance noted that Partnership 2000 contained "an action programme for social inclusion and equality involving additional expenditure of £525 million, again over three years".

---

[3] Budget Speech, 22 January 1997, p. 17.

5.3. The Growth of Taxation

The four factors identified in Section 4.2 have combined to shape the current configuration of taxation in Ireland. In broad terms, their individual effects can be summarised thus:

- Borrowing and debt strategy has not changed in substance since 1990. However, unexpectedly robust economic growth has led to improved performances on both fronts. Exchequer borrowing in 1997 had fallen to 0.5 per cent of Gross National Product while the General Government Account had moved from a deficit of 2.4 per cent of GDP in 1993 to a surplus equivalent to 0.9 per cent of GDP by 1997.

  The national debt/GDP ratio has fallen significantly because nominal GDP — the denominator in the debt equation — has been rising so rapidly. The ratio of General Government Debt to GDP declined from 96.3 per cent of GDP in 1993 to 66.3 per cent by 1997. In an environment of strong and sustained economic growth, the attainment of government deficit and borrowing targets has not, of itself, caused taxation to rise.

- Current government spending has risen swiftly since 1990. The very large year-to-year increases in current public spending have occurred despite low rates of consumer price inflation and virtually constant interest costs on government debt. The strongly expansionary tone of economic activity, and the related buoyancy in tax revenues, have allowed these exceptionally rapid increases in day-to-day public spending to be absorbed without recourse to higher tax rates. However, the rapidity of expenditure growth has ruled out cuts in average taxes on a scale that would otherwise have been possible.

  In short, the tax-enhancing impact of strong economic growth since 1990 has covered the cost of a multitude of economic sins. Continued economic expansion has raised incomes and profits while simultaneously increasing employment and consumer spending. Together, these factors have accelerated the flow of tax receipts into the Exchequer, even at declining tax rates. They have also permitted public spending to increase at a strong pace without breaching public borrowing targets. Hence, the tax revenue dividend paid out by consistently strong economic growth since 1990 has been absorbed principally by additional public spending; lesser amounts have been channelled towards cutting effective income tax rates.

- Collective national agreements have been broadened in scope since they resumed in Ireland in 1987. All of the four agreements concluded to date have recognised the links between taxes on income, rates of pay increase and national competitiveness. They have been innovative in explicitly trading reductions in income taxes for moderation in pay increases. The tax reductions proposed — and largely implemented — have been broadly successful in moderating the growth of private sector employee incomes, even as economic growth accelerated.

The evolution of the public finances since 1990 can be summarised in the following way. Government deficits and public borrowing have been restricted by the demands of common sense and the requirements of Maastricht. Current government spending has risen very rapidly. The increased bills for spending have been paid for by growth-induced additions to tax revenues. Sustained economic growth has allowed the additional tax revenues to be collected at unchanged, or in many cases reduced, tax rates. Collective bargaining agreements and government budgets have together directed a part of the proceeds of economic growth back to taxpayers in the form of tax reductions.

Nonetheless, this should not be allowed to obscure the fact that the government's receipts from taxation have risen very substantially. The scale of the increase in tax revenues between 1990 and 1997 is shown in Table 5.5.

As shown in Table 5.5, total tax revenues and tax revenues combined with PRSI contributions have increased by 81 per cent and 75 per cent respectively between 1990 and 1997. Over the same period, consumer prices increased by 16.9 per cent. Thus, tax revenues increased by four-and-a-half times the rate of retail price inflation between 1990 and 1997. As with spending, so with taxes.

TABLE 5.5: THE GROWTH OF TAX YIELDS BY CATEGORY, 1990–97

Category	1990 (£m)	1997 (£m)	Increase 1990–97 (%)
Income taxes*	3,149	5,407	+71.7
Corporation tax	474	1,699	+258.4
VAT	1,979	3,718	+87.9
Customs and excise	1,788	2,687	+50.3
Other	513	763	+48.7
Total Tax Revenue	7,903	14,274	+80.6
PRSI Contributions**	1,420	2,005	+41.2
Total Tax Revenues and PRSI	9,323	16,279	+74.6

* Income Tax, 1% Income Levy and 1% Training Levy.

** Includes both employer and employee contributions. The estimated yield for 1997 is as shown in the 1997 Budget Book (p. 123).

Sources: Budget Books, 1991–1997, Stationery Office; "Budget 1998: Statistics and Tables", December 1997, Table 2; "Exchequer Returns 1997", Department of Finance, January 1998.

The largest proportionate increase in revenues arose in the case of corporation tax. The yield from taxes on corporate income increased by over 258 per cent between 1990 and 1997, reflecting improved corporate earnings in existing enterprises, the creation of new profitable enterprises, particularly those located at the International Financial Services Centre (IFSC), and restrictions on corporate tax allowances.

Both income taxes and PRSI contributions increased at a slower pace than overall tax revenues. This reflected both the effectiveness of national collective bargaining in ameliorating the speed at which labour taxes were rising and a belated recognition by politicians that excessive tax loads on labour were damaging, politically as well as economically.

In the 1994 Budget, the Minister for Finance accepted that taxes on ordinary incomes were too high, not because tax rates were excessive, but because they were levied on relatively low incomes. In the course of his budget speech, the then Minister, Mr Bertie Ahern, observed:

> I would have to accept that our tax regime compares unfavourably, in terms of the usual international barometers, at the level of certain individual tax heads. It is indisputable that our income tax regime bears heavily on modest incomes. However, this is much more because tax, and the higher tax rate particularly, comes into play at relatively low thresholds, rather than on account of the rates as such; indeed, following the substantial progress made in recent years, these no longer stand out.[4]

In aggregate terms, given the strength of the economy over the first half of the 1990s, it is unsurprising that the growth in tax revenues significantly outpaced the rate of domestic price increases. However, it is surprising to find that total taxes rose faster than money Gross National Product over the period. This is shown in Table 5.6.

TABLE 5.6: SHARE OF TOTAL TAXES IN GROSS NATIONAL PRODUCT, 1990–97 (IN £ MILLION AT CURRENT PRICES)

Year	Money GNP	Total Taxes and PRSI	Total Taxes as % of GNP
1990	24,269	9,323	38.4
1991	25,427	9,887	38.9
1992	26,771	10,568	39.5
1993	28,698	11,506	40.1
1994	31,269	12,718	40.7
1995	34,129	13,294	39.0
1996	36,983	14,525	39.3
1997	40,525	16,279	40.2
Increase 1990–97	+67.0%	+74.6%	+1.8 points

Sources: Budget Books 1991–1997; "1996 National Income and Expenditure — First Results", CSO, June 1997, Table 5; "Budget 1998: Statistics and Tables", December 1997, Tables 1, 2.

---

[4] Budget 1994, Presented to Dáil Éireann, 26 January 1994, Budget Book, pp. 34–35.

Table 5.6 illustrates that not only have tax revenues increased substantially in absolute terms since the beginning of the 1990s, they have also risen as a proportion of GNP. Total tax revenues, including PRSI contributions, raised their share of Irish GNP from 38.4 per cent in 1990 to a peak level of 40.7 per cent four years later. Rapid growth in money GNP and a slight easing of the tax burden in recent years saw the share of taxes in GNP retreat to 40.2 per cent by 1997. However, this still left the share of total taxes in GNP 1.8 percentage points higher in 1997 than in 1990.

Thus, despite cuts in individual tax rates since 1990, some of significant depth, the national tax take has increased. This holds because the economy is now more profitably and fully employed than it was at the start of the decade. As economic activity picked up, more people were employed, more incomes were earned and spent and more profits were generated. All of these developments have broadened the base from which the Exchequer raises taxes.

Chapter 6

THE EVOLUTION OF PAY AND PRICES

6.1. Real Purchasing Power

The living standards of Irish households are shaped principally by the incomes they earn and the income transfers they receive from the state. Although work can be innately satisfying, and while employment may confer social status, the principal reason people go to work is to earn an income sufficient to support their material standard of living.

The size and structure of incomes across the economy results from the interaction of a complex set of factors. Skills and qualifications, economic rents and market power, labour scarcity and productivity, the nature of wage bargaining and the state of the economy all combine to produce a particular distribution of income and a specific set of pay differentials.

Those at work are essentially interested in the real spending power conferred by their earnings. Two factors act to diminish the real purchasing power of gross pay: inflation and income taxes. Since rising prices and increasing taxes erode real incomes, employees will usually seek compensation for both in the form of higher money wages.

The pace of inflation has been a particularly powerful force in shaping rates of pay increase in Ireland, since it very visibly erodes the purchasing power of money incomes. In the face of sharply rising prices, employees seek to protect their living standards by pursuing claims for compensating increases in their money wages. Rising income tax rates, since they also dilute the real purchasing power of money incomes, tend to induce a similar defensive response.

The experience of the past 25 years indicates that in Ireland, pay rises tend to track price increases. When inflation accelerates, the rate of increase in wages gathers pace; when inflation slows, pay rises moderate.

This tendency of pay to follow prices appears to hold whether or not national pay agreements are in force. Thus, the "National Understandings" of the late 1970s and early 1980s saw pay chasing prices upwards at a rapid pace. Despite the abandonment of national agreements after 1982, the deep domestic deflation of the early 1980s witnessed a sharp fall in inflation and a consequent moderation in rates of pay increase. The revival of collective national agreements from 1987 onwards has seen prices and pay both advance at very modest annual rates. The long-run tendency for prices and pay to march broadly in step is illustrated in Table 6.1, for the period 1979 through 1996.

The significant influence which inflation exerts on pay should not obscure the fact that other forces also play a part in determining rates of wage and salary increase. In the traded sector, Irish enterprises must sell their goods and services on competitive markets at home and abroad. Where Irish prices exceed international prices, markets are surrendered, profits are squeezed and, ultimately, jobs are lost. Labour costs constitute a large slice of value added in domestic Irish businesses. Hence, the demands of international competition set a ceiling for pay rises in the traded sector, which can be breached only at the expense of job losses.

Conversely, when the competitiveness of the Irish traded sector improves, or when domestic productivity growth is particularly rapid, output expands and profits swell. In these conditions, employees will seek to exploit the ability of employers to pay higher wages.

These underlying pressures on pay — inflation, direct taxes on employees' incomes, employers' inability to pay in bad times and wage drift in good times — will eventually manifest themselves, whether or not national agreements are in force. However, such collective agreements can dampen down rates of money wage increase through cutting employees' taxes, while they also provide a formal institutional structure within which disputes over distributional shares can be resolved in an informed and orderly manner without recourse to strikes.

The Evolution of Pay and Prices

TABLE 6.1: TRENDS IN CONSUMER PRICES AND MANUFACTURING PAY, 1979–96 (PERCENTAGE INCREASES ON PREVIOUS YEAR)

Year	Price Inflation (%)*	Wage Inflation (%)**	Average Hourly Pay Rates (£)**
1979	13.2	15.7	1.92
1980	18.2	21.4	2.33
1981	20.4	16.7	2.72
1982	17.1	14.7	3.12
1983	10.5	11.5	3.48
1984	8.6	10.9	3.86
1985	5.4	8.0	4.17
1986	3.8	7.2	4.47
1987	3.1	4.7	4.68
1988	2.1	4.3	4.88
1989	4.1	4.1	5.08
1990	3.3	4.5	5.31
1991	3.2	5.6	5.61
1992	3.1	4.6	5.87
1993	1.5	5.8	6.21
1994	2.4	1.8	6.32
1995	2.5	2.4	6.47
1996	1.6	2.6	6.64

* As measured by the Consumer Price Index. ** As measured by hourly earnings for all adults in manufacturing industry.

Sources: "Consumer Price Index" and "Industrial Earnings and Hours Worked", in *Statistical Bulletin*, Vol. LXXII, No 3, CSO, September 1997.

The annual number of days lost as a result of industrial disputes has fallen sharply since the peak year of 1979. While very high inflation and rising income taxes no doubt disturbed industrial relations in the late 1970s and early 1980s, the fall in days lost through disputes has gathered speed since the reintroduction of national agreements in 1988. This can be seen from Table 6.2.

TABLE 6.2: DAYS LOST THROUGH INDUSTRIAL DISPUTES, 1976–96 ('000S)

Year	Days Lost through Disputes	Year	Days Lost through Disputes
1976	777	1987	264
1977	442	1988	143
1978	613	1989	50
1979	1,465	1990	223
1980	412	1991	86
1981	434	1992	110
1982	434	1993	61
1983	319	1994	26
1984	386	1995	130
1985	418	1996	115
1986	309		

Source: Labour Market and Social Statistics Division, Central Statistics Office, Cork, September 1997.

The most remarkable aspect of these data is the extent to which days lost through disputes have been contained even as labour markets tightened and the income expectations of employees increased on the back of a booming economy.

6.2. The Renaissance of National Pay Agreements

The process of national pay bargaining was brought to an abrupt halt with the collapse in 1982 of the second "National Understanding". There followed a period of free collective bargaining that spanned five years. National pay agreements recommenced with the signing of the Programme for National Recovery (PNR) in October 1987. The new three-year national pay deal took effect from the beginning of 1988.

This process of national collective bargaining has proved durable. The PNR was followed by the Programme for Economic and Social Progress (PESP), covering the years 1991 to 1993 and the Programme for Competitiveness and Work (PCW), 1994–96/97. The fourth in the current series of national agreements, Partnership 2000, was ratified by the trade union movement in January

1997. From the outset, the new cycle of national agreements contained innovative and economically important features which differentiated it from previous exercises in national collective bargaining.

First, the Programme for National Recovery identified the pressing need to reduce the debt/GNP ratio, curb Exchequer borrowing and curtail public expenditure in order to recreate a healthy economy.[1] The fiscal correction achieved in the years 1988–90 laid the foundations for the rapid economic growth achieved in the years that followed.

Second, the links between pay moderation, competitiveness and employment growth were recognised explicitly from the start of the process and have been reiterated in each subsequent agreement. Thus, the Programme for National Recovery stated:

> The moderate pay agreements under the Programme will contribute significantly to our ability to compete more effectively and thus create more jobs. This discipline must be matched by better marketing and management and greater technological development.[2]

Partnership 2000 mirrors this analytic overview:

> The key objectives of the strategy are the continued development of an efficient modern economy capable of high and sustainable economic and employment growth and operating within the constraints of international competitiveness.[3]

Third, the agreements have sought to moderate the rate of increase in pay, thereby underpinning competitiveness, by explicitly trading income tax cuts for pay rises.

The basic pay terms and the most important features of the national agreements concluded since 1987 are summarised in Table 6.3.

---

[1] Programme for National Recovery, "Macroeconomic Policies", paragraphs 1–2, p. 9, October 1987.

[2] PNR, op. cit., paragraph 8, p. 17.

[3] Partnership 2000, paragraph 1.2, p. 5, December 1996.

TABLE 6.3: BASIC PAY TERMS OF NATIONAL PAY AGREEMENTS

Year	Basic Pay Increases	Other Pay and Tax Features
I. Programme for National Recovery, 1988–90 Inclusive		
1988	2.5%	Special pay awards for public servants deferred
1989	2.5%	Tax cuts of £225 million promised by government over three years
1990	2.5%	"Special consideration" for low-paid workers
II. Programme for Economic and Social Progress, 1991–93		
1991	4.0%	"Floor" weekly pay rises of £5.00 in year 1, £4.25 in year 2 and £5.75 in year 3 for the low paid
1992	3.0%	Local bargaining for "exceptional" increases of 3% permitted over the Agreement's term
1993	3.75%	Up to £400 million in tax cuts promised
III. Programme for Competitiveness and Work, 1994–96/97		
1994	2.0%*	Public service pay deal: 3.5 years: 5 month pause; 2% in year 1; 2% for year 2; 1.5% for next 4 mths; 1.5% for next 3 mths; 1% for final 6 mths
1995	2.5%*	Tax cuts unquantified but to be focused on low and middle earners
1996	2.5% for first 6 months* 1% for next 6 months*	"Floor" increases for low-paid in both public and private sectors from year 2
IV. Partnership 2000, 1997–2000		
1997	2.5%	Public service pay deal: Phase 1: 2.5% of first £220 basic for nine months, then 2.5% of the balance of full basic pay for 3 months. After first year: as private sector
1998	2.25%	Provision for local negotiation of further 2% rise in years 2 (private sector) and 3 (public sector)
1999	1.5% for 9 months	"Floor" cash increases to aid low-paid from year 2 onwards
	1.0% for 6 months	£1 billion on full-year cost basis to be made available for tax relief

* Private sector excluding construction; public service pay agreement terms are shown in parallel.

Sources: PNR, October 1987; PESP, January 1991; PCW, February 1994; Partnership 2000, December 1996.

The Department of Enterprise and Employment has argued that this cycle of national pay agreements has assisted in securing certain key economic objectives, including:

> (i) improving international competitiveness; (ii) transforming the fiscal position of our economy; and (iii) making the economy more employment-friendly through securing pay moderation (especially in the private sector) and reducing the threat of industrial action. . . . In times of significant economic growth, such agreements can also help to stem the growth in inflation. "Inability to pay" clauses have also played a significant role in the private sector by protecting vulnerable employment.[4]

The pay terms negotiated in national agreements over the past decade define increases in basic pay. Actual rates of pay increase can fluctuate around these basic terms for a number of reasons. In the private sector, average earnings may rise faster due to overtime working, local productivity deals and wage drift due to skills shortages. Conversely, private sector earnings may rise more slowly where enterprises plead inability to pay because of competitive pressures or where the basic pay terms are deferred. In the public service, actual pay rises faster than the basic negotiated increases because of annual increments, special pay awards and successful relativity claims.

However, while the official view is strongly supportive of the reinstatement of collective pay bargaining, such national pay deals have not been without their critics.

From an economic perspective, the objective of national pay deals is to restrain the growth of incomes below the levels they would have reached in the absence of such agreements. Where national pay deals are successful in slowing the rate of pay growth, the international competitiveness of Irish output is enhanced and employment prospects are improved. The critical issue is the extent to which the reintroduction of national bargaining has actually delivered pay restraint.

In the tables that follow, it will be seen that private sector incomes, from the shopfloor to the executive suite, have increased

---

[4] "Growing and Sharing Our Employment", April 1996, p. 51.

quite modestly in money terms over the years 1987 through 1996. Given the background of particularly robust economic growth, wage drift has been subdued on the shopfloor and only slightly more vocal at executive level.

However, public service pay has grown faster than its private sector counterpart over the period since 1987. This does not indicate that public service workers have breached the basic pay terms of national agreements introduced since 1987. Rather, it has been attributable to the interaction of basic increases, annual increments, and, above all, successful special pay claims.

Thus, the renewal of the collective bargaining experiment appears to have been far more successful in restraining income growth in the private than in the public sector. Critics of the reinstatement of national pay agreements thus argue that governments would have been better advised to direct their efforts to controlling public service pay while leaving private sector pay to be determined by market forces at enterprise level.

The logical force of this view is blunted by recognition of the locus of economic power in Ireland. Attempts to curb significantly the extent and incidence of special pay increases in the public service would have been met with stern resistance on the part of public service unions. In turn, this would have reversed the downward trend in days lost through industrial disputes. In broad terms, the reintroduction of national collective bargaining has delivered pay restraint in the private sector and, at considerable additional cost, industrial peace in the public sector.

6.3. Pay Levels in Ireland: Manufacturing Industry

While a plethora of price indices are produced in Ireland, reliable data on aggregate levels of pay across the economy are extremely limited. The trend in average earnings in manufacturing industry is the most commonly used indicator both of pay levels and changes in those levels over time. The trends in hourly pay rates and in weekly earnings for all industrial workers in manufacturing industry are shown in Table 6.4 for the years since 1987.

The Evolution of Pay and Prices

TABLE 6.4: PAY TRENDS IN IRISH MANUFACTURING SINCE 1987

Year	Hourly Rates	Increase (%)	Weekly Earnings	Increase (%)
1987	£4.68	+4.7	£193.64	+5.1
1988	£4.88	+4.3	£202.81	+4.7
1989	£5.08	+4.1	£210.98	+4.0
1990	£5.35	+5.3	£221.71	+5.1
1991	£5.61	+4.9	£228.72	+3.2
1992	£5.87	+4.6	£237.92	+4.0
1993	£6.21	+5.8	£250.70	+5.4
1994	£6.32	+1.8	£258.03	+2.9
1995	£6.47	+2.4	£263.75	+2.2
1996	£6.64	+2.6	£270.40	+2.5
Increase 1987–96	+£1.96	+41.9	£76.76	+39.6
1997e	£6.84	+3.0	£278.51	+3.0

e = estimate.

Source: "Industrial Earnings and Hours Worked" series, CSO; "Economic Review and Outlook 1997", Department of Finance, Summer 1997, p. 26.

The CSO industrial earnings data show that average hourly rates of pay for all workers in manufacturing industry increased from £4.68 in 1987 to £6.64 in 1996, a cumulative rise of 41.9 per cent. Over the same period, the average weekly earnings of industrial employees advanced by £76.76 or 39.6 per cent. Variations between the rates of increase in hourly and weekly earnings are explained by changes in the number of hours worked each week. In the summer of 1997, the Department of Finance, in its "Economic Review and Outlook 1997", estimated that manufacturing earnings would rise by about three per cent that year. This would have left average hourly earnings at £6.84 in 1997. Assuming no change in hours worked, average weekly earnings in manufacturing would have amounted to £278.51 in 1997, or £14,483 a year.

The CSO earnings data are derived from a sample drawn from all industrial establishments employing ten or more persons. The establishments in the sample cover roughly 70 per cent of all industrial employees. The industrial workers included in this series comprise operatives, maintenance workers, cleaners, storeroom staff, basic supervisory staff and apprentices.

The Central Statistics Office also separately estimates the weekly earnings of clerical and managerial employees in manufacturing industries. These are shown in Table 6.5 for the years since 1987.

Table 6.5 shows that the average weekly earnings of clerical workers in manufacturing industry rose by £105.68 or 49.2 per cent between 1987 and 1996. Over the same span, managerial employees in manufacturing on average saw their weekly pay cheques increase by over two-fifths, from £346.91 in 1987 to £497.78 in 1996.

The CSO earnings data constitute a valuable first approximation to determining pay levels and the structure of pay relativities in Ireland. However, two factors inhibit generalisation from earnings in manufacturing to pay levels throughout the economy.

TABLE 6.5: AVERAGE WEEKLY EARNINGS OF CLERICAL AND MANAGERIAL EMPLOYEES IN IRISH MANUFACTURING, 1987–96

Year	Clerical Employees	Rise (%)	Managerial Employees	Rise (%)
1987	£214.97	+6.4	£346.91	+6.5
1988	£225.77	+5.0	£365.41	+5.3
1989	£237.64	+5.3	£381.54	+4.4
1990	£248.97	+4.8	£396.38	+3.9
1991	£259.64	+4.3	£416.90	+5.2
1992	£273.66	+5.4	£442.73	+6.2
1993	£293.19	+7.1	£466.94	+5.5
1994	£300.32	+2.4	£476.54	+2.1
1995	£309.78	+3.1	£487.11	+2.2
1996	£320.65	+3.5	£497.78	+2.2
Increase 1987–96	£105.68	+49.2	£150.87	+43.5

Source: "Industrial Earnings and Hours Worked", Quarterly Series, Central Statistics Office, December 1997.

First, a relatively small proportion of those at work are employed in manufacturing industry. The 1997 Labour Force Survey estimated that 1.338 million people were at work in Ireland that year. Of the total, 271,000 were employed in manufacturing industry. Thus, the total manufacturing workforce accounted for just over one-fifth (20.3 per cent) of all those at work in Ireland.

Second, the CSO earnings data is drawn from a sample of the bigger manufacturing enterprises — those employing ten or more people. The earnings of those working in small firms employing less than ten people are therefore excluded. Since pay rates are likely to be higher in larger enterprises, the structure of the CSO earnings survey may tend to overstate average earnings in all Irish manufacturing enterprises, large and small.

6.4. Pay Levels in Ireland: The Public Sector

In a labour market context, the public sector is important in Ireland for two reasons. First, the government is a major Irish employer. The public sector workforce numbered 297,000 people at April 1997, accounting for 22.2 per cent of national employment. Between 1989 and 1997, the numbers working in the public sector increased by 11,000 or 3.8 per cent.[5]

The public sector workforce embraces two elements. The first consists of public service employees. In addition to civil servants, this group principally comprises those providing public education and health services, the defence forces and the Gardaí. Second, the wider public sector workforce also embraces those working in regional bodies, local authorities, state-sponsored bodies and state enterprises.

The second reason why the public sector workforce is important is that its pay bill must be financed principally by taxpayers. The public sector does not usually charge its clients and customers the full economic cost of the services it provides. Instead, the greater part of the pay of public sector employees is financed collectively through taxation. Given its size, the cost and rate of increase in the public sector pay bill is, therefore, an important determinant of the level of taxation in Ireland.

---

[5] 1997 Labour Force Survey, Appendix G, p. 104, CSO, October 1997.

Figures on the size of the public sector pay bill are not published at Budget time, nor are data yet available on the average levels of public sector pay in cash terms, though this is due to be remedied in the course of 1998. However, quarterly indices on the growth in average public sector earnings have been collected and published by the CSO since March 1988. These are shown in Table 6.6. Unfortunately, they exclude the earnings of those working in the public health sector.

TABLE 6.6: AVERAGE PUBLIC SECTOR EARNINGS INDEX (MARCH 1988 = 100; ANNUAL INDICES ARE AVERAGES OF FOUR QUARTERS)

Year	Total Public Sector*	Civil Service	Defence Forces	Education	Gardaí
1988	103.1	100.4	100.4	101.9	106.4
1989	107.7	105.5	109.0	106.7	112.1
1990	114.9	116.3	121.0	110.5	119.8
1991	121.5	123.2	137.0	119.2	128.5
1992	127.6	128.9	142.1	126.8	134.0
1993	135.3	133.2	149.1	134.6	144.1
1994	139.7	136.1	151.9	141.2	148.8
1995	144.2	139.0	157.0	145.1	151.5
1996	149.6	143.7	161.9	149.3	163.9
1997**	155.8	151.7	168.9	154.3	169.3

Notes: * Figures exclude the earnings of those employed by Health Boards and in voluntary hospitals. Since these are earnings data, they include overtime, where applicable; ** Indices as at June 1997.

Source: "Public Sector Average Earnings Indices", Central Statistics Office.

As can be seen from Table 6.6, average earnings for all public sector employees were 55.8 per cent higher in June 1997 than in March 1988, when the earnings index was constructed.

There were considerable variations in the rate of earnings growth as between different segments of the public sector. Over the nine-year period, the earnings of civil servants increased by 51.7 per cent, while average teachers' earnings moved ahead by 54.3 per cent. In the defence forces and the Gardaí, earnings were more than two-thirds higher in June 1997 than in March 1988.

Actual earnings of public sector employees, on which this index is constructed, are not published. As a result, no public data is available on the average levels either of earnings in the public sector or of average pay in the narrower public service.

An attempt to bridge this information gap is made in Table 6.7. The public service pay and pensions bill is published in each year's Budget book. It covers the pay of civil servants, providers of public education and health services, the defence forces and the Gardaí. It excludes the earnings of those working for local authorities and the employees of state-sponsored bodies.

Deducting pensions and dividing by the number of public servants should provide at least a first approximation to the size of average public service earnings. These computations are effected below.

TABLE 6.7: ESTIMATED LEVELS OF AVERAGE PUBLIC SERVICE PAY, 1987–96

Year	Public Service Pay Bill (£ million)	Public Service Numbers	Average Pay Per Year
1987	2,565	180,141	£14,239
1988	2,545	174,860	£14,555
1989	2,663	167,439	£15,904
1990	2,913	171,716	£16,964
1991	3,122	174,812	£17,859
1992	3,487	177,682	£19,625
1993	3,779	181,112	£20,866
1994	4,026	183,743	£21,911
1995	4,226	188,826	£22,380
1996	4,439	192,224	£23,093
Change 1987–96	+73.1%	+6.7%	+62.2%
1997e	4,887	192,555	£25,380

Notes: The public service pay bill excludes pensions. Public service numbers are those at 1 January each year. In 1995, public service numbers were raised both by increases and reclassifications of certain education posts.

Source: Budget Books; Department of Finance.

As Table 6.7 shows, the annual bill for public service pay increased by almost three-quarters, from £2.57 billion to £4.44 billion between 1987 and 1996. Over the same period, public service numbers rose by some 6.7 per cent. Dividing the public service pay bill by the number of public servants each year yields a tentative estimate of the annual average earnings of public servants. On this basis, average public service pay increased from £14,239 in 1987 to £23,093 in 1996, an increase of 62.2 per cent.

The particularly large increases in average public service earnings in the early 1990s reflects the impact of the "carryover" of special pay awards from the Programme for National Recovery. These special pay awards aimed at restoring pay relativities with comparable employments in the private sector.

Public service pay advanced at a notably rapid pace during 1997. The budgetary out-turn for 1997 indicates that the public service pay bill climbed by almost £450 million or 10.1 per cent to £4,887 million.[6]

As a result, the cost to the Exchequer of the public service pay bill increased by £2.3 billion or 90.5 per cent in the course of the decade ending 1997.

6.5. Pay Trends in Ireland: Executive Salaries

For many years, the Irish Management Institute has undertaken an annual survey of executive salaries in Ireland. The results of the 1996 survey, encompassing 8,930 Irish managers in 166 companies, are summarised in Table 6.8 by company size.

The executive incomes shown in Table 6.8 embrace salaries and other taxable remuneration such as bonuses and overtime, but exclude non-taxable fringe benefits. As might be expected, executive salaries rise not only as individuals ascend the corporate job ladder, but as the size of firm increases.

Since the respondents to each year's salary surveys differ, it is difficult to track long-run trend increases in executive salaries accurately. However, the IMI itself estimates annual year-on-year increases in average executive salaries, together with comparable annual inflation rates. These are shown in Table 6.9.

---

[6] Department of Finance, January 1998.

The Evolution of Pay and Prices

TABLE 6.8: EXECUTIVE SALARIES IN IRELAND BY SIZE OF COMPANY (AT APRIL 1996 IN £ PER ANNUM)

Job Category	Company Size Defined by Employee Numbers			
	20–50	51–100	101–250	251–500
Chief Executive	52,250	72,000	80,000	94,000
Head of Function	36,400	41,000	44,700	51,000
Middle Manager	21,350	28,000	32,000	34,700
Front-Line Manager	17,500	22,000	24,000	28,600

Notes: Heads of Function include Finance Director, Operations Director, Marketing/Sales Director; Middle Managers comprise Production Manager, Financial Accountant, Sales Manager, Employee Relations Manager; Front-Line Management encompasses Team Leader, Sales Executive, Payroll Supervisor, Recruitment Officer.

Source: "Executive Salaries in Ireland", IMI, March 1997.

TABLE 6.9: AVERAGE ANNUAL INCREASES IN EXECUTIVE SALARIES, 1987–96 (% INCREASE FOR THE 12 MONTHS TO APRIL EACH YEAR)

Year	Average Salary Increase (%)	Inflation Rate (%)
1988	+3.2	+1.9
1989	+1.6	+3.3
1990	+5.0	+4.2
1991	+4.2	+3.1
1992	+4.0	+3.6
1993	+4.2	+1.9
1994	+5.7	+2.7
1995	+5.3	+2.8
1996	+6.0	+2.0
Increase 1987–96	+46.7	+26.4

Sources: "Executive Salaries in Ireland, 1987–96", IMI, Dublin; CSO.

The cumulative increase in average Irish executive salaries over the period 1987 through 1996 amounted to 46.7 per cent. This cumulative increase is broadly in line with the CSO data for pay rises received by clerical and managerial employees in manufacturing industry, at 49.2 per cent and 43.5 per cent respectively, as shown in Table 6.5. While executive salaries have risen substantially over the past decade, the increases are not out of line with pay rises recorded by other occupational grades in the private sector. There has been no "Big Bang" in executive pay.

The data in Tables 6.8 and 6.9 allow the estimation of trends in executive salaries in cash terms over the years 1987 through 1996. These are shown in Table 6.10 and, since they are derived from the application of average general increases to specific management grades, should be treated as indicative only.

TABLE 6.10: TRENDS IN ANNUAL EXECUTIVE SALARIES, 1987–96 (£)

Year	Small Firms (20–50)		Large Firms (251–500)	
	CEO	*FLM*	*CEO*	*FLM*
1987	35,624	11,931	64,089	19,500
1988	36,764	12,313	66,140	20,124
1989	37,352	12,510	67,198	20,446
1990	39,220	13,136	70,558	21,468
1991	40,867	13,687	73,522	22,369
1992	42,502	14,235	76,463	23,264
1993	44,287	14,833	79,674	24,241
1994	46,811	15,678	84,216	25,623
1995	49,292	16,509	88,679	26,981
1996	52,250	17,500	94,000	28,600
Increase 1987–96	+46.7%	+46.7%	+46.7%	+46.7%

Notes: CEO: Chief Executive; FLM: Front-Line Manager.
Sources: Tables 6.8, 6.9; IMI.

6.6. Pay Trends in Ireland: National Income Data

Thus far, employee pay trends have been surveyed for those employed in manufacturing industry and in public sector. Together, these two groups account for over two out of every five members of the non-agricultural workforce. In addition, trends in executive salaries have been examined, using survey data collected by the Irish Management Institute.

In an effort to enhance the generality of the findings, estimates for average pay levels for the non-agricultural workforce as a whole are now derived using the National Income and Expenditure Accounts and Labour Force Surveys.

Item 10 of the annual national income accounts shows data for the wages, salaries and pensions of the non-agricultural workforce. This item not only includes basic pay, but overtime earnings, bonus payments, commissions and payments for piecework. However, pension payments and employers' contributions to pension funds are also included, imparting some upward bias to the pay estimates. Transfer payments, such as old-age pensions and unemployment benefits, are all excluded.[7] The national income data should therefore give a broad, rather than a precise, indication of average pay levels for the non-agricultural workforce.

The approximate size of the non-agricultural workforce can be gauged each year from the Labour Force Survey, undertaken by the Central Statistics Office every April. Dividing non-agricultural employee remuneration by the non-agricultural workforce yields estimates for the average pay levels of employees outside agriculture. The calculations for the decade are shown in Table 6.11.

Table 6.11 shows that the aggregate gross pay of Ireland's non-farm workforce increased by over £8.2 billion or 82.8 per cent between 1987 and 1996. The numbers at work outside agriculture rose by 243,000 or over one-quarter during this period. The average pay of all employees advanced from £10,874 in 1987 to £15,707 by 1996, representing an average gross income gain in excess of 44 per cent.

The substantial rise of more than four-fifths in aggregate employee income between 1987 and 1996 was driven both by increasing numbers at work outside farming and by large gains in average gross pay per employee. These two factors explain the sharp rise in the national tax take shown earlier in Table 5.5. More and larger incomes created more revenues from spending and income taxes for the Exchequer, even where tax rates were falling.

---

[7] See National Income and Expenditure 1995, CSO, Appendix 2, p. 50, July 1996, for coverage of Item 10.

TABLE 6.11: TRENDS IN NON-AGRICULTURAL PAY, 1987–96

Year	Non-Farm Pay Bill (£m)	Non-Farm Workforce	Average Pay (£)	Rise (%)
1987	9,961	916,000	10,874	—
1988	10,568	925,000	11,425	+5.1
1989	11,324	926,000	12,229	+7.0
1990*	11,961	965,000	12,395	+1.4
1991	12,740	979,000	13,013	+5.0
1992	13,627	991,000	13,751	+5.7
1993	14,760	1,008,000	14,643	+6.5
1994	15,767	1,046,000	15,074	+2.9
1995	16,923	1,105,000	15,315	+1.6
1996	18,204	1,159,000	15,707	+2.6
Increase 1987–96	+82.8%	+26.5%	+44.4%	+44.4%

* New series may influence 1989 to 1990 changes.

Sources: National Income and Expenditure 1994, 1995, 1996, CSO, Table 1; Labour Force Survey 1997, CSO, Appendix G, October 1997.

6.7. Irish Employee Incomes Compared, 1987–96

Seven sets of pay data have now been examined and discussed: executive salaries; the earnings of industrial workers, clerical employees and managers in manufacturing industry; indices for public sector earnings; average levels of pay in the public service; and average non-agricultural employee remuneration in the economy as a whole. Trends in executive salaries were illustrated in Tables 6.9 and 6.10, where it was shown that average cumulative increases have amounted to 46.7 per cent for the years spanning 1987–96. The progress of pay in each of the remaining categories has been tracked in Table 6.12.

The Evolution of Pay and Prices

TABLE 6.12: AVERAGE LEVELS OF NON-AGRICULTURAL EMPLOYEE PAY, 1987–96 (£)

Year	Economy-Wide*	Manufacturing			Public Service
		Industrial	Clerk	Manager	
1987	10,874	10,069	11,178	18,039	14,239
1988	11,425	10,546	11,740	19,001	14,555
1989	12,229	10,971	12,357	19,840	15,904
1990	12,395	11,529	12,946	20,612	16,964
1991	13,013	11,893	13,501	21,679	17,859
1992	13,751	12,372	14,230	23,022	19,625
1993	14,643	13,036	15,246	24,281	20,866
1994	15,074	13,418	15,617	24,780	21,911
1995	15,315	13,715	16,109	25,330	22,380
1996	15,707	14,061	16,674	25,885	23,093
Increase 1987–96	+44.4%	+39.6%	+49.2%	+43.5%	+62.2%

* Non-farm pay derived from national income data
Sources: Tables 6.4–6.7 above.

The data in Table 6.12 indicate that, nationally, average employee incomes outside agriculture rose by over two-fifths between 1987 and 1996. Clerical workers in manufacturing did a little better and industrial workers a little worse than average. Public service employees enjoyed a particularly rapid rise in pay, outperforming the average growth in employee incomes significantly.

In order to assess changing relativities in the pay levels of different groups, the data in Table 6.12 are re-stated in index numbers in Table 6.13. Managers' salaries, as shown in Table 6.9, are also included for comparative purposes. In all cases, base pay in 1987 is set equal to 100. This should not be taken to imply that the relative structure of pay in 1987 was in some way "correct". The objective is simply to trace the evolution of incomes over the period coinciding with the reintroduction of national collective bargaining agreements and the turnaround in the economy.

TABLE 6.13: THE EVOLUTION OF EMPLOYEE INCOMES IN IRELAND, 1987–96 (USING INDEX NUMBERS WITH BASE 1987 = 100)

Year	Economy-Wide	Manufacturing			IMI Survey	Public Service
		Industrial	Clerk	Manager		
1987	100.0	100.0	100.0	100.0	100.0	100.0
1988	105.1	104.7	105.0	105.3	103.2	102.2
1989	112.5	109.0	110.5	110.0	104.9	111.7
1990	114.0	114.5	115.8	114.3	110.1	119.1
1991	119.7	118.1	120.8	120.2	114.7	125.4
1992	126.5	122.9	127.3	127.6	119.3	137.8
1993	134.7	129.5	136.4	134.6	124.3	146.5
1994	138.6	133.3	139.7	137.4	131.4	153.9
1995	140.8	136.2	144.1	140.4	138.4	157.2
1996	144.4	139.6	149.2	143.5	146.7	162.2

Source: Tables 6.9, 6.12.

Table 6.13 makes clear that while the incomes of all managers and employees increased in the years since 1987, some rose more swiftly than others. In the incomes race, public servants out-sprinted all others.

6.8. Pay and Price Trends in Ireland Compared, 1987–97

Increases in money incomes do not, by themselves, determine the advances in the material living standards enjoyed by those at work. Employees are consumers as well as income earners. Therefore, the retail prices that income earners must pay for goods and services define the real purchasing power of their after-tax incomes. The restatement of income data in index number form in Table 6.13 facilitates a comparison with trends in consumer prices since 1987. This comparison is shown in Table 6.14.

TABLE 6.14: EMPLOYEE PAY AND CONSUMER PRICES COMPARED, 1987–97 (INDEX NUMBERS, ALL RE-BASED TO 1987 = 100)

1987	Consumer Prices	Employee Incomes*	Industrial Earnings	Public Service Pay
1987	100.0	100.0	100.0	100.0
1988	102.1	105.1	104.7	102.2
1989	106.3	112.5	109.0	111.7
1990	109.8	114.0	114.5	119.1
1991	113.3	119.7	118.1	125.4
1992	116.9	126.5	122.9	137.8
1993	118.5	134.7	129.5	146.5
1994	121.3	138.6	133.3	153.9
1995	124.4	140.8	136.2	157.2
1996	126.4	144.4	139.6	162.2
1997e	128.4	148.7	143.8	173.9**

* Economy-wide (NIE) measure; e= estimate. ** The Department of Finance estimates that public service pay on average increased by 7.2 per cent in 1997.

Sources: Table 6.7; "Consumer Price Index", Statistical Bulletin, CSO; "Economic Background to the Budget 1997", pp. 10, 15.

Inflation remained low throughout the period, with the price level rising by just over one-quarter between 1987 and 1996. As a result, average employees' gross incomes outpaced the rate of price increase — and by respectable margins. While some groups fared relatively better than others, the real incomes — money incomes adjusted for price changes — of all those at work have improved since the economy turned the corner out of recession in 1987.

These trends continued after 1996. Real income gains were consolidated in 1997. During that year, consumer price inflation was subdued, at just 1.5 per cent. The Department of Finance has estimated that average earnings in manufacturing moved ahead by 3 per cent. In the public service, average pay increased by 7.2 per cent in 1997.

This very rapid increase in per capita public service earnings during 1997 comprised an average general pay round increase of

3.2 per cent and average local bargaining increases of 3.9 per cent, according to the Department of Finance. The local bargaining increases, in many cases, contained an element of retrospection. These assessments provide the basis for the 1997 estimates in Table 6.14. Both indicate that earnings levels are stretching further ahead of inflation, raising real incomes in the process.

However, inflation is not the only force that siphons off the purchasing power of pay. Indirect taxes push up prices, thus confiscating the purchasing power of income earners. Taxes on income also take a chunk out of spending power. The depressing impact of direct taxes on real income is discussed in the next chapter.

Chapter 7

INCOME TAXES

7.1. The Evolution of the Tax Code Since 1987

This chapter traces the evolution of the Irish income tax code since 1987, based on the provisions and tax changes contained in annual budgets. The selection of 1987 as the base year is influenced by three factors.

First, the turnaround in Irish economic performance, although a gradual process rather than a specific event, is usually dated to 1987. Second, the current cycle of national pay agreements commenced in 1987 with the signing of the Programme for National Recovery. Third, there was a marked change in the disposition of fiscal policy following the formation of a new Government in March 1987. Cuts in current public spending, unrelieved initially by tax reductions, caused a sharp improvement in the government deficit. The deficit was further reduced by unexpectedly large inflows from the 1988 tax amnesty.

The approach adopted is narrow in perspective. It focuses primarily on changes in the taxation of labour income, touching only cursorily on the broader policy factors that influenced such changes. The discussion embraces 1998 budgetary tax changes and traces the evolution of the following variables over the past decade:

- Income tax exemption thresholds — the income levels below which households are not assessable for income tax

- Basic personal tax allowances for single people and married couples

- Adjustments to income tax bands and tax rates

- Changes in discretionary personal tax allowances

- Adjustments to Pay-Related Social Insurance rates of contribution and contribution ceilings for employers and employees.

While firm income data are available only as late as 1996, estimates and projections are provided for subsequent years in order to capture current trends.

7.2. Income Tax Exemption Thresholds

Income tax exemption thresholds are the levels of gross income below which households are exempted altogether from Income Tax. The thresholds are set with respect to marital status and household size. Income tax exemption thresholds for a selection of different household types are shown for the period since 1987 in Table 7.1.

TABLE 7.1: GENERAL INCOME TAX EXEMPTION THRESHOLDS, 1987–97 (IN £ PER YEAR AT CURRENT PRICES)

Year	Single Person	Married Couple	Married Couple + 2 Children	Married Couple + 4 Children
1987/88	2,650	5,300	5,300	5,300
1988/89	2,750	5,500	5,500	5,500
1989/90	3,000	6,000	6,400	6,800
1990/91	3,250	6,500	7,100	7,700
1991/92	3,400	6,800	7,400	8,400
1992/93	3,500	7,000	7,600	8,600
1993/94	3,600	7,200	7,900	9,000
1994/95	3,600	7,200	8,100	9,400
1995/96	3,700	7,400	8,300	9,600
1996/97	3,900	7,800	8,700	10,000
1997/98	4,000	8,000	8,900	10,200
1998/99	4,100	8,200	9,100	10,400
Increase 1987–97	+50.9%	+50.9%	+67.9%	+92.5%
Inflation 1987–97	+28.4%	+28.4%	+28.4%	+28.4%

Note: Marginal relief is afforded at 40% where income does not greatly exceed the relevant exemption limits.

Sources: Budget Books 1986–1997, Stationery Office; "Summary of 1998 Budget Measures", December 1997.

Consistent progress has been made over the past decade in the raising of exemption thresholds, below which households are liberated from income tax. In all cases, exemption thresholds have been raised significantly faster than inflation. This has allowed some among the low paid — particularly couples with larger families — to escape altogether from the income tax net.

The balance of advantage has been tilted firmly towards households with children. This follows the introduction in the 1989 Budget[1] of a child addition to the basic tax exemption limit. These child additions have been increased significantly in the intervening years, from £200 per child in 1989 to £650 for the third and subsequent children from 1994 onwards. As a result, a married couple with four children in 1997/98 could earn up to £10,200 annually without falling into the income tax net. For such a household, the income tax exemption threshold was lifted by over 90 per cent between 1987/88 and 1997/98.

However, in spite of sizeable improvements, without benefit of dependent children, the income tax exemption thresholds remain meagre relative to earnings. For those without children, only low-paid couples and very low-paid single people can gain exemption from income tax. In 1997/98, single people earning more than £76.92 a week — £4,000 annually — were liable to pay income tax.

Earlier, it was shown that the pay of an average industrial worker in manufacturing increased from £10,069 in 1987 to an estimated £14,483 in 1997. Over the same period, the income tax exemption threshold for a single person has been raised from £2,650 to £4,000. Hence, in both years, only single people earning just above a quarter of average manufacturing earnings were exempted from income tax. Relative to average earnings, tax exemption thresholds for single people have barely changed.

Where incomes of married couples without children exceeded 52.6 per cent of average manufacturing earnings in 1987, they lost their exemption from income tax. By 1997, that relative tax exemption threshold had moved up to just 55.2 per cent.

---

[1] Budget Book 1989, p. 68.

In summary, income tax exemption thresholds have been raised at a faster rate than inflation over the past decade. Large, low-paid households have clearly benefited as a result. Many such households have escaped from the income tax system altogether. For average earners without children, single or married, the changes in exemption thresholds have been of little consequence, since the ratio of the exemption threshold to average earnings has remained virtually static. Too many employees on low incomes remain trapped in the tax net.

7.3. The Evolution of Basic Personal Tax Allowances

The tax system plays a cruel trick on those it has trapped within its confines. Once income exceeds the income tax exemption threshold, it is assessable to income tax. But income up to the tax exemption threshold cannot be claimed as a personal tax allowance by newly recruited taxpayers. Instead, a different, and markedly lower, set of basic tax allowances are provided.

Hence, in 1997/98, single people earning less than £4,000 are exempt from income tax. But if they earn £6,000 annually, they cannot claim the exemption threshold of £4,000 as a tax allowance. Instead, as fully-fledged taxpayers, they are permitted a basic personal tax-free allowance of just £2,900.

Trends in basic personal tax allowances for single people and married couples, and including the PAYE and PRSI tax allowances, are shown in Table 7.2. No additional basic income tax allowances are granted in respect of children.

Over the period 1987/8 to 1995/6, basic personal tax allowances, for both single people and married couples, just about matched inflation. However, significant increases in personal tax allowances were granted in the budgets of 1996 and 1997. Between 1995/6 and 1997/8, basic personal tax allowances for both single people and married couples were increased by 16 per cent.

However, three factors have diluted the apparent generosity of the authorities in raising basic personal tax allowances. First, the PAYE income tax allowance, while increased from £700 to £800 per employee in the 1988 Budget, has languished at that level ever since. Second, the scaling down and subsequent abolition of the £286 PRSI income tax allowance in 1995/96 and 1996/97 acted as a counterweight to the increase in personal tax allowances in those years. Third, as will be seen later, the value of discretionary — as opposed to basic — personal tax allowances have been significantly eroded in recent years, most notably in the case of tax relief on mortgage interest.

In consequence, when all of these basic personal income tax allowances are combined, they barely kept pace with inflation over the decade 1987–97. In the case of single taxpayers, increases in basic tax allowances failed to match the rise in prices. More importantly, from the taxpayer's perspective, they lagged significantly behind increases in earnings. As a result, a larger slice of average employees' incomes was exposed to income tax in 1997/98 than a decade earlier.

TABLE 7.2: EVOLUTION OF BASIC PERSONAL TAX ALLOWANCES, 1987–97 (£)

Year	Single Person	Married Couple*	PAYE Allowance	PRSI Tax Allowance
1987/88	2,000	4,000	700	286
1988/89	2,050	4,100	800	286
1989/90	2,050	4,100	800	286
1990/91	2,050	4,100	800	286
1991/92	2,100	4,200	800	286
1992/93	2,100	4,200	800	286
1993/94	2,175	4,350	800	286
1994/95	2,350	4,700	800	286
1995/96	2,500	5,000	800	140
1996/97	2,650	5,300	800	Abolished
1997/98	2,900	5,800	800	0
1998/99	3,150	6,300	800	0
Change 1987/88–1997/98	+45.0%	+45.0%	+14.3%	−100.0%
Inflation 1987–97	+28.4%	+28.4%	+28.4%	+28.4%

* Available to married couples, whether one or both spouses are working.

Sources: Budget Books, 1986–1997; "Summary of 1998 Budget Measures", December 1997.

In combination, the basic personal allowances available to single employees increased from £2,986 in 1987/88 to £3,700 in 1997/98. This represented an increase of 23.9 per cent. For married couples, where one spouse was working, basic tax-free allowances rose from £4,986 to £6,600 over the same period, an advance of 32.4 per cent.

Thus, in spite of the generosity of the budgets of 1996 and 1997, the 23.9 per cent increase in single employees' core tax-free allowances failed to keep pace with the 28.4 per cent rate of inflation over the decade. Courtesy of the budgets of 1996 and 1997, the aggregated basic personal income tax allowances of one-income married couples just shaded inflation over the period.

In both cases, increases in basic tax-free allowances failed to keep pace with the rate of earnings growth over the decade. Those employees who saw their gross pay march in step with average earnings in manufacturing between 1987 and 1997 found a greater proportion of their income exposed to income tax. This is shown in Table 7.3.

TABLE 7.3: PROPORTIONS OF AVERAGE MANUFACTURING EARNINGS EXPOSED TO INCOME TAX, 1987–97*

Year	Single People	One Income Married Couples
1987	70.3	50.5
1988	70.3	50.8
1989	71.4	52.7
1990	72.8	55.0
1991	73.2	55.6
1992	74.2	57.3
1993	75.0	58.3
1994	74.4	56.9
1995	74.9	56.7
1996	75.5	56.6
1997f	74.5	54.4

* (Earnings minus basic allowances) divided by annual earnings and multiplied by 100; f = forecast.

Sources: Tables 6.4; 7.2.

Income Taxes

In essence, Table 7.3 shows that despite all the apparent tax concessions granted over the decade, the proportion of average employees' gross incomes exposed to income tax increased by around four percentage points. This holds whether the employees are single or married. This increased exposure resulted from earnings rising faster than aggregated basic tax allowances.

In 1987, after the deduction of basic allowances — the income tax, PAYE and PRSI tax allowances — from average manufacturing earnings, single people found that 70.3 per cent of their gross incomes were liable to income tax. Adjusting for increases in tax allowances and earnings in the intervening years, by 1997 exposure to income tax had climbed to 74.5 per cent of average single earnings. Similarly, over the same period, one-income married couples on average earnings saw the proportion of their incomes exposed to income tax rise from 50.5 per cent in 1987 to 54.4 per cent in 1997.

In summary, despite much trumpeting by successive governments, there was little relief for average taxpayers on the tax allowances front in the decade after 1987. With upward adjustments in basic allowances lagging behind the rate of earnings growth, average employees — single and married — found a larger slice of their gross incomes exposed to income tax.

In mitigation, the phasing out of the £286 PRSI income tax allowance was accompanied by the introduction of a new PRSI exemption. Under this initiative, in 1995/96, the first £50 of employees' weekly gross income was exempted from PRSI contributions. This exemption was extended to the first £80 of weekly gross income in 1996/97, and to the first £100 of weekly gross income for 1998/99.

7.4. Income Tax Bands and Income Tax Rates

It is the interplay of tax allowances, tax rates and the tax bands to which they apply that determines the actual amount of cash which taxpayers must hand over to the Exchequer. As has been seen, taken together, the basic income tax allowances available to employees have trailed some way behind increases in earnings. As a result, the average proportion of gross employee income exposed to taxation — taxable income — has risen over time, though again, this has been partially corrected in the very recent past.

Income tax allowances are deducted from gross income to ascertain the amount of taxable income, that portion of gross income assessable to income tax. Once the extent of taxable income has been defined, actual tax payments will be determined by tax rates and the slices of taxable income to which those tax rates apply.

This interaction between tax rates and tax bands is particularly important in Irish circumstances. Of themselves, Irish income tax rates are not excessively high relative to rates prevailing in competitor countries. However, Irish tax bands are very narrow. The compression of tax bands, allied to steeply progressive income tax rates, gives rise to the two defining features of the Irish income tax code:

- Irish individuals and households bear high average direct tax burdens at modest levels of gross income

- Ordinary taxpayers face very high marginal income tax rates on any additional income they earn.

These features are particularly pronounced in the tax treatment of single people, as can be seen from Table 7.4. This shows that in 1987/88, single individuals earning taxable incomes in excess of £7,500 were liable to income tax at 58 per cent on any additional pay. While improvements were effected in the intervening years, for 1998/99, such single individuals still face marginal tax rates of 46 per cent on any taxable earnings above £10,000. Taxable earnings are defined as gross pay less basic personal tax allowances and any discretionary allowances claimed, such as tax relief on mortgage interest. Moreover, the tax treatment described in Table 7.4 effectively extends beyond single people. Where both spouses in a marriage are working and earning average incomes, they will bear broadly the same tax burden as two single people.

In the years since 1987, when the first of the current series of national agreements was concluded, the tax rates and tax bands as they apply to single people have evolved as follows:

1. The standard rate of income tax — also the initial rate — has been reduced from 35 to 24 per cent in the 1998 budget;

2. The width of the standard rate tax band has been more than doubled from £4,700 to £10,000;

Income Taxes

3. The top rate of tax, 58 per cent in 1987/88 was progressively reduced prior to its abolition in 1992/93; since then, there have been only two tax rates;

4. The 48 per cent rate remained unchanged for a decade before being cut to 46 per cent in the 1998 budget.

TABLE 7.4: INCOME TAX RATES AND TAX BANDS FACING SINGLE PEOPLE (AS LEVIED ON TAXABLE INCOME* FOR THE YEARS 1987–99)

Year	Standard Tax Rate	Middle Tax Rate	Top Tax Rate
1987/88	35% on first £4,700	48% on next £2,800	58% above £7,500
1988/89	35% on first £5,700	48% on next £2,900	58% above £8,600
1989/90	32% on first £6,100	48% on next £3,100	56% above £9,200
1990/91	30% on first £6,500	48% on next £3,100	53% above £9,600
1991/92	29% on first £6,700	48% on next £3,100	52% above £9,800
1992/93	27% on first £7,475	48% above £7,475	Abolished
1993/94	27% on first £7,675	48% above £7,675	—
1994/95	27% on first £8,200	48% above £8,200	—
1995/96	27% on first £8,900	48% above £8,900	—
1996/97	27% on first £9,400	48% above £9,400	—
1997/98	26% on first £9,900	48% above £9,900	—
1998/99	24% on first £10,000	46% above £10,000	—

* Taxable income = gross income less basic personal tax allowances and discretionary tax allowances.

Sources: Budget Books 1987–1997, Stationery Office; "Summary of 1998 Budget Measures", December 1997.

Over the decade to 1997, the incomes of married couples, where only one spouse is earning, were taxed with a much lighter touch than either single people or working married couples. This easier tax treatment arises from the fact that income tax liabilities in Ireland are determined not only by income, but by marital status. By virtue of marriage, couples gain access not only to a double set of basic personal tax allowances, but to a double set of tax bands. This holds whether one or both spouses earn incomes.

TABLE 7.5: INCOME TAX RATES AND TAX BANDS FACING MARRIED COUPLES (ON TAXABLE INCOMES WHETHER ONE OR BOTH EARNING)

Year	Standard Tax Rate	Middle Tax Rate	Top Tax Rate
1987/88	35% on first £9,400	48% on next £5,600	58% above £15,000
1988/89	35% on first £11,400	48% on next £5,800	58% above £17,200
1989/90	32% on first £12,200	48% on next £6,200	56% above £18,400
1990/91	30% on first £13,000	48% on next £6,200	53% above £19,200
1991/92	29% on first £13,400	48% on next £6,200	52% above £19,600
1992/93	27% on first £14,950	48% above £14,950	Abolished
1993/94	27% on first £15,350	48% above £15,350	—
1994/95	27% on first £16,400	48% above £16,400	—
1995/96	27% on first £17,800	48% above £17,800	—
1996/97	27% on first £18,800	48% above £18,800	—
1997/98	26% on first £19,800	48% above £19,800	—
1998/99	24% on first £20,000	46% above £20,000	—

* Taxable income = gross income less basic personal tax allowances and discretionary tax allowances.

Sources: Budget Books 1987–1997, Stationery Office; "Summary of 1998 Budget Measures", December 1997.

Where both spouses are working outside the home and earning average or above average incomes, this concession makes little effective difference to the household's total income tax liabilities. However, where the household depends on one income only, the weight of the tax burden is lightened appreciably. The evolution of tax rates and tax bands for married couples since 1987 is shown in Table 7.5.

In summary, married couples have enjoyed the same cuts in income tax rates as single people since 1987. However, one-income married couples have benefited doubly from the broadening of single people's tax bands. Combining the data in Tables 7.2, 7.4 and 7.5, the swiftness with which taxpayers hit the higher tax rate is illustrated in Table 7.6. From 1987/88 to 1997/98, the higher rate of income tax remained unchanged at 48 per cent. It was reduced to 46 per cent for the 1998/99 tax year.

TABLE 7.6: EXPOSURE TO HIGHER RATE OF INCOME TAX, 1987–99 (ANNUAL GROSS INCOME LEVELS (£) ABOVE WHICH HOUSEHOLDS ARE EXPOSED TO INCOME TAX ABOVE THE STANDARD RATE)

Year	Single Person	Married Couple Both Earning*	Married Couple One Earning
1987/88	7,686	15,372	14,386
1988/89	8,836	17,672	16,586
1989/90	9,236	18,472	17,386
1990/91	9,636	19,272	18,186
1991/92	9,886	19,772	18,686
1992/93**	10,661	21,322	20,326
1993/94	10,936	21,872	20,786
1994/95	11,636	23,272	22,186
1995/96	12,340	24,680	23,740
1996/97	12,850	25,700	24,900
1997/98	13,600	27,200	26,400
1998/99	13,950	27,900	27,100

* A married couple where both are at work and earn similar incomes are essentially taxed as two single working people; ** top tax rate abolished. Note: the higher tax rate was cut from 48 to 46 per cent in the 1998 budget.

Sources: Budget Books 1987–1997; "Summary of 1998 Budget Measures", December 1997.

In 1987/88, single taxpayers strayed into the 48 per cent tax zone when their annual gross incomes exceeded £7,686. Married couples, both of whom were working and earning broadly similar incomes, found themselves in a similar position. Where their joint household incomes edged above £15,372, any extra cash earned attracted income tax at 48 per cent. One-income married couples fell into the 48 per cent net in 1987/88 when annual household earnings passed £14,386.

By 1997/98, progression through the tax code had become less rapid, at least in money terms. Single people could earn up to £13,600 and two-income married couples could gross £27,200 before hitting the 48 per cent tax rate. One-income married couples needed to earn above £26,400 before becoming liable to income tax at the top rate.

For the 1998/99 tax year, single employees earning more than £13,950 will find themselves paying income tax at 46 per cent on any additional earnings. Two-income married couples will face the new 46 per cent of income tax on marginal income above £27,900 a year.

To discount any effects of "money illusion", the point at which households become liable to income tax at the higher rate is shown as a percentage of average manufacturing earnings in Table 7.7.

Table 7.7 signals two important trends. First, over the ten years since 1987/88, progression through the income tax code has become less rapid for all taxpayers. Second, despite the relative lightening of the tax load over the past decade, the steps in the income tax structure remain very steep for most income earners. In recent years, the incomes of single people are still exposed to the top rate of income tax when they are earning just over 90 per cent of average manufacturing earnings.

This fate is shared also by two-income married couples, a fact that has merited insufficient attention in the past. Where both are working, they too can find themselves liable to the highest rate of income tax when their individual incomes exceed 94 per cent of average manufacturing earnings. Married couples where one spouse only is earning escape exposure to the top rate of income tax until household income reaches about 180 per cent of average manufacturing earnings.

TABLE 7.7: PERCENTAGE OF AVERAGE MANUFACTURING EARNINGS AT WHICH LIABILITY TO INCOME TAX AT THE HIGHER RATE BEGINS

Year	Single Person	Married Couple, One Earning
1987/88	76.3	142.9
1988/89	83.8	157.3
1989/90	84.2	158.5
1990/91	83.6	157.7
1991/92	83.1	157.1
1992/93	86.2	163.6
1993/94	83.9	159.5
1994/95	86.7	165.3
1995/96	90.0	173.1
1996/97	91.4	177.1
1997/98e	93.9	182.3

e = estimate.
Sources: Tables 6.4, 7.4, 7.5.

In summary, while taxpayers' incomes do not become exposed to the higher rate of income tax as quickly as a decade ago, progression through the tax system remains too rapid. The fact that single people and two-income married couples can find themselves paying tax at the top rate on less than average manufacturing earnings remains the Irish tax code's besetting sin.

Thus, the OECD pointed out in 1997:

> Ireland, though, is marked by very high marginal rates at low-income levels. In 1996, a single person entered the top tax bracket at an annual income that was almost 10 per cent below the level of average earnings. Consequently, such workers face maximum marginal tax rates, including payroll taxes, of 55.8 per cent. In contrast, in the United Kingdom, which has an average tax wedge that is very close to that in Ireland, a worker begins to pay the top 40 per cent rate at an earnings level that is almost double the average production worker's wage.[2]

---

[2] "OECD Economic Surveys 1997 — Ireland", op. cit., p. 79.

7.5. Changes in Discretionary Tax Allowances

Taxpayers have traditionally been able to reduce their exposure to income tax by claiming extra discretionary tax allowances in addition to their basic personal tax allowances. Traditionally, the most popular discretionary tax allowances have included income tax reliefs on mortgage interest, Voluntary Health Insurance (VHI) contributions, life assurance premiums and covenants.

Such discretionary tax allowances, in an undiluted form, are highly tax-efficient. Not only do they raise the total tax allowances that can be claimed by taxpayers, but by so doing, they engineer savings at taxpayers' highest marginal rates of income tax. They are therefore of significantly greater advantage to top-rate taxpayers than to those paying tax at the standard rate. They are of no benefit whatsoever to those exempt from income tax.

Over the past decade, these discretionary tax allowances have been pared back, gradually but continuously. For many households, increasing restrictions on discretionary tax allowances have caused a larger slice of personal income to be exposed to taxation. The principal changes in the four major discretionary tax reliefs introduced since 1987 are outlined below.

1. The largest of these discretionary tax allowances is the tax relief afforded on mortgage interest payments. In the 1987 Budget, the Minister for Finance restricted relief to 90 per cent of mortgage interest paid, subject to the existing interest ceilings of £2,000 for a single person and £4,000 for a married couple.[3] This restriction was further tightened to 80 per cent of existing ceilings in the 1989 Budget.[4] A temporary respite was afforded by the interest rate and currency crises of 1992/93. Ceilings for tax relief on mortgage interest were raised to £2,500 and £5,000 in the 1993 Budget, while the proportion of existing mortgage interest qualifying for tax relief was raised temporarily from 80 per cent to 90 per cent.[5] However, the 1994 Budget restricted income tax relief on mortgage interest

---

[3] 1987 Budget Book, p. 58.

[4] 1989 Budget Book, p. 66.

[5] 1993 Budget Book, pp. 29–30.

to the standard income tax rate over a four-year period. As a result, from 1997/98, tax relief on mortgage interest is allowed only at the lowest rate of income tax, 24 per cent in 1998/99.[6] The standard rate relief applies to 80 per cent of mortgage interest payments up to a maximum interest ceiling of £2,500 less £100 for a single person and £5,000 less £200 for a married couple.

2. The Minister for Finance also announced in the 1994 Budget that tax relief on Voluntary Health Insurance contributions would be restricted to the then standard 27 per cent income tax rate by 1996/97.[7]

3. Income tax relief on life assurance premiums was curbed to 80 per cent of existing levels in the 1989 Budget. Further restrictions on life assurance relief were introduced in the 1990 and 1991 budgets. Finally, in the 1992 Budget, tax allowances in respect of life assurance premiums were abolished altogether.[8]

4. The 1995 Budget abolished, from 6 April 1996, all tax relief on covenants except those benefiting the elderly, the incapacitated, designated teaching and research and covenants in favour of UN-recognised human rights organisations. However, covenants for maintenance payments between separated spouses remain unaffected by these changes.[9]

The withdrawal and restriction of discretionary tax reliefs since 1987 has been systematic and continuous. The restrictions imposed on discretionary tax allowances and reliefs have produced two principal effects.

First, taxpayers can avail of fewer and smaller discretionary tax allowances in seeking to postpone their exposure to income tax at the top rate. Second, the value of most discretionary tax allowances that remain has been reduced, since they can now be

---

[6] 1994 Budget Book, pp. 40–41.

[7] 1994 Budget Book, p. 41.

[8] 1992 Budget Book, p. 65.

[9] 1995 Budget Book, p. 49.

claimed only at the standard rate rather than at the higher rate of income tax.

7.6. Other Taxes on Employee Income

Direct taxes on employees' incomes do not cease with income tax. Since 1987, as many as four other direct taxes have been deducted from employees' pay. The four hidden taxes imposed on employee income over the past decade comprise:

- Employee Pay-Related Social Insurance contributions
- Health contributions
- Employment and Training levies
- Temporary income levies.

The changing effects of these other taxes on employee income in the years since 1987 are examined below.

7.6.1. Employee Pay-Related Social Insurance Contributions

Most of those working in the private sector pay employee PRSI contributions at the full rate. Employees in the public service pay reduced rates of contribution on the grounds that they cannot avail of all the benefits provided by the social insurance fund. From 1987 to 1996, the full rate of employee PRSI contribution remained unchanged at 5.5 per cent of eligible gross pay. This rate was cut from 5.5 per cent to 4.5 per cent in the 1997 Budget. Contributions are not open-ended; there is an income ceiling beyond which PRSI contributions are no longer exacted. This ceiling has been raised in every budget since 1987, exposing larger slices of employee income to PRSI. The raising of these ceilings is shown in Table 7.8.

For much of the past decade, PRSI contributions were levied on the gross pay of employees without benefit of any allowances or exemptions. As a result, many low-paid workers often found themselves exempt from Income Tax proper and still liable to PRSI. An attempt was made to address this problem as far back as the 1990 Budget, when earnings of less than £60 a week were exempted altogether from PRSI contributions. However, because of the very low income threshold selected, the numbers benefiting from this concession were small.

TABLE 7.8: EMPLOYEE PRSI: CONTRIBUTION RATES AND CEILINGS, 1987–99

Year	Full-Rate PRSI (%)	Contribution Ceiling (£)
1987/88	5.5	15,500
1988/89	5.5	16,200
1989/90	5.5	16,700
1990/91	5.5	17,300
1991/92	5.5	18,000
1992/93	5.5	19,000
1993/94	5.5	20,000
1994/95	5.5	20,900
1995/96[1]	5.5	21,500
1996/97[2]	5.5	22,300
1997/98[2]	4.5	23,200
1998/99[3]	4.5	24,200

[1] First £50 of weekly income exempt from contributions; [2] first £80 of weekly income exempt from contributions; [3] first £100 of weekly income exempt from contributions.

Sources: Budget Books, 1988–1997; "Summary of 1998 Budget Measures", December 1997.

More realistic and concerted attempts to overcome this anomaly, and to reduce total direct taxes on the low-paid, have been made in recent years. In the 1995 Budget, the first £50 of weekly income — £2,600 annually — was exempted from PRSI for all full-rate contributors. The exemption was extended to the first £80 of weekly earnings — £4,160 annually — in the 1996 Budget. The amount of income exempted from employees' PRSI was raised to £100 per week in the 1998 Budget.

The PRSI load on all full-rate contributors was further lightened in the 1997 Budget, when the contribution rate was cut from 5.5 per cent to 4.5 per cent.

Together, these initiatives have significantly reduced the effective rates of total income taxes levied on the low-paid. They have

7.6.2. Health Contributions

The health contribution rate was raised from 1 per cent to 1.25 per cent in the 1987 Budget.[10] It has remained at this rate ever since. As in the case of PRSI contributions, the health contribution was subject to an income ceiling. This ceiling was abolished in the 1991 Budget.[11]

In an effort to reduce the weight of the direct tax burden on the low-paid, the 1994 Budget[12] exempted employees earning less than £173 a week and the self-employed earning less than £9,000 a year from health contributions. These exemption thresholds have been raised in each subsequent budget.

In the 1998 Budget, the gross income thresholds for the payment of the health contribution in 1998/99 was raised to £10,750 or £207 per week. Those earning less do not pay health contribution; those earning more pay the contribution on all of their gross income. As a result, health contributions at 1.25 per cent are now levied on all gross income where such income exceeds the exemption threshold. The health contribution acts to increase the direct taxes paid by average employees. It also raises all marginal tax rates by 1.25 per cent where income exceeds the exemption threshold.

7.6.3. Employment and Training Levies

Until 1993/94, an Employment and Training Levy of 1 per cent of all gross pay was collected from all employee incomes. As with the health contribution, the 1994 Budget exempted those earning less than £173 a week or £9,000 annually from the training levy. The exemption thresholds for both charges since 1994 are shown in Table 7.9.

---

[10] 1987 Budget Book, p. 17.

[11] 1991 Budget Book, p. 20.

[12] 1994 Budget Book, p. 38.

Income Taxes

TABLE 7.9: EXEMPTION THRESHOLDS FOR HEALTH AND TRAINING LEVIES

Year	Exemption Threshold
1994/95	£9,000 annually or £173 per week
1995/96	£9,250 annually or £178 per week
1996/97	£9,750 annually or £188 per week
1997/98	£10,250 annually or £197 per week
1998/99	£10,750 annually or £207 per week

7.6.4. Temporary Income Levy

In the wake of the currency and interest rate crises of 1992/93, a 1 per cent temporary levy on incomes was introduced in the 1993 Budget.[13] Those holding medical cards and those earning less than £173 a week or £9,000 annually were exempted from the temporary levy. The prompt recovery of the economy in the aftermath of the 10 per cent devaluation of the Irish pound allowed the temporary income levy to be rescinded in the 1994 Budget.

7.7. Employers' Pay-Related Social Insurance Contributions

Just as the direct taxation of employee incomes does not stop at income tax, neither does the taxation of labour income cease with the direct taxes paid by employees.

In addition to gross wages, enterprises must meet the cost of Pay-Related Social Insurance contributions made on behalf of their employees. The standard rate of employers' PRSI contribution has remained anchored above 12 per cent since 1987. Further, the maximum ceiling on which employers' PRSI is charged has been raised from £15,500 in 1987/88 to £29,000 for 1998/99, an increase of 87 per cent in the height of the ceiling over the period. In combination, these two factors add substantially to the cost of hiring labour, and especially skilled labour. The evolution of employers' PRSI since 1987 is shown in Table 7.10.

---

[13] 1993 Budget Book, pp. 27–28.

TABLE 7.10: EMPLOYERS' PRSI RATES AND CONTRIBUTION CEILINGS, 1987–99

Year	Standard Rate (%)	Income Ceiling (£)	Lower Rate (%)
1987/88	12.33	15,500	None
1988/89	12.4	16,200	None
1989/90	12.2	18,000	None
1990/91	12.2	18,600	None
1991/92	12.2	19,300	None
1992/93	12.2	20,300	None
1993/94	12.2	21,300	None
1994/95	12.2	25,800	9% on incomes below £9,000
1995/96	12.2	25,800	9% on incomes below £12,000
1996/97	12.0	26,800	8.5% on incomes below £13,000
1997/98	12.0	27,900	8.5% on incomes below £13,520
1998/99	12.0	29,000	8.5% on incomes below £14,040

Sources: Budget Books 1987–1997, Stationery Office; "Summary of 1998 Budget Measures", December 1997.

Budgets since 1994 have recognised the employment-inhibiting effects of high rates of employers' PRSI. A new low 9 per cent rate of employers' PRSI was introduced in the 1994 Budget for employees earning up to £9,000 annually. The reach of the reduced rate was extended in the 1995 Budget, when the income limit was raised to £12,000. In the 1996 Budget, the lower rate was cut to 8.5 per cent and the income limit further extended to £13,000. The income threshold to which the low employers' PRSI rate applies was raised again to £13,500 in the 1997 Budget. In the 1998 budget, the earnings limit for the lower 8.5 per cent rate of employers' PRSI was further extended from £260 to £270 per week, the latter being equivalent to over £14,000 annually.

These initiatives — the disregarding of a significant slice of initial income from employees' PRSI; the cut in the rate of employers' PRSI; the introduction of exemption thresholds for both health contributions and training levies; and the launching of a reduced PRSI rate for employers hiring low-paid labour — have made the labour market far more employment-friendly since 1994.

Chapter 8

INCOMES, TAXES AND PRICES SINCE 1987

8.1. Methodology

Data on wages and salaries in a range of non-agricultural employments were presented in Chapter 6. The evolution of taxes on labour income in the years since 1987 was traced in Chapter 7. This Chapter fits together the pieces of the real disposable income jigsaw. It applies changes in the direct tax code introduced since 1987 to the trends in earnings over the same period. The patterns of disposable incomes that emerge are then adjusted for changes in consumer prices to ascertain trends in real disposable incomes.

Since the period covered corresponds with the reintroduction of national collective bargaining, the data permit a review of pay, price and tax trends during the currency of the four national agreements to date.

The methodology adopted is straightforward. It consists of the following steps:

1. Average industrial earnings in manufacturing industry has been selected as the base for calculations. It is a long-running, readily accessible series and is the most frequently used barometer of average non-agricultural pay. The data in Table 6.12 indicate that trends in industrial earnings do not deviate too far from data on average non-agricultural incomes derived from the national accounts. It is a reasonable proxy for average earnings.

2. To broaden the scope of the investigation, three income variants are examined — average industrial earnings, twice average industrial earnings and half average industrial earnings.

This allows the impact of tax and price changes on the spending power of the better-off and of the low-paid to be assessed.

3. Basic tax-free allowances — personal tax allowances, the PAYE and PRSI income tax allowances — are deducted from gross pay to ascertain taxable income. While the restriction of discretionary tax allowances in recent years has been noted in the last Chapter, such allowances differ too much in individual cases to be included in a general analysis. Discretionary tax allowances are thus excluded from consideration.

4. The tax allowances, tax rates and tax bands prevailing in each year are then applied to the figures for taxable income. Basic income tax liabilities are derived as a result.

5. The additional taxes on employee incomes — employees' PRSI, health contributions, the employment and training levy and the temporary 1 per cent income levy — are calculated as appropriate. These are added to income tax liabilities to derive the total direct tax deductions from employees' taxable incomes.

6. Disposable income is estimated by subtracting all direct tax deductions from gross pay.

7. Total direct tax deductions are shown as a percentage of gross pay. This represents the average or effective rate of income tax (ATR) at each income level for each year.

8. The marginal tax rate (MTR) represents the amount of additional direct taxation deducted from each additional £1 earned. It comprises not only income tax itself, but also employees' PRSI contributions, health contributions and the training levy.

9. Employers' PRSI contributions are calculated and added to gross pay to determine the cost to the employer of hiring labour.

10. The direct tax wedge is computed by subtracting employees' after-tax incomes from the total cost to the employer, including PRSI, of hiring those employees. In effect, the tax wedge

is the amount of direct taxation levied by the government on each job.

11. Trends in the tax wedge are expressed first as a proportion of the gross cost of labour to the employer, then as a percentage of employees' take-home pay. These wedges illustrate the size of the gap that separates the cost of labour to employers and the gains from working to employees.

12. Finally, employees' after-tax incomes are expressed in constant 1987 Irish pounds to trace changes in real disposable incomes over time.

Not all of these individual steps are shown in the tables that follow or are referred to in the text. That would prove excessively tiresome for readers. Instead, the principal results are shown in condensed form for three groups:

1. Average earners, both single and married
2. The better-off (those earning twice average pay)
3. The low-paid (households with earned incomes pegged at just half the level of average industrial earnings).

8.2. Living Standards of Average Earners, 1987–97

Trends in the gross pay, taxes and real disposable incomes of single people receiving average industrial earnings is shown in Table 8.1 for the years since 1987.

Single people on average industrial earnings gained an estimated 43.8 per cent in their gross money incomes between 1987 and 1997. Over this period, the average direct tax rate borne by such employees fell by 9.3 percentage points, from 35.5 per cent to 26.2 per cent. Pay increases, combined with lower taxes, raised average after-tax earnings by almost two-thirds between 1987 and 1997. However, while annual inflation was modest, the cumulative increase in consumer prices still amounted to 28.4 per cent over the decade. Inflation thus significantly reduced the purchasing power of disposable money incomes. When adjusted for changes in prices, the spending power of single people on average earnings increased by 28.2 per cent between 1987 and 1997.

TABLE 8.1: PAY, TAXES AND REAL INCOMES OF AVERAGE SINGLE EARNERS

Year	Gross Pay (£)[1]	Average Tax Rate (%)[2]	Marginal Tax Rate (%)[3]	After-Tax Income (£)[4]	Real Income (£)[5]
1987	10,069	35.5	55.75	6,499	6,499
1988	10,546	34.4	55.75	6,913	6,768
1989	10,971	33.1	55.75	7,336	6,901
1990	11,529	32.5	55.75	7,777	7,080
1991	11,893	32.2	55.75	8,065	7,115
1992	12,372	30.7	55.75	8,574	7,335
1993	13,036	32.4	56.75	8,816	7,438
1994	13,418	30.6	55.75	9,309	7,674
1995	13,715	29.0	55.75	9,733	7,824
1996	14,061	28.3	55.75	10,081	7,975
1997e	14,483	26.2	54.75	10,694	8,329
Change 1987–97	+43.8%	–9.3 points	–1.0 point	+64.5%	+28.2%

Notes and Sources:

e: estimate.

[1] Average industrial earnings as shown in Table 6.4;
[2] Total direct deductions as a percentage of gross pay;
[3] Tax rate on next pound earned;
[4] Gross pay less all direct taxes;
[5] Real disposable income: after-tax income deflated by the consumer price index shown in constant 1987 pounds.

This gain in real purchasing power derived from two factors: money incomes rose faster than prices while direct taxes took a smaller bite of those rising money incomes.

However, while the real incomes of single people on average earnings have improved substantially since 1987, they remain heavily taxed. In 1997, single people earning average pay were still losing over one-quarter of their earnings in direct taxes.

More importantly, single people on average pay were trapped in the higher income tax bracket throughout the period. In consequence, the marginal tax rates they faced on any additional earnings remained punitively high in 1997 at 54.75 per cent — a drop of just one percentage point on the marginal tax rates they faced a decade earlier.

The 1998 Budget allows for a further lightening of the tax load on average single earners. It raised the single person's basic tax allowance by £250 a year while cutting the standard tax rate from 26 per cent to 24 per cent, and the top rate from 48 per cent to 46 per cent. Nonetheless, despite the reduction in average tax rates, even single people earning less than average pay will remain trapped in the top rate band during 1998/99. This follows the decision in the Budget to widen the standard tax rate band by a meagre £100 to £10,000. As a result, a higher proportion of all taxpayers will pay tax at the top rate in 1998/99 than in 1997/98.

Again, it should be emphasised that the tax code for single people in effect also applies to dual income working couples. Where both partners in a marriage are earning reasonable incomes, together they bear broadly the same tax burden as two single people. The tax code works to the advantage of married couples only in single income households.

Table 8.2 shows the tax treatment of a one-income married couple over the years 1987 through 1997.

Married couples, where only one spouse is working and earning average industrial pay, have also experienced substantial real income gains over the past decade. Between 1987 and 1997, the real disposable incomes of such households advanced by 20.7 per cent, propelled by money wage increases that outpaced inflation, coupled with a declining average tax rate.

The tax code treats one-income married couples with far greater leniency than single people, as can be seen by comparing Tables 8.1 and 8.2. In 1997, average single earners lost more than one-quarter of their gross incomes in direct taxes whereas one-income married couples on the same pay gave up just one-fifth of their incomes in direct tax deductions. Further, the marginal tax rates faced by the two sets of taxpayers were markedly different. Average single workers faced total direct taxes of 54.75 per cent on any extra cash earned, while for one-income married couples on similar pay, the marginal tax rate was 22 percentage points lower.

TABLE 8.2: TAX TREATMENT OF ONE-INCOME MARRIED COUPLES, 1987–97 (WHERE INCOME IS EQUIVALENT TO AVERAGE INDUSTRIAL EARNINGS)

Year	Gross Pay (£)	Average Tax Rate (%)	Marginal Tax Rate (%)	After-Tax Income (£)	Real Income (£)
1987	10,069	25.4	42.75	7,509	7,509
1988	10,546	25.5	42.75	7,853	7,689
1989	10,971	24.6	39.75	8,270	7,780
1990	11,529	24.3	37.75	8,733	7,951
1991	11,893	23.9	36.75	9,055	7,989
1992	12,372	23.2	34.75	9,500	8,127
1993	13,036	24.5	35.75	9,844	8,305
1994	13,418	23.1	34.75	10,317	8,505
1995	13,715	22.0	34.75	10,697	8,599
1996	14,061	21.4	34.75	11,051	8,743
1997e	14,483	19.6	32.75	11,642	9,067
Change 1987–97	+43.8%	–5.8 points	–10.0 points	+55.0%	+20.7%

Notes: As in Table 8.1.

This reflects the fact that, in Ireland, income tax liabilities are determined not only by income but also by marital status. A married couple enjoys access to two sets of single tax allowances and two sets of tax bands, even where only one spouse is earning an income. As a result, a married couple's progress through the graduated income tax code is much slower. Such couples pay less tax in consequence.

In 1987, the average direct tax rate faced by one-income married couples on average incomes was 25.4 per cent, a full ten percentage points below the effective tax rates paid by single people on similar incomes. Similarly, the marginal tax rates faced by married couples, at 42.75 per cent, was 13 percentage points below the marginal rates confronting single people in similar circumstances.

However, a comparison of Tables 8.1 and 8.2 reveals that the gap in average tax rates separating single people and one-income married couples narrowed between 1987 and 1997, though it still remained substantial. The ten percentage point gap in average tax rates that prevailed in 1987 had diminished to under seven percentage points by 1997. The real purchasing power of single people — and two-income married households — increased faster than one-income married couples over the period.[1]

This narrowing of the tax gap separating single earners from one-income married couples arises because single people are particularly highly taxed. As a result, they have benefited more than proportionately from the tax concessions introduced, particularly from 1994 onwards.

8.3. Pay, Taxes and Real Incomes of the Better-off

For the purposes of this analysis, the "better-off" are defined as those earning twice average industrial earnings in manufacturing industry. This would equate to the average earnings of middle managers in manufacturing industry, while the average pay of public servants would not trail far behind. The rich have been excluded, not because they are different, but because they are few. The rich are also better advised. They have access to legal tax avoidance devices which can reduce their average tax rates below those borne by single people on average earnings.

The position of single people earning twice average pay through the period 1987 to 1997 is examined in Table 8.3.

Single people on twice average earnings have gained significantly from the cuts in top tax rates engineered since 1987. Gradual reductions in the top rate of income tax, 58 per cent in 1987, culminating in its abolition in 1992, powered considerable gains in the after-tax incomes of better-off single people.

Between 1987 and 1997, an increase of more than two-fifths in money incomes supported by a reduction of 9.2 percentage points in average tax rates, raised the disposable incomes of single people earning twice average pay by almost 70 per cent. Discounting

---

[1] This does not imply any neglect of households with children. Untaxed monthly Child Benefit payments have been increased from £15.80 per month for each of the first two children in 1992 to £31.50 per month for each of the first two children from September 1998. See 1993 Budget Book, p. 20; "Summary of 1998 Budget Measures", p. 17.

for a 28.4 per cent increase in the general level of prices, the real purchasing power of such single people moved ahead by close to one-third over the decade.

TABLE 8.3: TAX TREATMENT OF SINGLE PEOPLE ON TWICE AVERAGE EARNINGS, 1987–97

Year	Gross Pay (£)	Average Tax Rate (%)	Marginal Tax Rate (%)	After-Tax Income (£)	Real Income (£)
1987	20,138	48.8	59.0	10,309	10,309
1988	21,092	47.9	59.0	10,983	10,753
1989	21,942	46.3	57.0	11,785	11,086
1990	23,058	44.7	54.0	12,757	11,614
1991	23,786	44.4	54.25	13,214	11,658
1992	24,744	41.9	50.25	14,365	12,289
1993	26,072	43.3	51.25	14,787	12,475
1994	26,836	42.0	50.25	15,573	12,838
1995	27,430	41.2	50.25	16,127	12,964
1996	28,122	40.9	50.25	16,622	13,150
1997e	28,966	39.6	50.25	17,507	13,635
Change 1987–97	+43.8%	–9.2 points	–8.75 points	+69.8%	+32.3%

Notes: As Table 8.1.

Again, better-off single people saw their living standards advance swiftly, both because pay rises outpaced price increases and because average direct taxes declined. Moreover, the improvement in their relative income position reflects the fact that they were very heavily taxed at the beginning of the period and thus stood to benefit disproportionately from cuts in tax rates.

But despite the advances of the past decade, single people on twice average earnings remain heavily taxed. By 1997, such individuals were still losing two-fifths of their gross incomes in direct taxes. And they faced deductions of more than 50 per cent on any additional income they earned.

However, such high single earners stand to gain substantially from the provisions of the 1998 Budget. The cuts in tax rates, and especially in the top rate of tax, will swell their salary cheques through 1998/99.

In summary, single people on twice average earnings have effected a signal improvement in their tax position over the 1987–97 decade. They have moved from being penally taxed in 1987 to being just heavily taxed a decade later. Again, it should be emphasised that this tax impact extends beyond high-earning single people. It holds also, and with almost equal force, for two-income married couples, where both are earning twice average manufacturing pay.

This is significant. Two-income married couples are no longer an unusual feature of the Irish labour market. Material living standards have risen in many households over the past two decades because the number of incomes flowing into such households has increased. As was seen in Chapter 2, the proportion of Irish women working outside the home has been advancing continuously in recent years. Labour force participation rates amongst Irish women of working age are now approaching 50 per cent.

In terms of income tax, working married couples broadly share the same fate as single people. The tax position of better-off married couples, where only one spouse is earning an income, is quite different, as illustrated in Table 8.4.

For higher-earning married couples, where one spouse only was in employment outside the home in the years since 1987, effective tax cuts reinforced the purchasing power gains derived from money incomes rising faster than prices.

Between 1987 and 1997, such households saw their average tax rates fall to under 30 per cent, translating a 43.8 per cent gain in gross income into an advance of 64.3 per cent in after-tax income. Allowing for inflation over the decade, the real purchasing power of one-income married couples on twice average earnings increased by almost 28 per cent.

Nonetheless, by 1997, such households were still losing 27.2 per cent of gross income in direct taxes while the tax charge on any additional earnings remained above 50 per cent. As with all higher earners, the tax-cutting provisions of the 1998 Budget ensured lower tax charges on such households in 1998/99.

TABLE 8.4: TAX TREATMENT OF ONE-INCOME MARRIED COUPLES EARNING TWICE AVERAGE INDUSTRIAL PAY, 1987–97

Year	Gross Pay (£)	Average Tax Rate (%)	Marginal Tax Rate (%)	After-Tax Income (£)	Real Income (£)
1987	20,138	36.3	59.0	12,830	12,830
1988	21,092	35.3	49.0	13,643	13,358
1989	21,942	33.9	49.0	14,513	13,652
1990	23,058	33.1	49.0	15,427	14,045
1991	23,786	33.0	50.25	15,927	14,052
1992	24,744	31.5	50.25	16,942	14,494
1993	26,072	32.4	51.25	17,637	14,880
1994	26,836	31.3	50.25	18,423	15,188
1995	27,430	30.0	50.25	19,196	15,431
1996	28,122	29.4	50.25	19,868	15,718
1997e	28,966	27.2	50.25	21,077	16,415
Change 1987–97	+43.8%	–9.1 points	–8.75 points	+64.3	+27.9%

Notes: As Table 8.1.

8.4. The Tax Treatment of the Low Paid

The focus on direct tax reductions in recent years has been directed particularly at the low-paid. For the purposes of this analysis, the low paid are defined as those earning half average industrial earnings in manufacturing industry. This approximated to £140 per week during 1997. Table 8.5 assesses the extent to which the attempts to alleviate taxes on low-paid single people have been successful.

Given the priority afforded by successive governments to improving the lot of the low-paid, the most startling fact about single people on half average manufacturing earnings is that they remain liable to income tax at all.

Yet, despite the increases in income tax exemption thresholds over the past decade, single people being paid half of average manufacturing earnings are still securely trapped in the income tax net. In 1997/98, only those single people earning less than £4,000 annually were exempt from income tax.

While the marginal tax rates they face have tumbled over the past ten years — falling by 12.25 percentage points — the decline in average tax rates has been far less dramatic. In 1987, single people earning half the average industrial salary lost over one-fifth of their gross incomes in direct taxes. A decade later, single individuals in similar circumstances were still surrendering almost 15 per cent of their money wages in direct tax deductions.

TABLE 8.5: ALLEVIATING THE TAX BURDEN ON LOW-PAID SINGLE PEOPLE

Year	Gross Pay (£)	Average Tax Rate (%)	Marginal Tax Rate (%)	After-Tax Income (£)	Real Income (£)
1987	5,035	22.0	42.75	3,928	3,928
1988	5,273	21.9	42.75	4,116	4,030
1989	5,486	21.5	39.75	4,308	4,053
1990	5,765	21.4	37.75	4,529	4,123
1991	5,947	21.2	36.75	4,686	4,134
1992	6,186	20.8	34.75	4,897	4,189
1993*	6,518	21.2	34.75	5,135	4,332
1994	6,709	18.7	32.5	5,456	4,498
1995	6,858	16.9	32.5	5,701	4,583
1996	7,031	16.0	32.5	5,906	4,672
1997e	7,242	14.6	30.5	6,182	4,815
Change 1987–97	+43.8%	−7.4 points	−12.25 points	+57.4%	+22.6%

* Those earning less than £9,000 annually (£173 per week) were exempted from the 1 per cent temporary income levy.

Notes: As Table 8.1.

Given the thrust of tax policy, it is little short of extraordinary that single employees earning about £140 a week in 1997 were paying over £1,000 a year in direct taxes.

While the low-paid gained through their exemption from health contributions and training levies and from cuts in their effective rates of PRSI contributions, the abolition of the top rate of income tax benefited them not at all. And while cuts in the standard rate of income tax proved useful, the relatively modest increases in basic tax allowances left large slices of their income exposed to income tax. As a result, while the purchasing power of low-paid single individuals advanced by 22.6 per cent over the past ten years, their proportionate gains in real income were considerably smaller than their single counterparts further up the income ladder.

The income difficulties faced by single people in low-paid employment are compounded by the fact that no wide-ranging income subsidies are available to low-paid single workers in Ireland.[2] Such subsidies, in the form of Family Income Supplement, are only available to married households.

Married couples, where one spouse only is earning an income in low-paid employment, were exempt from income tax throughout the period. However, while escaping income tax, the earning spouse remained liable to pay employees' PRSI, health contributions and the 1 per cent employment and training levy on all gross income until 1994.[3] The exemptions and reliefs for those on low incomes — introduced in the 1994 Budget and reinforced thereafter — have almost lifted low-income couples out of the tax net altogether. This is illustrated in Table 8.6.

Paradoxically, because such married couples were exempt from income tax throughout the period, they gained nothing from any income tax concessions that were introduced. As a result, their real incomes advanced very slowly until 1993. It was only with their exemption from health and training levies in 1994, and the exclusion of initial income from employees' PRSI contributions from 1995, that low-income married couples reaped any real benefits from tax-cutting programmes directed specifically at improving their circumstances.

This is reflected in the data in Table 8.6. As can be seen, the real purchasing power of low-paid one income married households advanced by just 5 per cent between 1987 and 1992. In the ensu-

---

[2] The Back to Work Allowance is available only to single people moving back into jobs from unemployment. It does not cover those already in employment.

[3] Those earning less than £173 per week or £9,000 annually were, however, exempted from the 1 per cent Temporary Income Levy introduced in the 1993 Budget.

Incomes, Taxes and Prices since 1987

ing five years to 1997, the inflation-adjusted gain in disposable income for such households is estimated at over 13 per cent.

TABLE 8.6: TAX TREATMENT OF ONE-INCOME MARRIED COUPLES EARNING HALF AVERAGE INDUSTRIAL PAY, 1987–97

Year	Gross Pay (£)	Average Tax Rate (%)	Marginal Tax Rate (%)	After-Tax Income (£)	Real Income (£)
1987	5,035	7.75	7.75	4,645	4,645
1988	5,273	7.75	7.75	4,864	4,762
1989	5,486	7.75	7.75	5,060	4,760
1990	5,765	7.75	7.75	5,318	4,842
1991	5,947	7.75	7.75	5,487	4,841
1992	6,186	7.75	7.75	5,707	4,882
1993	6,518	7.75	7.75	6,013	5,073
1994	6,709	5.5	5.5	6,340	5,227
1995	6,858	3.4	5.5	6,624	5,325
1996	7,031	2.2	5.5	6,873	5,438
1997e	7,242	1.9	4.5	7,103	5,532
Change 1987–97	+43.8%	−5.85 points	−3.25 points	+52.9%	+19.1%

Notes: As Table 8.1. e = estimate. Family Income Supplements have been excluded (see Chapter 10).

Nonetheless, over the decade as a whole, the real net spending power of low-paid one-income households increased by just 19.1 per cent. This is the smallest real income gain recorded in any of the six cases surveyed. The reason is straightforward. Low-income married couples did not benefit from income tax cuts because they did not pay income tax at the start of the period. It was only when the focus shifted to relieving the low-paid from the other, hidden, taxes imposed on employees' incomes that such households began to reap some of the rewards of tax reform.

Further, it is important to note that since these calculations trace the interaction only of trends in employee earnings, prices and direct taxes, they do not take account of income subsidies, such as those delivered through the Family Income Supplement programme. These are assessed in Chapter 10.

8.5. Who Fared Best since 1987?

This chapter has traced the evolution of real disposable incomes — purchasing power — for six types of households over the years 1987 through 1997. The estimates for real incomes presented take account of average pay increases, budgetary tax changes and consumer price rises over the period.

In terms of additions to real spending power and reductions in taxes, who fared best? Tables 8.7 and 8.8 rank the gains in spending power and effective tax cuts over the last decade by household type. Further, the changes over the decade are decomposed into two sub-periods, 1987–92 and 1992–97, in order to answer two questions.

First, how did real incomes and taxes evolve over the years when fiscal correction was at its most forceful and successful? This covers the years after 1987 and embraces the return to national collective bargaining under the PNR and its successor, the PESP.

Second, to what extent were governments successful when they focused on seeking to improve the position of the low-paid? This broadly corresponds to the years from 1993 onwards. Since this period also encapsulates the post-devaluation boom, it allows an assessment of how the fruits of accelerated growth have been distributed to taxpayers.

TABLE 8.7: CHANGES IN REAL PURCHASING POWER BY HOUSEHOLD TYPE, 1987–97 (RANKED BY SIZE OF GAIN IN %)

	Household Type	1987–92	1992–97	1987–97
1.	Single people earning twice average pay	+19.2	+11.0	+32.3
2.	Single people earning average pay	+12.9	+13.6	+28.2
3.	One-income married couples earning twice average pay	+13.0	+13.3	+27.9
4.	Single people earning one-half of average pay	+6.6	+14.9	+22.6
5.	One-income married couples earning average pay	+8.2	+11.6	+20.7
6.	One-income married couples earning half average pay	+5.1	+13.3	+19.1

Sources: Condensed from Tables 8.1–8.6.

The principal conclusion to be drawn from Table 8.7 is that, in 1997, all households were significantly better off in terms of real purchasing power than they had been a decade earlier. As a result of the combined effects of pay increases, subdued inflation and tax reductions, the gains in the real purchasing power of households broadly ranged from one-fifth to one-third over the decade.

The second major finding is that those who were most heavily taxed in 1987 had gained the biggest additions to their purchasing power by 1997. Thus, single people earning twice average industrial pay saw their real spending power surge by almost one-third in the ten years to 1997.[4] Conversely, one-income married couples where household income came to just one-half of average manufacturing earnings, managed a real income gain of just 19.1 per cent over the decade. They did not benefit from any of the reductions in income tax, since they were exempt from such direct taxes throughout the period.

Third, the timing of gains in purchasing power by different types of household varied greatly. Low-income households made meagre real income advances between 1987 and 1992. On the one hand, the cuts in top tax rates were of no use to them. On the other, the failure of basic tax allowances to march upwards in step with pay rises during these years exposed a larger slice of low-paid single people's incomes to taxation, albeit at a declining standard rate. Moreover, they continued, during these years, to bear the full brunt of the hidden taxes on income. In contrast, the better-off, and especially better-off single people and dual-income married couples, benefited substantially from successive reductions in the top 58 per cent rate of income tax after 1988 and from its abolition in 1992/93. Given the background of fiscal contraction, the real income gains captured by the better-off in the five years after 1987 were of substantial magnitude.

Fourth, the redirection of policy between 1993 and 1997 has improved the relative position of the low-paid, but not by much. The biggest gains in real purchasing power over the years 1992 through 1997 have been recorded by single people on half average manufacturing earnings. In this respect, the most important ini-

---

[4] This conclusion applies with equal validity to two-income married couples where both were earning twice average industrial pay.

tiatives were the discounting of the first £80 of weekly income for employees' PRSI contribution purposes and the introduction of exemption thresholds for the payment of health and training levies. However, except in the case of exemption thresholds, all income groups have been able to cash in on these concessions, diluting their distributional impact.

This point is illustrated more graphically in Table 8.8. This table shows the reductions achieved in average direct tax rates — total income taxes as a percentage of gross income — for different income groups over the past decade. Over the decade as a whole, Table 8.8 shows that the largest tax cuts were enjoyed by those who initially paid the highest taxes. Single people on average manufacturing earnings and above and one-income married couples earning twice average pay were the biggest beneficiaries of the last decade's tax reductions.

TABLE 8.8: REDUCTIONS IN AVERAGE TAX RATES BY HOUSEHOLD TYPE, 1987–97 (PERCENTAGE POINTS)

Household Type	1987–92	1992–97	1987–97
1. Single people earning average pay	–4.8	–4.5	–9.3
2. Single people earning twice average pay	–6.9	–2.3	–9.2
3. One-income married couples earning twice average pay	–4.8	–4.3	–9.1
4. Single people earning one-half of average pay	–1.2	–6.2	–7.4
5. One-income married couples earning half average pay*	0	–5.85	–5.85
6. One-income married couples earning average pay	–2.2	–3.6	–5.8

*Excluding the impact of FIS.

Sources: Condensed from Tables 8.1–8.6.

However, the shift in the distributional impact of tax reductions over time is startling. Those on low incomes gained little or nothing in terms of average tax reductions between 1987 and 1992. This period witnessed systematic cuts in the top rate of income tax and so the principal beneficiaries were those exposed to tax at the highest rate.

Between 1993 and 1997, the low-paid fared best in terms of tax reductions, though those higher up the income distribution also gained from most of the concessions targeted on low-paid taxpayers.

The income tax provisions of the 1998 Budget will favour those on average incomes and above. The two percentage point cut in both the standard and higher rates of tax will indeed benefit the rich, but given the compression of the Irish tax code, it will also benefit single people and two-income married couples earning average wages. Both of these sets of taxpayers are currently exposed to the highest rates of income tax. This leads to the highly unusual outcome whereby cuts in the top rate of tax benefit not only the rich, but also many ordinary taxpayers in Ireland.

Yet again, this demonstrates the fundamental flaw in the Irish tax system: ordinary employees progress to the top rate of income tax far too rapidly.

Moreover, as a result of the 1998 Budget, the Government has been forced to admit that a higher proportion of taxpayers will pay income tax at the top rate in 1998/99 than in 1997/98. In the immediate aftermath of the 1998 Budget, in response to a Dáil question, the Minister for Finance, Mr Charles McCreevy, revealed that an expected 38.2 per cent of taxpayers would pay tax at the top rate in 1998/99 compared to 37.0 per cent in 1997/98.[5]

This is perhaps the most incisive commentary of all on the tardiness of Ireland's tax reform programme. After more than a decade of unparalleled, non-inflationary growth, almost two out of every five taxpayers in Ireland will be paying tax at the top rate in 1998/99. Even allowing that the top tax rate has been cut from 58 per cent to 46 per cent since 1987, this still constitutes a signal reproach to successive Ministers for Finance.

---

[5] Minister for Finance, written Dáil reply to Mr Paul McGrath, TD, reported in *The Irish Times*, 11 December 1997.

Chapter 9

THE TAX WEDGE AND THE LABOUR MARKET

9.1. The Nature of the Direct Tax Wedge

The imposition of direct taxes on incomes prevents employees from receiving the gross wages they are paid by employers. In the case of employees taxed on a Pay As You Earn (PAYE) basis, direct taxes are subtracted at source from incomes. The higher the direct tax charge, the lower will be the level of disposable income derived from a given gross wage. High direct tax charges on employees' gross incomes both exert upward pressure on money wages and weaken the incentive to work.

Two sets of responses to the imposition or raising of direct taxes are possible. First, employees will, through concerted action, attempt to restore their real incomes by seeking increases in money wages that compensate for the direct taxes imposed. In this instance, the response to higher direct taxes is similar to that induced by an acceleration of inflation. Efforts are made to shift the incidence of taxes on to employers by negotiating wage increases to compensate for tax increases. Where such efforts are successful, they will raise employers' labour costs and diminish the competitiveness of the output they produce. As a result, even where successful, efforts to gain cash compensation for tax hikes will result in slower growth in employment, as businesses will respond to the increase in costs by reducing the amount of labour hired.

Second, where efforts to gain compensation for higher income taxes through additional money wages fail, the disposable incomes — and hence the real wages — of employees will fall. Declining real wages may act as a disincentive to employment, not only for existing workers, but particularly, for prospective recruits. This effect may be quite pronounced where the opportunity cost of unemployment is low because of the availability of high replacement incomes from the social welfare system.

However, taxes deducted from employee incomes are not the only direct taxes levied on labour. In addition, social insurance contributions must be paid by employers on behalf of their employees. This raises the direct cost of labour to employers well above the levels of gross wages they pay to employees. Such increases in direct labour costs weaken employers' demand for labour.

In combination, the direct taxes levied on employee incomes and the payroll taxes imposed on employers act to drive a direct wedge between the costs to employers of hiring labour and the after-tax incomes received by employees.

This tax wedge widened substantially through the 1980s. The Department of Enterprise and Employment's 1996 "Strategy Paper on the Labour Market" reviewed the evidence of the impact of this widening tax wedge on employment:

> It has been estimated that in the traded sector, each 1 per cent increase in the tax wedge is associated with a 0.24 per cent wage increase in the short term and 0.5 per cent in the long term (Bradley, Whelan and Wright, 1993).
>
> Work carried out by Professor P. Geary found that in most studies, a 1 per cent real increase in labour costs was associated with a decline of between 0.6 per cent and 1 per cent in employment.
>
> Murphy (1987) estimated that a 1 per cent increase in the tax wedge reduces employment by 0.2 per cent.
>
> Barry (1991) concluded that the increase in the tax wedge was capable of explaining up to 30 per cent of the fall in manufacturing employment which occurred throughout the first half of the 1980s.
>
> McGettigan and Browne (1993) of the Central Bank concluded that the growth of the combined tax and exchange rate wedge in the first half of the 1980s accounted for an estimated 50,000 (43.8 per cent) of the 114,000 actual increase in unemployment between 1979 and 1989.

The National Economic and Social Council, in its November 1993 Report "A Strategy for Competitiveness, Growth and Employment" concluded that the growth of the tax wedge has played a significant role in Ireland's unemployment.[1]

The balance of the evidence indicates clearly that widening tax wedges have, in the past, diminished employment and contributed to raising unemployment in Ireland.

Following their substantial widening through the 1980s, this Chapter seeks to trace the evolution of Irish tax wedges during the first half of the 1990s. The first elements in the tax wedge equation — the direct taxes borne by employees on their incomes — were calculated in the preceding chapter. The second set of elements — the cost of employers' Pay-Related Social Insurance (PRSI) contributions — are integrated into the analysis below.

The rates and contribution ceilings for such employers' PRSI contributions were shown in Table 7.10. As indicated, the standard rate has changed little over the past decade. It has declined from 12.33 per cent in 1987/88 to 12.0 per cent in 1997/98. However, a reduced rate of contribution, currently 8.5 per cent, was introduced in 1994/95 for those employing low-paid workers.

Employers' PRSI contributions directly raise the cost to employers of hiring labour, and by substantial amounts. Such contributions swell the size of the initial tax wedge driven between employers' gross pay costs and employees' take-home pay by the direct taxes imposed on employees' incomes.

9.2. Calculating the Irish Tax Wedge

The total tax wedge is calculated in three stages. First, employers' PRSI contributions at the relevant rates, as shown in Table 7.10, are added to employees' gross wages to ascertain the total direct cost of employing workers. This is shown in the tables that follow as the "cost to employer".

Second, the direct taxes charged on employee incomes are deducted from gross wages and salaries to derive take-home pay or

---

[1] "Growing and Sharing Our Employment — Strategy Paper on the Labour Market", Department of Enterprise and Employment, Stationery Office, April 1996, p. 56.

after-tax income. These calculations were effected for a range of households in Tables 8.1 through 8.6. The results show the levels of disposable income which households retain from their gross earnings.

Third, the total tax wedge is the gap that separates the cost of labour to employers from the take-home pay of employees. This gap thus represents the direct tax charge which governments levy on every job, since it comprises the income taxes, PRSI contributions and levies borne by employees and the PRSI contributions paid by employers on their behalf.

The total tax wedge, or the tax charge per job, can then be expressed either as a proportion of total labour costs to employers or as a percentage of employees' take-home pay. Both are illustrated in the Tables that follow.

9.3. The Tax Wedge and Average Single Employees, 1987–97

The tax wedge as it applies to single employees receiving gross remuneration equivalent to average manufacturing earnings over the past decade is shown in Table 9.1. Again, it is important to emphasise that the tax wedges illustrated in Table 9.1 apply with almost equal force to married couples, both of whom are working and both of whom are earning average pay.

The first point to notice from the data in Table 9.1 is that the tax wedges relating to single people on average earnings were very wide at the beginning of the period surveyed. In 1987/88, the total taxes levied on the jobs of average single earners were equivalent to 42.5 per cent of the total direct labour costs to employers of hiring such employees. At the same time, the tax wedge amounted to almost three-quarters of the cash single people took home in their paypackets from average gross earnings.

Second, the tax wedge has narrowed appreciably over the past decade, and particularly since the post-1993 devaluation boom got under way. By 1997, the estimated tax wedge in this instance had declined to around one-third of employers' direct labour costs.

TABLE 9.1: THE TAX WEDGE AND SINGLE EMPLOYEES ON AVERAGE EARNINGS

Year	Cost to Employer (£)	Employee Net Pay (£)	Tax Wedge (£)	Wedge as % Employer Cost	Wedge as % Take-Home Pay
1987	11,311	6,499	4,812	42.5	74.0
1988	11,854	6,913	4,941	41.7	71.5
1989	12,309	7,366	4,973	40.4	67.8
1990	12,936	7,777	5,159	39.9	66.3
1991	13,344	8,065	5,279	39.6	65.5
1992	13,881	8,574	5,307	38.2	61.9
1993	14,626	8,816	5,810	39.7	65.9
1994	15,055	9,309	5,746	38.2	61.7
1995	15,388	9,733	5,655	36.7	58.1
1996	15,748	10,081	5,667	36.0	56.2
1997e	16,221	10,694	5,527	34.1	51.7

Sources: Tables 7.10, 8.1.

However, the rapidity with which the tax wedge has retreated over the past decade should not be allowed to obscure the fact that it still remains extremely wide in the case of single employees on average earnings. By 1997, the tax wedge still stood equivalent to more than half the after-tax incomes of average single earners.

9.4. The Tax Wedge and Average One-Income Couples

The tax wedge as it applies in the case of married couples where one spouse is working and earning average pay is shown in Table 9.2. In this instance, both the initial width of the tax wedge and its subsequent paring back are thinner than in the case of single people earning similar incomes.

In 1987/88, the tax wedge for average married workers whose spouses were not earning amounted to half the take-home pay they received and one-third of the cost to the employer of hiring them. In the succeeding decade, the tax wedge contracted to two-fifths of the married worker's take-home pay, a decline of over ten percentage points. However, for the employer, the tax wedge fell by just over five percentage points.

TABLE 9.2: THE TAX WEDGE AND ONE-INCOME COUPLES ON AVERAGE EARNINGS

Year	Cost to Employer (£)	Employee Net Pay (£)	Tax Wedge (£)	Wedge as % Employer Cost	Wedge as % Take-Home Pay
1987	11,311	7,509	3,802	33.6	50.6
1988	11,854	7,853	4,001	33.7	50.9
1989	12,309	8,270	4,039	32.8	48.8
1990	12,936	8,733	4,203	32.5	48.1
1991	13,344	9,055	4,289	32.1	47.4
1992	13,881	9,500	4,381	31.6	46.1
1993	14,626	9,844	4,782	32.7	48.6
1994	15,055	10,317	4,738	31.5	45.9
1995	15,388	10,697	4,691	30.5	43.9
1996	15,748	11,051	4,697	29.8	42.5
1997e	16,221	11,642	4,579	28.2	39.3

Sources: Tables 7.10, 8.2.

The smaller proportionate reduction in the tax wedges facing married workers in one-income households relative to single workers on similar incomes is explained by the differential impact of cuts in the top rate of income tax. Since married households were initially less exposed to income taxes at the higher marginal rates, they gained less in terms of tax cuts when the top rate of tax was reduced and, ultimately, abolished.

9.5. The Tax Wedge and Better-Off Single Employees

Despite the reductions in direct taxation effected in the past decade, the tax wedges separating employer labour costs from the take-home pay of better-off single employees remain substantial. As late as 1989, the tax wedge on the incomes of single people receiving twice average manufacturing earnings was larger, in cash terms, than the take-home pay of such employees.

Reductions in income tax rates and the broadening of income tax bands have narrowed the tax wedge for higher-earning single people. By 1997, it is estimated that the government's total direct tax take from the jobs of single people on twice average earnings amounted to 84.6 per cent of their take-home pay. This represents a reduction of one-quarter in the width of the tax wedge over the past decade, as shown in Table 9.3.

TABLE 9.3: THE TAX WEDGE AND SINGLE PEOPLE EARNING TWICE AVERAGE PAY

Year	Cost to Employer (£)	Employee Net Pay (£)	Tax Wedge (£)	Wedge as % Employer Cost	Wedge as % Take-Home Pay
1987	22,049	10,309	11,740	53.2	113.9
1988	23,101	10,983	12,118	52.5	110.3
1989	24,138	11,785	12,353	51.2	104.8
1990	25,327	12,757	12,570	49.6	98.5
1991	26,141	13,214	12,927	49.5	97.8
1992	27,221	14,365	12,856	47.2	89.5
1993	28,671	14,787	13,884	48.4	93.9
1994	29,984	15,573	14,411	48.1	92.5
1995	30,578	16,127	14,451	47.3	89.6
1996	31,338	16,622	14,716	47.0	88.5
1997e	32,314	17,507	14,807	45.8	84.6

Sources: Tables 7.10, 8.3.

Nonetheless, the fact remains that the direct taxes collected on jobs paying single people twice average manufacturing earnings stand equivalent to 85 per cent of their disposable incomes. Nor can such single people be classed amongst the super-rich. Their gross, pre-tax earnings during 1997 are estimated at less than £30,000.

As a percentage of the cost to the employer, the tax wedge in this case has declined by a decidedly modest seven percentage points, from 53.2 per cent in 1987 to 45.8 per cent a decade later.

The principal reason for the small scale of this decline is the sharp increase in employers' PRSI contributions in respect of such workers. Over the past decade, the ceiling for employers' PRSI contributions has been raised from £15,500 in 1987/88 to £27,900 in 1997/98. This represents an 80 per cent raising of the roof for employers' PRSI contributions over the decade. In consequence, employers' standard PRSI contributions on behalf of employees earning twice average manufacturing earnings have risen from £1,911 in 1987/88 to £3,348 in 1997/98, an increase of over 75 per cent.

Thus, in the case of more skilled and educated employees, the cash cost of employers' PRSI contributions has advanced at a much faster pace than the growth in earnings — 43.8 per cent over the period — while it has outdistanced the 28.4 per cent rate of inflation over the decade. The proximate cause of this sharp ascent in employers' PRSI costs lies in the lifting of the ceiling for contributions by 80 per cent over the decade. In the 1998 Budget, the contributions ceiling was raised again, to £29,000 for 1998/99.

9.6. The Tax Wedge and Better-Off One-Income Couples

Reflecting their lower exposure to income tax at the top rate, the tax wedges relating to better-off one-income couples are smaller than those associated with their single counterparts on comparable earnings. The trend in the tax wedges dividing employer costs from the disposable incomes of married couples where one spouse is paid twice average manufacturing earnings is shown in Table 9.4.

From Table 9.4, it can be seen that the tax wedge as a percentage of after-tax income has fallen from over 70 per cent in 1987 to just over 50 per cent a decade later. This decline reflects both the growth in earnings over the period and the lower average tax charges exacted from income.

However, the tax wedge as a proportion of employers' costs in hiring such workers has exhibited only a modest decline of seven percentage points over the period. This again reflects the impact on employers' costs of the steep increase in PRSI contribution ceilings. In the case of highly paid workers, the raising of these ceilings extended considerably the gross income base on which employers' payroll taxes became chargeable.

TABLE 9.4: THE TAX WEDGE AND ONE-INCOME COUPLES EARNING TWICE AVERAGE PAY

Year	Cost to Employer (£)	Employee Net Pay (£)	Tax Wedge (£)	Wedge as % Employer Cost	Wedge as % Take-Home Pay
1987	22,049	12,830	9,219	41.8	71.9
1988	23,101	13,643	9,458	40.9	69.3
1989	24,138	14,513	9,625	39.9	66.3
1990	25,327	15,427	9,900	39.1	64.2
1991	26,141	15,927	10,214	39.1	64.1
1992	27,221	16,942	10,279	37.8	60.7
1993	28,671	17,637	11,034	38.5	62.6
1994	29,984	18,423	11,561	38.6	62.8
1995	30,578	19,196	11,382	37.2	59.3
1996	31,338	19,868	11,470	36.6	57.7
1997e	32,314	21,077	11,237	34.8	53.3

Sources: Tables 7.10, 8.4.

9.7. The Tax Wedge and Low-Income Single Workers

From 1993 onwards, a determined and sustained effort has been made by successive governments to reduce taxes and tax wedges as they affect the low-paid. As indicated earlier, this effort has culminated in exempting low-paid workers from health contributions and training levies, disregarding the first £4,160 of annual income for PRSI contribution purposes and introducing a new low rate of 8.5 per cent for employers' PRSI contributions for those employees earning up to £260 per week in 1997/98. The result has been a significant slimming of the tax wedge as it applies to single people earning half average manufacturing pay, as can be seen from Table 9.5.

As shown in Table 9.5, between 1987 and 1993, the tax wedge as a proportion of take-home pay remained virtually static for single people earning half average industrial pay. Thereafter, it fell sharply, dropping by over 15 percentage points to an estimated 27.1 per cent by 1997.

TABLE 9.5: THE TAX WEDGE AND LOW-INCOME SINGLE WORKERS

Year	Cost to Employer (£)	Employee Net Pay (£)	Tax Wedge (£)	Wedge as % Employer Cost	Wedge as % Take-Home Pay
1987	5,656	3,928	1,728	30.5	44.0
1988	5,927	4,116	1,811	30.6	44.0
1989	6,155	4,308	1,847	30.0	42.9
1990	6,468	4,529	1,939	30.0	42.8
1991	6,673	4,686	1,987	29.8	42.4
1992	6,941	4,897	2,044	29.4	41.7
1993	7,313	5,135	2,178	29.8	42.4
1994*	7,313	5,456	1,857	25.4	34.0
1995	7,475	5,701	1,774	23.7	31.1
1996	7,629	5,906	1,723	22.6	29.2
1997e	7,858	6,182	1,676	21.3	27.1

Sources: Tables 7.10, 8.5.

* Employers' PRSI rate reduced from 12.2 per cent to 9.0 per cent for low-paid workers. Current low rate now stands at 8.5 per cent.

A similar stasis was evident in this tax wedge as a proportion of employers' total labour costs between 1987 and 1993. Again, there was a concerted contraction in succeeding years, with the width of the wedge narrowing by well over one-quarter between 1993 and 1997.

Thus, policy has been successful in reducing both direct tax rates — for employers as well as employees — and tax wedges in the case of low-paid single workers. As a result, judged in isolation, taxation policy in recent years has worked to strengthen employment incentives at the bottom of the labour market. The only remaining conundrum is why people on such low wages should be trapped in the tax net at all.

9.8. The Tax Wedge and Low-Paid One-Income Couples

Low-paid one-income couples have been exempt from income tax throughout the period surveyed. Recent initiatives have also released them from health contributions and training levies. As a result of the exemption of the first £4,160 from employees' PRSI contributions, the amounts they pay in social insurance have been significantly reduced. On the employers' side the introduction of the low 8.5 per cent PRSI contribution rate has reduced the total cost of hiring low-paid workers. These changes are reflected in Table 9.6.

TABLE 9.6: THE TAX WEDGE AND LOW-PAID ONE-INCOME COUPLES

Year	Cost to Employer (£)	Employee Net Pay (£)	Tax Wedge (£)	Wedge as % Employer Cost	Wedge as % Take-Home Pay
1987	5,656	4,645	1,011	17.9	21.8
1988	5,927	4,864	1,063	18.8	21.9
1989	6,155	5,060	1,095	17.8	21.6
1990	6,468	5,318	1,150	17.8	21.6
1991	6,673	5,487	1,186	17.8	21.6
1992	6,941	5,707	1,234	17.8	21.6
1993	7,313	6,013	1,300	17.8	21.6
1994	7,313	6,340	974	13.3	15.3
1995	7,475	6,624	851	11.4	12.8
1996	7,629	6,873	756	9.9	11.0
1997e	7,858	7,103	755	9.6	10.6

Sources: Tables 7.10, 8.6.

As can be seen, since 1987 the tax wedge as a proportion of the net take-home pay of such households has been halved and is now hovering around 10 per cent. In terms of employer costs, the tax wedge on low-paid married workers has dipped into single digits.

In broad terms, the policy of cutting direct taxes on the incomes and the employment of the low-paid has been pushing in the right direction. This has been important to the functioning of the labour market for two reasons.

First, many facing low pay in the labour market are potential young labour market entrants with few qualifications or skills. If they are deterred by high taxes and low after-tax pay from accepting offers of employment on leaving the educational system, they become candidates for early graduation into long-term unemployment.

Second, reducing the direct tax take on low incomes assists in recruiting the unemployed, and particularly the long-term unemployed, back into the workforce. The initial wages earned by those returning to the workforce after a prolonged absence will be low in the majority of cases. Minimising the tax take from low-paying jobs is therefore central to encouraging the acceptance of job offers by the long-term unemployed.

The case for cutting taxes on low-paying jobs is reinforced by the fact that taxed work is not the only potential source of income available to the unemployed. If the returns from work are suppressed by taxes, then the relative attractions of untaxed income from not working or from working in the black economy are necessarily enhanced.

Chapter 10

POVERTY AND UNEMPLOYMENT TRAPS

10.1. Explaining Poverty and Unemployment Traps

In answer to a Parliamentary Question in April 1997, the Minister for Finance produced figures showing that a married man, with a wife and one child, earning £167.50 a week would be £10 a week worse off if his employer gave him a £20 a week pay rise. While the employee's weekly after-tax pay would increase from £163.56 to £177.26 on foot of the £20 a week pay increase, his total weekly income would fall from £211.38 to £201.36 because of the curtailment of entitlements to state benefits, principally rent subsidies and access to a medical card.[1]

This paradox illustrates graphically that, even in the case of those at work, real living standards are not solely determined by the interplay of pay, prices and taxes. The state is not only a taker of taxes; it is a provider of benefits in cash and in kind. The extent and incidence of the benefits it provides can exert considerable influence on the behaviour of the labour market.

While the influence of the state is pervasive, its hand is most visible in the lower reaches of the labour market. The state's actions are informed by good intentions. Through Unemployment Assistance, it provides means-tested and untaxed cash incomes for the long-term unemployed. It issues medical cards, providing free health care, to unemployed and low-paid households. It varies the rents of local authority housing in line with household circumstances, labour market status and ability to pay. It gives fuel al-

---

[1] Written reply by the then Minister for Finance, Mr Ruairi Quinn to Mr Noel Ahern TD, reported in *The Irish Times*, 10 April 1997.

lowances, butter vouchers and back-to-school clothing and footwear allowances to those in need.

This type of social provision, in cash, goods and services, is the distinguishing mark of a civilised community. It constitutes an explicit recognition that, collectively, individuals in a society have a responsibility to those who are poor or disadvantaged.

However, such actions by the state's visible hand can produce labour market consequences that were not part of its original intention. This arises because of the dual role assumed by the state in the sphere of income determination. On the one hand, it taxes, at progressive rates, the incomes of those in employment. On the other, it supports the incomes of the poor, particularly the low-paid and the unemployed.

These two objectives collide in the labour market. High taxes on work increase the costs of, and reduce the returns to, labour. The range of available social welfare benefits, in cash and kind, cushion the cost of not working. The interaction of an income tax system that taxes low incomes and a social welfare system that provides a wide array of untaxed benefits to the unemployed can cause severe dislocation in the lower reaches of the labour market.

That dislocation is of two types. First, "unemployment traps" arise where "a person's financial circumstances if unemployed compare favourably with his/her net take-home pay from employment such that there is a disincentive for unemployed people to take up employment or for people in low-paid employment to remain in it".[2] Where unemployment benefits "replace" a high proportion of net earnings from employment, then there is little immediate financial reward to be derived from taking a job.

Second, those in employment can fall into "poverty traps" where net income falls as gross income increases. "Poverty traps" arise where the acceptance of an increase in money wages leaves an employee with a lower after-tax income due to the effects of a higher tax bill and the simultaneous withdrawal of means-tested state benefits.

---

[2] "Report of the Expert Working Group on the Integration of the Tax and Social Welfare Systems", Stationery Office, Dublin, June 1996, p. 14.

Much of the policy debate in recent years has focused on how such traps can be eliminated or minimised, thereby improving the functioning of the labour market, but without interfering with the integrity of social support systems for those in need. This chapter seeks to quantify the depth of both traps in Ireland.

10.2. Unemployment Assistance and Unemployment Traps

Clearly, given the scale and complexity of the safety net provided by the social security system, a wide array of potential incomes from unemployment now exist. These are shaped, inter alia, by duration of unemployment, marital status and household size.

In order to keep the analysis to manageable proportions, the focus is directed at households that have suffered prolonged spells of unemployment and are in receipt of maximum rates of Unemployment Assistance. For the reasons adduced in previous chapters, members of such households regaining a foothold in the workforce are likely to be offered only low rates of pay in the first instance.

As a result, the analysis initially compares the returns to work at half average manufacturing earnings against income from unemployment. It seeks to estimate the proportion of disposable income derived from half average manufacturing earnings that is replaced by Unemployment Assistance.

Maximum rates of long-duration Unemployment Assistance for all household types have risen much faster than inflation over the past decade. The rates of increase in maximum weekly rates are shown in Table 10.1.

Over the decade 1987–97, the level of consumer prices is estimated to have increased by some 28 per cent. Relative to this increase in retail prices, the maximum rate of Unemployment Assistance available to single people has increased by 78.6 per cent while, for claimants with adult dependants, the rate has increased by 65.4 per cent. For married couples with two children, the maximum rate of has increased by a lower 59.0 per cent, but this has been supplemented by very extensive increases in Child Benefit, particularly after 1992.

Hence, the purchasing power of maximum payments for all households has risen sharply over the past ten years.

TABLE 10.1: MAXIMUM WEEKLY RATES OF UNEMPLOYMENT
ASSISTANCE, 1987–98 (£; LONG-TERM)

Year	Single Person	Married Couple, No Children	Married Couple, Two Children
1987*	37.80	65.00	84.20
1988	42.00	70.00	90.40
1989	47.00	76.00	97.00
1990	52.00	83.00	105.00
1991	55.00	88.00	112.00
1992	57.20	91.50	116.50
1993	59.20	94.70	120.30
1994	61.00	97.60	124.00
1995	62.50	100.00	126.40**
1996	64.50	103.00	129.40
1997	67.50	107.50	133.90
Increase 1987–97	+78.6%	+65.4%	+59.0%
1998	70.50	111.70	138.10

* Increases in rates announced in the budget usually become effective in the following Summer; ** Following substantial increases in Child Benefit ("children's allowances") in 1995, UA child dependent allowances have remained unchanged. Child Benefit is excluded from the calculations since it is universally available to all households with children, so that its labour market impact is neutral.

Sources: Budget Books 1987–97; "Summary of 1998 Budget Measures", December 1997.

10.3. Basic Income Replacement Ratios

For given levels of gross pay, income replacement ratios (IRRs) measure the proportion of net, after-tax income from employment that is "replaced" by unemployment benefits for those who are out of work.

Basic income replacement ratios measure the proportion of after-tax income replaced by cash unemployment benefits for hypothetical households. More sophisticated IRRs also take account of the "secondary" benefits available to those out of work and on low pay, employment subsidies, where applicable, and work-related expenses, such as travel costs.

For single people being paid half average industrial earnings, the basic income replacement ratio, as measured by the relationship between net, after-tax income and Unemployment Assistance, is shown in Table 10.2.

TABLE 10.2: BASIC INCOME REPLACEMENT RATIOS FOR SINGLE PEOPLE ON HALF AVERAGE MANUFACTURING EARNINGS, 1987–97

Year	After-Tax Income (£)*	Unemployment Assistance (£)**	UA as % of Net Pay
1987	3,928	1,966	50.1
1988	4,116	2,184	53.1
1989	4,308	2,444	56.7
1990	4,529	2,704	59.7
1991	4,686	2,860	61.0
1992	4,897	2,974	60.7
1993	5,135	3,078	59.9
1994	5,456	3,172	58.1
1995	5,701	3,250	57.0
1996	5,906	3,354	56.8
1997e	6,182	3,510	56.8

*Data as in Table 8.5; ** Annualised data in Table 10.1. Christmas bonus excluded.

As can be seen, in the case of low-paid single earners, the basic Income Replacement Ratio climbed by over ten percentage points from 50.1 per cent to 61.0 per cent between 1987 and 1991. This advance was attributable to relatively generous budgetary increases in maximum rates of Unemployment Assistance over these years.

After 1991, the income replacement ratio began to fall, partly because annual increases in UA were lower in absolute terms than in the 1987–91 period, partly because the cuts in the direct taxes levied on low-paid single workers raised the take-home pay of those at work. In consequence, the basic IRR for single people on half average earnings declined by over four percentage points to an estimated 56.8 per cent by 1997.

In other words, for single people, Unemployment Assistance replaces a little more than half the cash income they would receive from jobs paying half average earnings. Given that the non-cash supports available to unemployed single people are relatively limited, unemployment payments alone cannot be seen as a strong disincentive to employment amongst single people at income bands above half average industrial earnings.

Below these levels, however, disincentive effects become more pronounced. In 1996, basic income replacement ratios for single people on gross weekly wages ranging from £80 to £140 were calculated by the Department of Enterprise and Employment. The results are summarised in Table 10.3.

TABLE 10.3: INCOME REPLACEMENT RATIOS FOR LOW-PAID SINGLE PEOPLE, 1996

Category	Gross Weekly Income			
Gross Pay	£80.00	£100.00	£120.00	£140.00
Net Pay	£78.00	£89.81	£103.31	£116.61
Unemployment Assistance	£64.50	£64.50	£64.50	£64.50
Basic IRR	83%	72%	62%	55%
"Adjusted" IRR	91%	80%	68%	59%

Notes: The Basic IRR shows Unemployment Assistance as a proportion of Net Pay. The Adjusted IRR takes account of non-cash benefits, such as medical cards, and of work and job-search related spending such as travel. It excludes, however, the impact of Back to Work Allowances.

Source: "Growing and Sharing Our Employment — A Strategy Paper on the Labour Market", Department of Enterprise and Employment, April 1996, condensed from Table 3.5, p. 64.

As shown in Table 10.3, the lower the level of gross income earned by single people, the larger the segment of after-tax income that is replaced by state unemployment benefits.

Commenting on these results, the Department of Enterprise and Employment noted that, even in the aftermath of the 1996 Budget:

> ... the problems remain serious. The incentive for single persons to take up low-skill jobs at gross wage levels consistent with their educational and skill levels is blunted... Thus, a conscious decision by some to opt for out-of-work income support creates a cycle: persons who can only command a low wage because of their limited value-added potential face a high replacement rate and little incentive to seek work.[3]

In the case of one-income married couples with no children, where the working spouse is earning half manufacturing earnings, basic income replacement ratios increased from 72.8 per cent in 1987 to reach a peak at 83.4 per cent in 1991 and 1992. Thereafter, as

TABLE 10.4: INCOME REPLACEMENT RATIOS FOR LOW-PAID MARRIED COUPLES (WHERE THE WORKING SPOUSE IS EARNING HALF AVERAGE EARNINGS)

Year	Net Pay (£)	Unemployment Assistance (£)	UA as % of Net Pay
1987	4,645	3,380	72.8
1988	4,864	3,640	74.8
1989	5,060	3,952	78.1
1990	5,318	4,316	81.2
1991	5,487	4,576	83.4
1992	5,707	4,758	83.4
1993	6,013	4,924	81.9
1994	6,340	5,075	80.0
1995	6,624	5,200	78.5
1996	6,873	5,356	77.9
1997e	7,103	5,590	78.7

Sources: Tables 7.10; 8.6; 9.1.

---

[3] "Growing and Sharing Our Employment", p. 65.

the gross incomes of the low-paid were relieved of PRSI and levies, the basic IRR declined, falling back to 78.7 per cent by 1997. Falling average taxes on low-paid employment, rather than benefit cuts, have been the decisive factor in causing IRRs to decline after 1992.

The rise and fall of the basic income replacement ratio for single-earning low income married households over the past decade has been dictated by two factors. First, between 1987 and 1992, the IRR increased because of significant annual additions to Unemployment Assistance. Since such households were exempt from income tax throughout the period, the reductions in income tax rates and the broadening of income tax bands conferred no benefits on them. As a result, basic IRRs increased.

Second, the progressive exemption of low-income households from health and training levies after 1992, coupled with the introduction of exemption thresholds for employee PRSI contributions, significantly raised after-tax incomes from employment. As a result, basic IRRs for such households began to decline once again.

The analysis of basic income replacement ratios gives rise to the following conclusions:

1. For single people earning half average industrial pay — around £7,100 in 1996 — or more, cash unemployment benefits do not constitute a significant disincentive to accepting offers of employment, since, at best, they replace slightly over half of after-tax earnings.

2. Below this level, where the gross incomes of single people range from £80 to £120 a week, disincentive effects for single workers gather strength. At these rates of gross pay, cash unemployment benefits replace between three-fifths and four-fifths of net income from employment. When non-cash benefits are factored in, the income replacement ratio rises to between two-thirds and nine-tenths. While the gross pay levels in this range are low, they are not untypical of the offers likely to be made to young people entering the labour market with no skills or minimal educational qualifications.

Poverty and Unemployment Traps

3. At pay levels around half average manufacturing earnings, over three-quarters of net income from employment is replaced by cash unemployment benefits for a working spouse with an adult dependant. While this does not constitute an insurmountable financial barrier to accepting employment, it comes close.

10.4. Income Replacement Ratios including "Secondary" Benefits

Basic income replacement ratios, while instructive, provide only a first approximation to quantifying the scale of unemployment traps. Not only do they take insufficient cognisance of "secondary" benefits — particularly important to married households with children — they also neglect the growing importance of employment subsidies that are available to low-paid workers.

This section examines income replacement ratios adjusted for the inclusion of secondary social welfare benefits. Clearly, access to secondary benefits will differ considerably from household to household. To take account of this diversity, two sets of examples are shown. First, replacement ratios for 1995/96 for five household types are illustrated in Table 10.5. At each level of gross income from employment, Table 10.5 shows the extent to which the social welfare system replaces the net after-tax income derived from work. The results can be summarised thus:

At gross income levels of £5,000, equivalent to roughly one-third of average industrial earnings, the social welfare system replaced 88 per cent of the net income a single person would have earned from working in 1995/96. For one-income married couples with children claiming the Family Income Supplement (FIS) wage subsidy, total unemployment payments would have replaced some 90 per cent of net employment income. For married couples with children not claiming FIS, unemployment payments, including secondary benefits, would have yielded incomes ranging between 150 per cent and 175 per cent of net pay from work.

At gross income levels of £7,000, approximating to half average industrial earnings, all unemployment benefits would have replaced two-thirds of a single person's net income from employment in 1995/96. For one-income married couples claiming the

FIS wage subsidy, unemployment payments would have compensated for between 82 and 86 per cent of after-tax earned income, depending on the number of children in the household. At this gross income level, net incomes from employment were easily eclipsed by social welfare unemployment benefits for married couples with children not claiming FIS.

TABLE 10.5: INCOME REPLACEMENT RATIOS WITH SECONDARY BENEFITS, 1995/96 (PERCENTAGE OF NET INCOME FROM WORK REPLACED BY ALL SOCIAL WELFARE BENEFITS AT EACH LEVEL OF GROSS PAY*)

Gross Income (£)	Single Person (%)	Married Couple Plus FIS (%)		Married Couple, No FIS (%)	
		2 Children	4 Children	2 Children	4 Children
5,000	88.3	88.3	91.8	149.2	175.7
6,000	75.7	85.2	89.1	125.9	149.4
7,000	66.3	81.8	86.0	109.0	129.9
8,000	58.9	82.6	83.6	101.4	114.9
9,000	53.1	82.7	80.9	93.2	103.0
10,000	49.3	85.0	85.5	89.1	103.0
11,000	45.3	84.0	87.6	84.0	97.4
12,000	41.8	79.4	88.4	79.4	92.4
13,000	39.5	75.3	88.0	75.3	88.0
14,000	37.7	71.0	83.9	71.0	83.9
15,000	36.0	66.9	80.1	66.9	80.1
20,000	29.4	52.1	63.9	52.1	63.9

* Table 10.5 shows the percentage of net after-tax income, including Family Income Supplement where applicable, at each gross income level, that is replaced by the net weekly incomes of unemployed households, taking account of Unemployment Assistance, the value of medical cards, differential rents, free fuel allowance and other minor allowances and subsidies. Travel and work-seeking expenses are accounted for in all cases.

Source: "Report of the Expert Working Group on the Integration of the Tax and Social Welfare Systems", Stationery Office, June 1996, Appendix 3, pp. 155–159.

At gross income levels of £14,000 in 1995/96, then almost equivalent to average industrial pay, the total package of unemployment benefits replaced just over one-third of the after-tax earned income of a single person. However, in the case of one-income married couples with two children, who were not claiming FIS, social welfare benefits made up 71 per cent of the net income from employment. Where there were four children, benefits replaced 84 per cent of net earnings.

The Expert Group concluded:

> ... successive governments over the past twenty years have significantly increased social welfare benefits in real terms. This arose from a social consensus to deal with the problem of poverty. During the same period the burden of taxation was increased substantially. This combination of policies has resulted in a reduction in the incentive for the unemployed to accept relatively low-paid work or for those on low pay to remain in employment.[4]

In the second example, replacement rates for single people have been derived for 1997/98 tax and benefit rates, drawing on an informative model developed by the Irish National Organisation of the Unemployed.[5] This model is particularly useful because it includes the cost of private sector rented accommodation.

As shown in Table 10.1, the maximum rate of Unemployment Assistance available to single people in 1997/98 amounted to £3,510 annually or £67.50 a week.

Assuming that single people pay £40 a week for private rented accommodation, the INOU calculates the value of weekly secondary benefits to the long-term unemployed as follows: rent allowance (maximum) £31.90; fuel allowance: £2.50; medical card: £1.34; butter vouchers and the value of the Christmas bonus: £1.03. Thus, assuming rental costs of £40 a week, the total value of secondary benefits amounts to £36.77. This leaves the long-

---

[4] "Report of the Expert Working Group", op. cit., p. 26.

[5] "Welfare to Work — Research on the Financial Benefits of Taking Up Employment", Irish National Organisation of the Unemployed (INOU), March 1997.

term unemployed with net disposable incomes after rent of £64.27 a week or £3,342 annually.

To ascertain adjusted income replacement ratios, including secondary benefits, this net social income is compared against a range of net incomes derived from employment in Table 10.6.

In Table 10.6, direct taxes comprise income tax and employees' PRSI, having allowed for a personal tax allowance of £2,900, the PAYE tax allowance of £800 and a rental allowance of £500 in 1997. Weekly rents cost £40 or £2,080 annually. The adjusted income replacement ratio represents primary and secondary social welfare benefits — including rent allowances — as a proportion of income from employment after deduction of direct taxes and rent.

TABLE 10.6: SINGLE PEOPLE: ADJUSTED INCOME REPLACEMENT RATIOS, 1997/98 (ANNUAL 1997/98 INCOMES IN £)

Gross Pay	Direct Taxes	Rent	Net Income from Work After Rent	Social Income After Rent*	IRR (adj.) (%)
6,000	551	2,080	3,369	3,342	99.2
7,000	856	2,080	4,064	3,342	82.2
8,000	1,161	2,080	4,759	3,342	70.2
9,000	1,466	2,080	5,454	3,342	61.3
10,000	1,771	2,080	6,149	3,342	54.4

* Primary and secondary state benefits.

Sources: Previous Tables; INOU (1997), Table 5 (b), p. 10, for gross pay ranges £8,000–£10,000. Other calculations are author's own.

On the stated assumptions, primary and secondary state benefits replace all the net disposable income that would be derived from gross employment incomes of up to £6,000 a year for the single long-term unemployed.

Put another way, in this model there is no financial incentive for the long-term unemployed to return to work at jobs paying £6,000 or less when secondary social welfare benefits are taken into consideration. Even on gross employee incomes of £7,000 a year, the total benefit package supplied by the state replaces more than four-fifths of the net disposable income derived from working.

For those who are single and long-term unemployed, primary and secondary social welfare benefits are replacing 77.2 per cent of the net disposable income of jobs paying £7,382 in 1997 — half prospective manufacturing earnings.

The addition of secondary benefits thus raises the income replacement rate for people who are single and long-term unemployed. This can be seen by comparing Tables 10.2 and 10.6. In effect, it sets an income floor at around £6,000 in 1997, below which there is no financial incentive to seek employment or re-employment.

The corollary of high adjusted income replacement ratios is very low incremental income from returning to work. Thus, the single long-term unemployed person returning to a job at £9,000 a year for a 40-hour week will earn £1 extra an hour for working compared to remaining unemployed.

By replacing a high proportion of after-tax income, the social welfare system dims the attractions of low-paid employment, particularly for married couples with child dependants. In turn, this can weaken the intensity of job search efforts, lengthening the duration of unemployment and providing a partial explanation of the persistence of long-term unemployment.

Browne and McGettigan have stated that:

> the persistence of high unemployment may have been underpinned by rather high replacement ratios which are also of indefinite duration, and the labour security legislation in place.[6]

10.5. Poverty Traps

Where high replacement ratios may discourage the unemployed from seeking to re-enter the workforce, "poverty traps" penalise those at work for raising their incomes. In brief, the joint impacts of the income tax and social welfare codes conspire to ensure that employees receive less net income as gross income rises. This is shown for a one-income married couple with two children in the 1995/96 tax year in Table 10.7.

---

[6] Quoted in "Report of the Expert Working Group", p. 177.

TABLE 10.7: THE POVERTY TRAP IN 1995/96: LESS INCOME FOR MORE PAY (MARRIED COUPLE, TWO CHILDREN, ONE EARNER)

Annual Earnings (£)	Net Weekly Income* (£)
5,000	142
6,000	147
7,000	153
8,000	152
9,000	151
10,000	147
11,000	149
12,000	158
13,000	166
14,000	176
15,000	187

* Includes non-cash benefits. Full take-up of Family Income Supplement is assumed.

Source: "Report of the Expert Working Group on the Integration of the Tax and Social Welfare Systems", June 1996, Table 2.1, p. 14.

As Table 10.7 demonstrates, if the working spouse in this household managed to increase gross earnings from £7,000 to £11,000 in 1995/96 — representing a 57 per cent increase in gross pay — the household's net weekly income would have fallen from £153 to £149. A doubling of gross pay, from £7,000 to £14,000 annually, would have yielded an addition of just £23 to the household's net weekly income.

These extraordinary outcomes result, on the one hand, from the deduction of taxes and levies from gross income and, on the other, from the phased withdrawal of state income supports, most notably Family Income Supplement.

10.6. Employment Subsidies for the Low Paid

Over the past decade or so, there has been a growing implicit recognition amongst policymakers that high income replacement ratios can stifle the incentive to work, particularly amongst the long-term unemployed. The combination of real improvements and extensions in social welfare benefits for the unemployed and high taxes on low pay reduced the attractions of taking a job.

This politically sensitive issue has been addressed in an extremely careful and gradualist manner. In essence, the approach adopted has been to introduce employment subsidies for the low-paid while at the same time reducing the direct tax burden on low-paid employment. Simultaneously, successive governments have continued to effect annual increases in the real value of unemployment benefits. In other words, governments have moved gradually from subsidising unemployment to subsidising low-paid employment.

The first initiative in the employment subsidy sphere was the introduction, in September 1984, of Family Income Supplement. Since then, FIS has acted to top up the net incomes of low-paid married workers with children. The size of the weekly Supplement is shaped by gross earnings and the number of children in the household. In essence, the Department of Social Welfare makes a tax-free payment each week equivalent to 60 per cent of the difference between actual gross earnings[7] — less PRSI and levies — and defined income ceilings, which depend on the number of children in the household.

As was shown in Table 10.4, where childless married couples suffered prolonged spells of unemployment, the financial incentives for either partner to seek low-paid work were weak. Since they have no children, such households would not qualify for Family Income Supplement. However, where there are children, FIS greatly strengthens work incentives by providing direct and untaxed cash subsidies to such households.

The INOU has calculated that a long-term unemployed household, consisting of a married couple with two children, receives a net income of £134.42 a week or £6,990 annually after meeting local authority rent bills. This weekly income comprises long-term Unemployment Assistance payments of £133.90, secondary benefits valued at £12.10 and a local authority rent charge of £11.58.

---

[7] "Family Income Supplement will be assessed on earnings net of income tax from October 1998", Summary of 1998 Budget Measures, December 1997, p. 18.

Clearly, in the absence of employment subsidies, there is no financial incentive for adult members of the household to return to work at pay levels of less than £7,000 annually. The extent to which FIS strengthens financial incentives to work can be seen from Table 10.8. The table is instructive on a number of counts. In a very real sense, it represents in microcosm the problems embedded in the joint operation of the Irish tax code and social welfare systems even in the face of efforts at reform.

TABLE 10.8: THE IMPACT OF FIS ON THE NET INCOME OF A MARRIED COUPLE WITH TWO CHILDREN, 1997/98 (£ PER ANNUM)

Gross Pay	Direct Taxes	Rent (LA)	Net Pay from Work (After Rent)	FIS	Total Income	Social Wage*
8,000	173	1,083	6,744	2,340	9,364**	6,990
9,000	258	1,135	7,607	1,768	9,375	6,990
10,000	703	1,129	8,168	1,177	9,345	6,990
11,000	1,395	1,112	8,493	753	9,246	6,990
12,000	1,862	1,117	9,021	260	9,280	6,990

Notes: Rent (LA) = Local Authority Rent. * Primary and secondary unemployment and social welfare benefits after deduction of differential local authority rent. ** Net pay after rent plus FIS, includes £280 as value of a household medical card.

Source: "Welfare to Work", Irish National Organisation of the Unemployed, March 1997, Tables 7a and 7b, p. 11.

First, in the absence of Family Income Supplement, clear unemployment traps confront long-term unemployed couples with children at gross income levels up to £8,000 per year. Nor are all households entitled to FIS availing of it. The Department of Finance estimates that 60 per cent of those households eligible for FIS are still not claiming it, more than a decade after its introduction.[8]

Second, for those returning to work at £8,000 a year, all of their net income gain is attributable to FIS payments. Without FIS, it simply would not be worth working. Even in jobs paying £9,000 an-

---

[8] Budget Book 1997, p. 56.

nually, net income from unemployment would only be about £700 ahead of the social wage available from remaining unemployed.

Third, while FIS relieves initial unemployment traps, its operation actually accentuates poverty traps. As can be seen from Table 10.8, the household's net disposable income is actually lower if it earns £12,000 a year gross than if pre-tax earnings from employment amount to just £8,000. Thus, for a 50 per cent increase in gross earnings, the household is left worse off. Even on gross earnings of £15,000 a year, the household is less than £25 a week better off than if it were earning £8,000 a year and £70 a week better-off than if it had remained unemployed. Thus, the difference between remaining long-term unemployed and returning to a job paying average manufacturing earnings is in the region of £70 a week.

Fourth, this perverse outcome is the result of three forces which still operated in 1997/98. First, taxes continue to rise very rapidly as pay increases, even on the incomes of low-paid married couples. Remaining unemployed attracts no tax charge. Returning to work at £8,000 a year imposes a minimal average tax charge of 2.2 per cent. But at £12,000 a year, the average direct tax rate has risen to 15.5 per cent or almost £1,900 annually. While taxes are rising, Family Income Supplement is waning and it disappears altogether by the time gross earnings reach £13,000 annually. Finally, as gross income rises, access to secondary benefits, particularly to medical cards, is lost.

In partial response to these deep-rooted problems, recent budgets have sought to mitigate the disincentive effects of high income replacement ratios and the loss of cash and non-cash benefits sustained by low income earners on their return to work by strengthening the Back to Work Allowance Scheme.

The Scheme is open to the long-term unemployed over the age of 23 years who are returning to employment or self-employment. To qualify, the jobs must be new, must not displace existing workers and must span at least 20 hours a week. There must be a likelihood that the employment created will become self-sustaining over time.

For those eligible, the Back to Work Allowance Scheme permits participants to retain 75 per cent of their existing social welfare cash payments in year one, 50 per cent in year two and 25 per cent in year three. Direct cash subsidies of this type cease after three years. These employment subsidies are exempt from income tax and PRSI deductions. In addition, participants on the Scheme can retain their entitlements to all "secondary" social welfare benefits as long as gross pay does not exceed £250 a week.

The numbers availing of the Back to Work Allowance have increased rapidly. By early 1996, some 10,000 participants had signed up for the Scheme. In the 1997 Budget, the Government provided for an increase in participant numbers from 17,000 to 22,000 in 1997.[9] The numbers were further increased to 27,000 in the 1998 Budget.

As shown earlier, when both primary and secondary social welfare benefits were claimed, long-term unemployed single people had little incentive to return to work where the gross annual earnings offered were £6,000 or less. However, where the single long-term unemployed are eligible for the Back to Work Allowance, work becomes much more attractive financially, even at low rates of gross pay. This can be seen from Table 10.9.

TABLE 10.9: IMPACT OF THE BACK TO WORK ALLOWANCE: LONG-TERM UNEMPLOYED SINGLE PEOPLE RETURNING TO WORK, 1997/98 (£)

(1) Gross Pay	(2) After-tax Income	(3) Rent	(4) Net Pay After Rent	(5) BTWA + Benefits	(6) Net Income from Work
6,000	5,449	2,080	3,369	4,544	7,913
7,000	6,144	2,080	4,064	4,544	8,608
8,000	6,839	2,080	4,759	4,544	9,303
9,000	7,534	2,080	5,454	4,544	9,998
10,000	8,229	2,080	6,149	4,544	10,693
14,000	11,009	2,080	8,929	2,702	11,631

Notes: (1) Gross pay from work; (2) Gross pay less income tax and PRSI; (3) Private sector rental costs; (4) Net income after tax and rent; (5) Back-to-work allowance at 75% of Unemployment Assistance (£67.50) plus retention of secondary benefits until weekly income exceeds £250; (6) Net income from work = (4) + (5).

Sources: Table 10.5; INOU (1997), Table 1 (b).

---

[9] Budget Book 1997, p. 20.

Poverty and Unemployment Traps

Clearly, the effects of retaining 75 per cent of Unemployment Assistance payments in the first year and of holding on to secondary social welfare benefits once weekly earnings do not exceed £250 makes working a rewarding option relative to remaining unemployed.

The labour market perspective of single people amongst the long-term unemployed has been completely changed by the advent of the Back to Work Allowance Scheme. As Table 10.10 shows, faced with a job offer at £6,000 a year, a single long-term unemployed person would previously have been financially indifferent between employment and unemployment.

In the absence of the Back to Work Allowance package, long-term unemployed people returning to jobs paying gross wages of £6,000 a year would have been left with a net annual income of just £3,369 after meeting direct taxes and private rented accommodation costs of £40 a week. This is just £27 a year more than such people would have received in Unemployment Assistance and other benefits, even after meeting the weekly rent bill of £40. In these circumstances, returning to work from the dole would have yielded a weekly dividend of 50p.

TABLE 10.10: THE RETURNS TO WORK UNDER THE BTWA SCHEME, 1997/98 (FOR A SINGLE LONG-TERM UNEMPLOYED PERSON OVER 23 YEARS AFTER ALLOWING FOR RENT AT £40 PER WEEK)

(1) Gross Pay	(2) Net Wages after Rent	(3) Net Wages + BTWA	(4) Social Wage	(5) IRR 1 (4) as % (2)	(6) IRR 2 (4) as % (3)
6,000	3,369	7,913	3,342	99.2	42.2
7,000	4,064	8,608	3,342	82.2	38.8
8,000	4,759	9,303	3,342	70.2	35.9
9,000	5,454	9,998	3,342	61.3	33.4
10,000	6,149	10,693	3,342	54.4	31.3
14,000	8,929	11,631	2,702	30.3	23.2

Notes: (1) Gross pay from work; (2) Net pay after taxes and weekly rent of £40; (3) Net pay after taxes and rent + Back to Work Allowance and value of secondary benefits retained; (4) Unemployment assistance + rent allowance less rental costs; (5) & (6) Income replacement ratios.

Sources: Tables 10.5; 10.7; INOU (1997).

With the introduction of the BTWA Scheme, jobs paying a gross wage of £6,000 a year now offer an annual net disposable income of £7,913 to participants, when the continuance of secondary social welfare benefits and of tapering UA payments are included.

Put another way, in the absence of the BTWA package, the social wage for the long-term unemployed almost matched the net income after rent from a job paying £6,000. With the BTWA scheme in operation, the social wage now replaces just 42.2 per cent of net income from being employed.

The returns to work are patently at their most advantageous during the first year, since 75 per cent of previous Unemployment Assistance payments are retained. But even allowing for the subsequent tapering off of such payments, the breaking of the unemployment barrier and the securing of an initial foothold in the jobs market is of immense importance.

The employment incentives provided by the Back to Work Allowance Scheme are similarly strong in the case of long-term unemployed married couples with children. As seen earlier, such households with two children, living in local authority rented accommodation, receive a net weekly disposable income of £134.42 after rent payments, equivalent to £6,990 annually. The financial consequences of one spouse returning to work under the BTWA Scheme are illustrated in Table 10.11.

TABLE 10.11: NET INCOME OF MARRIED SPOUSE RETURNING TO WORK UNDER BTWA

Gross Pay	Taxes/ Rent	Work Income*	BTWA + MC**	Total Income	Social Wage
8,000	1,688	6,312	5,502	11,814	6,990
9,000	1,910	7,090	5,502	12,592	6,990
10,000	2,438	7,562	5,502	13,064	6,990
11,000	2,966	8,034	5,502	13,536	6,990
12,000	3,494	8,506	5,502	14,008	6,990

* Work Income excludes any Family Income Supplement. **BTWA + MC is the combined value of the Back to Work Allowance in the first year and of a Medical Card.

Source: INOU (1997), derived from Table 3(b).

Access to the Back to Work Allowance together with the retention of secondary benefits clearly lifts income from employment well above the social welfare entitlements of the long-term unemployed.

Without claiming FIS and without access to the BTWA Scheme, a long-term unemployed spouse in a married household supporting two children would be financially indifferent to employment until gross annual earnings rose above £9,000.

Participation in the Scheme makes virtually any job attractive, at least in the short-term. Because it has raised participants' net income from employment so far ahead of unemployment benefits, the Back to Work Allowance has broken a logjam in the labour market. It has reduced, by large margins, the amount of employment income replaced by primary and secondary unemployment benefits, thereby significantly strengthening the financial attractions of taking a job.

While the financial incentives offered by the Scheme taper off over time, initially they provide the long-term unemployed with large rewards for regaining a foothold in the workforce. And that is more than half the battle in reintegrating the long-term unemployed back into the national workforce.

Both Family Income Supplement and the Back to Work Allowance Scheme subsidise employment rather than unemployment. Both measures actively promote the re-entry of the unemployed into the workforce by sharpening the financial incentives to accept offers of work on the open labour market. In this, they differ from traditional practice, which concentrated on providing passive and open-ended income support for those who were out of work.

This active strengthening of work incentives for the unemployed has been buttressed in three ways in the 1998 Budget.

First, from October 1998, FIS payments will be calculated by reference to net after-tax earnings rather than to gross pay.

Second, from January 1998, the number if places on the BTWA scheme has been increased by 5,000 to 27,000.[10]

Third, an additional tax-free allowance is available for the long-term unemployed returning to work in 1998/99. Those who have been out of work for a year or more and who regain employ-

---

[10] "Summary of 1998 Budget Measures", Department of Finance, 3 December 1997, p. 18.

ment after April 1998 will gain an additional annual tax-free allowance of £3,000 plus a further tax allowance of £1,000 for each child in the household. Two-thirds of these extra allowances will be retained in the second year of employment and one-third in the third year.

Employers recruiting the long-term unemployed from April 1998 onwards will be entitled to a double wages deduction, in respect of each additional worker hired, in the calculation of the employer's taxable income. This double deduction is available for up to three years while the long-term recruits remain in employment.

At last, governments are taking cognisance of the reality that the unemployed are as responsive to financial incentives as the rest of the working population.

Chapter 11

COMPLETING THE SUPPLY-SIDE REVOLUTION

11.1. The Reasons for Rapid Growth

The Irish economy has enjoyed a decade of unparalleled economic progress. Irish economic growth has been unmatched in the European Union. Material living standards have risen appreciably for the majority of Irish citizens. Social safety nets have been strengthened. The exodus of people from the country has ceased. The population is growing, having reached a post-Independence peak at the 1996 census.

Above all, there are now more people gainfully employed in Ireland than at any time since the foundation of the state. In the 10 years to April 1997, the numbers at work have risen by a quarter of a million people. Throughout the 1990s, rapid output growth has paid handsome employment dividends.

Nor has the rapid pace of economic advance placed unmanageable strains on the Irish economic system. In the face of continuing economic expansion, inflation has remained mild. The current balance of payments has stayed in surplus. The Exchequer's accounts are back in the black. This restoration of macroeconomic stability was an essential precondition for economic revival.

How did Ireland attain these very high rates of employment-rich, low-inflation growth over the better part of the last decade?

The answer lies in two areas. In the first place, the economy's supply-side — its capacity to produce goods and services efficiently — has been expanded and modernised. In the second, price competitiveness has been regained, allowing Irish goods and services to be sold profitably at home and abroad. Like the blades of a scissors, both have been necessary for success.

The structure of the Irish economy has been transformed by a stealthy supply-side revolution. This quiet revolution has raised the economy's growth ceiling. As a result, sustained high rates of expansion have been achieved without the economy running into capacity constraints.

Three principal agents have been responsible for Ireland's supply-side revolution.

11.2. Education as a Catalyst for Growth

First, the education system has been a catalyst for economic and social change. More young people are going to school and college, and for longer. Participation rates in the higher levels of secondary education and at third level have risen continuously for 30 years. This has widened and deepened the knowledge base of Irish society. The economy's productive potential has been much enhanced by this accumulation of human capital.

At present, over three-quarters of all young people complete the senior cycle of second-level education. Of the 66,500 school-leavers of all ages in 1996, two out of five entered higher education, one in four proceeded to further education or training and just one in three entered the labour market directly.

The participation rates and attainment levels of the age cohorts now progressing through the education system bear comparison with the leading industrial countries. In turn, this is gradually, but continuously, upgrading Ireland's stock of human capital amongst the population of working age. In recent years, the domestic stock of human capital has been augmented by the cessation of net emigration. Talented, highly qualified young Irish people are now finding remunerative work at home.

Continuous improvements in the quantity and quality of the Irish human capital stock, supported by growing state commitments to investment in education even in times of budgetary austerity, have been the fulcrum on which the economy's growth potential has been levered upwards. Not only have continuing investments in human capital directly enhanced the long-run productivity of Irish labour, they have been a major causal factor in triggering the second principal agent of the supply-side revolution.

11.3. Foreign Industrial Enterprises

That second agent has been the scale and quality of foreign direct investment in both industry and international services. Like investments in education, foreign industrial capital has been flowing into Ireland, principally from US corporations, since the 1960s. Traditionally, the magnets attracting such inflows were low rates of corporation tax on manufactured exports, free profit repatriation and unhindered access to the markets of the European Union.

In seeking to induce inward investment, Irish governments have always acted as committed supply-siders. For 30 years, they have been resolute and undeviating in their belief that low corporate taxes pull foreign investors, their know-how and their technology, to Ireland. They have been rewarded not only by a continuing inflow of sophisticated new foreign projects, but also by enhanced corporation tax receipts. Revenues from corporation tax increased three-and-a-half-fold between 1990 and 1997, with annual inflows into the Exchequer rising from £474 million to £1,699 million over this seven-year stretch.

Moreover, policymakers have been highly imaginative in keeping corporate taxes low for inward investors. When the zero tax rate on manufactured exports was challenged, they substituted a 10 per cent corporation tax rate. To reduce investment risk, the time horizon was extended. The 10 per cent rate is now guaranteed by government to remain in force until the year 2010 for enterprises in manufacturing and internationally traded services. Policymakers also showed their innovative capacity in building the Dublin International Financial Services Centre (IFSC) on the foundations of a 10 per cent corporation tax rate, applicable, in the first instance, to the year 2005.

Most recently, they have demonstrated their ingenuity in warding off EU objections to the continuance of the low corporation tax regime after 2010, not by undertaking to raise the rate towards the European average, but by undertaking to reduce all Irish corporation tax rates on trading income to 12.5 per cent for a period of 15 years after the expiry of existing guarantees. This was confirmed in the 1998 Budget speech.[1]

But if low corporate taxes and EU market access were initially the most significant incentives in attracting foreign investors to Ireland, the ready availability of highly-qualified labour has matched, if not surpassed, these initial incentives in recent years.

The importance of foreign direct investment is not restricted to the direct jobs, output and export earnings it generates in Ireland. At a more fundamental level, such industrial investment has been a powerful force for modernisation.

Investment inflows have been concentrated in high-technology, knowledge-based industry sectors — electronics, computers, software, pharmaceuticals, financial services. The jobs they offer have thus fully exercised the capacities of those emerging from the education system. The interplay of sophisticated imported technology and modern management techniques with a labour force of improving quality has resulted in significant gains in total factor productivity in Ireland. Critical-mass industry clusters have formed in many of these segments and the economic benefits, in terms of sub-supply, have spilled over their boundaries into the indigenous economy.

While the transfer-pricing strategies of multinational companies operating in Ireland may result in an overstatement of their contribution to Irish output, exports and economic growth, this should not be allowed to obscure the reality that their direct and indirect contribution to Irish economic development has been very substantial.

In effect, while Ireland has modernised its indigenous industry through trade liberalisation, it has extended its industrial and technology base by importing it ready-made from abroad. Moreover, such additions to supply-side productive capacity have been purchased at a relatively modest cost through the judicious use of tax incentives, backed by grant aid. As a result, the creation of a modern industrial base has been accomplished without placing strains on either domestic capital markets or the balance of payments.

---

[1] Budget speech, Minister for Finance, 3 December 1997, p. 16.

11.4. EU Infrastructural Inflows

The third agent of supply-side expansion has been the greatly enhanced inflow of infrastructural investment funds from the European Union since 1989. The structural fund initiatives since then have been designed to improve Ireland's infrastructural base to allow it to compete on an equal footing with its more prosperous partners in the EU Single Market. Such inflows are estimated to stand equivalent to about 2.5 per cent of annual Irish GNP over the years 1994–99.

In summary, the revolution on Ireland's supply side has been driven by mutually reinforcing elements: domestic human capital accumulation allied with an expanding physical capital and technology base financed principally by foreign capital. Together, they have combined to effect a significant expansion both of the economy's productive capacity and its productivity.

The principal instruments utilised to expand the economy's supply-side capability have been high levels of government investment in education and low tax rates on foreign private investors reinforced by a large quantum of free infrastructural investment funds from the European Union.

If both the emphasis on education and the attraction of foreign direct investment date back to the 1960s, it might legitimately be asked: why did Ireland's supply-side revolution take so long to mature? The answer is that Ireland so comprehensively mismanaged its economy from the early 1970s through to the mid-1980s that it put the supply-side revolution on hold. During these years, the Irish economy became deeply uncompetitive.

11.5. Competitiveness Regained

The regaining of national competitiveness has been an essential precondition for relaunching the Irish economy over the past decade. Other things being equal, for small open economies such as Ireland, if the price is right, demand will take care of itself. The problem for Ireland during the 1970s and into the 1980s centred on the fact that it allowed its costs and prices to go astray.

The two oil shocks of the 1970s were met with an orthodox Keynesian response. Demand levels in the domestic economy were pumped up through additions to government spending and borrowing. Such policies only purchased a temporary respite from recession, and at great cost.

In a recessionary Europe, deficit-induced additions to demand simply seeped out of the economy through the balance of payments. By 1981, the current balance of payments deficit was approaching 15 per cent of Gross National Product. Inflation spiralled above 20 per cent, dragging wages upwards in its wake. The real exchange rate became dangerously overvalued. All of these factors combined to render Irish output deeply uncompetitive on home and foreign markets.

At the same time, financing extra public spending, including a rapid escalation in public service pay costs, stretched the public finances almost to the limit. By 1981, public sector borrowing had reached almost one-fifth of national income. Government debt, accumulated since the foundation of the state, climbed from £4.2 billion in 1977 to £14.4 billion six years later.

Severe deflation was the only available antidote for this strain of fiscal profligacy. Much of the deflationary corrective was externally imposed by the growing uncompetitiveness of Irish output. Reinforced by initial attempts to curtail government capital borrowing and by sharp tax increases, the economy stalled in the first half of the 1980s.

This prompted a sharp fall in employment and an even larger rise in unemployment. The decline in employment during the first half of the 1980s was accentuated by the increasing taxation of labour. Taxes on employee incomes grew heavier, inciting demands for compensating pay increases. The cost of labour to employers was further raised by payroll taxes. As the weight of labour taxes increased and as tax wedges widened, total employment in the economy fell sharply. Unemployment increased from less than 100,000 in 1980 to 226,000 by 1985. The empirical economic studies relating to these years indicate that domestic policy factors, including increases in the taxes on labour, caused almost half the rise in unemployment. The country is still living with the consequences of the unemployment shock experienced in the first half of the 1980s.

This severe deflation, however painful, generated two payoffs. First, inflation decelerated remarkably rapidly, with the annual rate of price increase falling from 20.4 per cent in 1981 to 2.1 per cent by 1988. Second, and equally important, the political elite's flirtation with fiscal activism came to an abrupt end.

Public aversion to the taxation consequences of the borrow-and-spend policies of the late 1970s and early 1980s forced politicians, whatever their ideological coloration, back on the road of fiscal orthodoxy. Promising lower taxes on income and broadly balanced budgets became both popular and politically profitable.

11.6. Good Housekeeping

In the late 1980s, improvements in domestic economic housekeeping were introduced which released the economy's suppressed supply-side potential. These improvements included:

1. Gains in international competitiveness, dictated by the sustained fall in Irish inflation rates, and buttressed in 1986 by a unilateral devaluation of the Irish pound.

2. A moderation in the growth in money wages, due both to the easing of inflation and the reintroduction of national pay agreements from 1988 onwards. The novel character of the new series of national pay agreements, where governments explicitly traded tax cuts for pay restraint, caused money wages to grow slowly in the private sector. Powered by special pay deals, public service pay continued to increase at a faster pace, though this was countered by significant reductions in days lost through industrial disputes.

3. Governments reasserted control over the public finances, restoring the credibility of Irish public policy. Sharp cuts in current public spending between 1987 and 1989, aided by accelerated tax inflows and a broadened tax base as a result of the 1988 tax amnesty effected a significant improvement in the public finances. By 1990, the General Government Deficit had been reduced to 2.2 per cent of Gross Domestic Product while Exchequer borrowing was running at just 1.9 per cent of Gross National Product. The Exchequer returns for end-December 1997 reveal that the General Government Balance shifted into surplus during 1997 to the tune of 0.9 per cent of Gross Domes-

tic Product. The debt-to-GDP ratio had been reduced to 66 per cent by the end of 1997.

The sustained boom that has characterised the Irish economy in the 1990s was interrupted only once — by the European-wide exchange rate crises of 1992/93. However, the unilateral devaluation of the Irish pound by 10 per cent within the European Exchange Rate Mechanism in January 1993 quickly returned the economy to its growth path.

11.7. The Persistence of Unemployment

While consistently strong rates of economic growth have translated into rapid employment expansion throughout the 1990s, reductions in unemployment have been relatively limited. While total employment rose by more than a quarter of a million between 1987 and 1997, this was not matched by a fall in unemployment of a similar scale. Almost three-quarters of the substantial increase in the demand for labour between 1987 and 1997 was met, not by reductions in unemployment, but by additions to the labour supply.

The increase in the labour supply reflects three forces: an increase in the population of working age due to past population growth; a rise in labour force participation rates amongst women; and the cessation of the heavy net emigration that marked the last years of the 1980s.

Moreover, there is an interdependence between supply and demand in the labour market. As domestic job opportunities became more plentiful, many amongst those who would otherwise have emigrated decided to remain at home, swelling the size of the domestic labour supply in the process. Similarly, the strengthening of labour demand increased labour force participation rates amongst the population of working age, and particularly amongst women. In these ways, it can be seen that the labour supply is not a fixed quantity, but its size is highly responsive to the strength of labour demand. As a result, increases in employment do not result in equivalent reductions in unemployment.

Nonetheless, the unprecedented expansion of Irish employment during the 1990s is now beginning to exhaust the supply of labour at prevailing wage rates. A FÁS/IMS Survey taken in October 1996 indicated that vacancies were significant in number, difficult to fill and generalised across the economy. These vacancies were not confined to highly qualified jobs in modern industries, but extended to cleaners, operatives and assemblers.

11.8. Ireland's Labour Market Paradox

The Irish labour market thus presents an apparent paradox: high unemployment — 179,000 at April 1997 — co-existing with an increasing incidence of vacancies which, according to employers, are difficult to fill.

This apparent paradox can be explained in two ways. First, the Irish labour market exhibits a high level of structural unemployment. Structural unemployment arises where there is a mismatch between the supply and demand for labour. In essence, those who are structurally unemployed do not possess the skills or qualifications that employers wish to hire. In Ireland, structural unemployment can be proxied by the scale of long-term unemployment. Over half of those out of work have been unemployed for over a year, while two out of every five have been out of work for more than two years. By its nature, structural unemployment cannot be relieved in the short-run by increases in the demand for labour. Employers will not hire those who cannot do the jobs they offer.

However, it is clear that, when vacancies for cleaners and assemblers are becoming difficult to fill, not all of the unemployment in the Irish labour market is structural in character. The second explanation for Ireland's labour market paradox can be traced to the fact that low-paid jobs are financially unrewarding because of the interaction of the tax and benefit codes.

Much of the financial correction achieved through the 1980s was engineered through sharp increases in taxation. During these years, the Irish tax code acquired two distinctive features, which remain, in diluted form, to this day. First, heavy tax loads were levied on employee incomes, even on those earning less than average pay. Second, any extra pay earned by ordinary workers was taxed at punitive marginal rates.

But at the same time as taxes on ordinary incomes were rising rapidly, the real value of untaxed cash benefits for the unemployed was increasing substantially. The material circumstances of the unemployed were further improved by an extensive array of "secondary" benefits, ranging from rent subsidies and free medical cards to free butter and fuel vouchers.

11.9. Unemployment Traps

This combination of circumstances created deep "unemployment traps", particularly for large households, where working in low-paid jobs could be an unrewarding alternative to drawing the dole. More formally, the proportion of net income from employment replaced by the full package of social welfare benefits available to unemployed households rose to quite high levels.

The problems posed by "unemployment traps" was recognised as early as 1984, when Family Income Supplement was introduced. This provided effective wage subsidies to low-income working households with children. It represented the first significant attempt on the state's part to subsidise employment rather than unemployment.

Direct taxes on all households have declined fairly significantly through the 1990s. Since 1992, concerted attempts have been made to ease the tax burden on the low-paid. Average tax rates on those earning low incomes have declined. Single people earning half average industrial pay lost 22 per cent of their gross incomes in direct taxes in 1987; by 1997, their average tax rate had fallen to around 15 per cent. Innovative schemes such as the Back to Work Allowance have been introduced, which permit the long-term unemployed to retain their benefits on a reducing basis for three years after returning to work.

Targeting tax cuts on the low-paid and the more extensive use of wage subsidies has caused income replacement ratios to fall in recent years.

In short, policy is at last heading down the right road, but the pace of its advance is too slow. The labour market paradox, where high unemployment and labour shortages coexist, needs to be resolved, not explained. Increasing labour scarcity in an economy characterised by a large labour surplus constitutes not only an affront to economic logic but also a threat to future economic performance, and for three reasons.

First, competition between employers for scarce labour will drive wages above existing pay norms. Such "wage drift" will undermine competitiveness and reduce the pace of future employment expansion.

Second, the easy availability of highly skilled labour has proved one of the principal incentives attracting foreign industry to Ireland in the past. The emergence of persistent labour shortages in the future would thus act as a strong disincentive to foreign investors choosing Ireland as a location for industrial investment.

Third, recent Irish economic growth has been powered by increased inputs of factors of production, especially labour. If such factor inputs become scarce, then national output growth will falter.

11.10. A Modest Proposal

To obviate the emergence of performance-threatening labour shortages and to mount an attack on the persistence of long-term unemployment, two planks of present policy require further strengthening.

First, while reinforcing the national emphasis on education and training, resources must be directed particularly towards those who are falling out of society, from illiterate school dropouts to those trapped in unemployment for prolonged spells. A social contract with school-leavers should guarantee all a job, a training slot or a place in further education. For the long-term unemployed, counselling, advice and the fashioning of individual pathways back to education, training and the workforce offer the best, and perhaps the last, hope of preventing the emergence of a permanent underclass, divorced from the rest of Irish society.

Second, taxes on the low-paid, and particularly on low-paid labour market entrants, must be cut to reduce the depth of unemployment traps. Those earning half of average industrial earnings should simply not be in the tax system at all. The potential for tax reform created by the economic boom should be utilised to help those on the bottom rungs of the pay ladder. That means concentrating resources on raising basic tax allowances, on broadening the standard rate tax band and on introducing a new, low, initial rate of income tax. On this score, the provisions of the 1998 Budget must be counted as disappointing.

Over the long haul, Irish policymakers have been singularly successful in pursuing a low-tax, supply-side strategy in the corporate domain. But they have denied to ordinary income earners what they have countenanced for corporations. It is now time to complete Ireland's supply-side revolution by extending low taxes to the ordinary working people of the country.

BIBLIOGRAPHY

Books and Articles

Arrow, Kenneth J. (1997), "Economic Growth Policy for a Small Country", in Alan W. Gray (ed.), *International Perspectives on the Irish Economy*, Dublin: Indecon.

Barry, F. and J. Bradley (1991), "On the Causes of Ireland's Unemployment", UCD Centre for Economic Research, Working Paper No. WP 91/1, January.

Barry, Frank and Aoife Hannan (1997), "Education, Deprivation, Hysteresis, Unemployment", Paper presented to the Dublin Economics Workshop, Kenmare, October.

Becker, Gary (1964), "Human Capital", National Bureau for Economic Research.

Bradley, John, John FitzGerald, Patrick Honohan and Ide Kearney (1997), "Interpreting the Recent Irish Growth Experience" in *ESRI Medium-Term Review 1997–2003*, April, Dublin: The Economic and Social Research Institute.

de la Fuente, Angel and Xavier Vives (1997), "The Sources of Irish Growth" in Alan W. Gray (ed.), *International Perspectives on the Irish Economy*, Dublin: Indecon.

Durkan, Joe (1997), "Reducing Long-term Unemployment in Ireland", Paper read to Dublin Economics Workshop, Kenmare, October.

Englander, Steven and Andrew Gurney (1994), "Medium-Term Determinants of OECD Productivity", *OECD Economic Studies*, No. 22, Spring, Paris: OECD.

Fahey, Tony and John FitzGerald (1997), "The Educational Revolution and Demographic Change", in *ESRI Medium-Term*

Review 1997–2003, April, Dublin: The Economic and Social Research Institute.

Fox, Roger (1996), "Company Training in Ireland 1993", *Labour Market Review*, Vol. 5, No. 2, Dublin: FÁS.

Gillmor, D.A. (1985), *Economic Activities in the Republic of Ireland*, Dublin: Gill and Macmillan.

Gray, Alan W. (1997), "Irish Economic Challenges and International Perspectives", in Alan W. Gray (ed.), *International Perspectives on the Irish Economy*, Dublin: Indecon.

Honohan, Patrick (ed.) (1997), *EU Structural Funds in Ireland — A Mid-term Evaluation of the CSF 1994–1999*, ESRI Policy Research Series, No. 31, July, Dublin: The Economic and Social Research Institute.

Kennedy, Kieran A. (1993), *Facing the Unemployment Crisis in Ireland*, Cork: Cork University Press.

Krugman, Paul R. (1997), "Good News from Ireland: A Geographical Perspective", in Alan W. Gray (ed.), *International Perspectives on the Irish Economy*, Dublin: Indecon.

Layard, Richard, Ken Mayhew and Geoffrey Owen (eds.) (1994), *Britain's Training Deficit*, Avebury: Centre for Economic Performance.

Leddin, Anthony J. and Brendan M. Walsh (1990), *The Macroeconomy of Ireland*, Dublin: Gill and Macmillan.

Leddin, Anthony and Brendan Walsh (1997), "Economic Stabilisation, Recovery and Growth: Ireland 1979–1996", *Irish Banking Review*, Summer.

Lee, George (1991), "Hysteresis — A New Concept in Irish Unemployment", *Labour Market Review*, Summer, Dublin: FÁS.

McAleese, Dermot (1997), *Economics for Business*, Englewood Cliffs, NJ: Prentice Hall.

Murphy, Antoin (1998), *The Celtic Tiger: the Great Misnomer — Economic Growth and the Multinationals in Ireland in the 1990s*, Dublin: MMI.

Nolan, Brian, Tim Callan, Christopher Whelan and James Williams (1994), "Poverty and Time: Perspectives on the Dynamics of Poverty", ESRI General Research Series, No. 166, December, Dublin: The Economic and Social Research Institute.

O'Connell, Philip and Maureen Lyons (1995), *Enterprise-related Training and State Policy in Ireland: The Training Support Scheme*, ESRI Policy Research Series, No. 25, May, Dublin: The Economic and Social Research Institute.

O'Connell, Philip J. and Frances McGinnity (1997), *Working Schemes? Active Labour Market Policy in Ireland*, Aldershot: Ashgate Publishing.

Ó Gráda, Cormac (1994), *Ireland: A New Economic History 1780–1939*, Oxford: Clarendon Press.

Porter, Michael (1990), *The Competitive Advantage of Nations*, London: Macmillan.

Tansey, Paul (1991), *Making the Irish Labour Market Work*, Dublin: Gill and Macmillan.

Tansey, Paul and Colm McCarthy (1996), "Human Capital as a Mechanism for Reducing Long-term Unemployment in Ireland", unpublished study for DG V, Brussels: European Commission.

Walsh, Brendan (1997), *How Fast Can the Irish Economy Grow?*, Paper delivered to the Dublin Economics Workshop, Kenmare, October.

Official Reports and Data Sources

Central Bank of Ireland
Quarterly Bulletins and Annual Reports, 1986–1997.

Central Statistics Office
Census of Population, quinquennial. The latest census was taken in 1996.

Consumer Price Index, Quarterly, *Statistical Bulletin*.

Industrial Earnings and Hours Worked, Quarterly, *Statistical Bulletin*.

Labour Force Surveys, annual, 1986–1997. The latest, relating to April 1997, was published in October 1997.

"Live Register Coverage and Analysis", *Statistical Bulletin*, Volume LXXI, No. 1, March 1996.

Live Register Unemployment, data published monthly, collected in the *Statistical Bulletin*, Quarterly.

"Live Register Unemployment by Duration of Continuous Registration", surveyed in April and October each year, results published in the *Statistical Bulletin*, Quarterly.

"Population and Labour Force Projections 1996–2026", April 1995.

"Population and Migration Estimates — April 1997", October 1997.

"Public Sector Average Earnings Indices", Quarterly since March 1988.

"Revised Economic Indicators Since 1960".

National Income and Expenditure, annual, 1986–1997.

"Unemployment Statistics: Study of the Differences between the Labour Force Survey (LFS) Estimates of Unemployment and the Live Register", September 1996.

Department of Education

"Charting Our Education Future", White Paper on Education, Stationery Office, 1995.

"International Adult Literacy Survey: Results for Ireland", Education Research Centre, St Patrick's College Dublin, results published by the Department of Education, September 1997.

Statistical Report 1993/94, Dublin, 1995.

Department of Enterprise and Employment

"Growing and Sharing Our Employment — Strategy Paper on the Labour Market", Stationery Office, April 1996.

"Human Resource Development", White Paper, May, 1997.

Department of Finance

Budget Books, annual, 1986–1997.

Budget Speech 1998; "Budget 1998: Economic Background"; "Budget 1998: Statistics and Tables"; "Summary of 1998 Budget Measures", December 1997.

"Economic Background to the Budget 1997", January 1997.

"Economic Review and Outlook", various years, published each summer.

"Exchequer Returns 1997", January 1998.

Economic and Social Research Institute (ESRI)

"ESRI Medium-Term Review 1997–2003", April 1997.

"EU Structural Funds in Ireland — A Mid-term Evaluation of the CSF 1994–1999", Policy Research Series, No. 31, July 1997.

"The Economic Status of School-leavers 1994–96", December 1997.

European Commission

"Employment in Europe 1996", Directorate General for Employment, Industrial Relations and Social Affairs, Brussels, 1996.

EU Statistics, Eurostat and DG II, December 1996.

FÁS
"A Strategy for Training the Employed", 1994.

"Survey of Current Vacancies in Selected Sectors of the Irish Economy", FÁS/IMS, August 1997.

Forfás
"Shaping Our Future", 1996.

"Government Response to the Moriarty Task Force on the Implementation of the Culliton Report", Stationery Office, April 1993.

"Investment in Education", Stationery Office, 1966.

Irish Management Institute
"Executive Salaries in Ireland", annual surveys, 1987–96.

Irish National Organisation of the Unemployed (INOU)
"Welfare to Work — Research on the Financial Benefits of Taking Up Employment", March 1997.

National Economic and Social Council
"The Association between Economic Growth and Employment Growth in Ireland", Report No. 94, December 1992.

"Education and Training Policies for Economic and Social Development", Report No. 95, 1993.

National Economic and Social Forum
"Ending Long-Term Unemployment", Forum Report No. 4, June 1994.

"Early School Leavers and Youth Unemployment", Forum Report No. 11, January 1997.

Operational Programme for Human Resources Development 1994–99, Stationery Office, 1995.

Organisation for Economic Co-operation and Development
"Economic Outlook", biannual, various years.

"Economic Surveys 1995 — Ireland", June 1995.

"Economic Surveys 1997 — Ireland", 1997.

"Education at a Glance", 1996.

"Employment Outlook 1996", July 1996.

Partnership 2000, Stationery Office, December 1996.

Programme for Competitiveness and Work, Stationery Office, February 1994.

Programme for Economic and Social Progress, Stationery Office, January 1991.

Programme for National Recovery, Stationery Office, October, 1987.

Report of the Expert Working Group on the Integration of the Tax and Social Welfare Systems, Stationery Office, June 1996.

INDEX

agriculture, 11, 35, 37

Back to Work Allowance, 208, 243–7, 258
balance of payments, 16, 25, 254
birth rate, 67, 70
budgets, 16, 50, 177, 178, 188–9, 191, 192, 193, 194, 201, 204, 208, 247–8; *see also* fiscal policy; government policy; social welfare; tax

child benefit, 177, 229, 230
competitiveness, 1, 4, 16, 17, 19, 20, 21, 47, 50, 97, 109, 113, 154, 253–5
current public spending, 6, 16, 17, 25, 141–5, 148, 175

debt, national, 6–7, 27, 28, 141, 157, 254, 256

economic
    boom, *xix*, 11–32, 249–60
    growth, 1, 2, 6, 11, 16–26, 24, 25, 43–4, 97, 103–4, 145–6, 148–9, 249, 259
        and employment, 45–6, 79
        and unemployment, 79–80
        models of, 98
        trends, 11–16

education, *xx*, 5–6, 13, 22, 49, 89–90, 97, 100–101, 106–21, 131, 133, 137, 250, 259
    and earnings, 110–11
    and employment, 81–3, 84, 85, 89, 109–10
    and lifetime income, 111–14
    attainment levels, *xix*, *xxi*, 5, 76, 82, 109–10, 116, 250
    participation, 5, 72, 111, 113, 114–17, 250
    public spending on, 117–18
    returns to, 99, 110–11
    vocational, 119–20, 121
    weaknesses in, 118–20
    see also skills; training
emigration, 1, 29, 33, 34–5, 67, 68–70, 139; *see also* immigration; population
employment, 33–50, 64, 109–10, 254
    expansion, 2, 28–9, 35–50, 62, 65–6, 77–80, 249
    intensity, 43–4
    historical trends in, 2, 33–5
    part-time, 2, 39–40
    ratio, 76–7, 78
    schemes, 38–9, 61, 81, 136
    subsidies, 81, 135, 240–8, 258
    see also labour market; unemployment; work incentives

European Union, 2, 12–13, 18–21, 25, 29–32, 42–6, 73–4, 77, 78, 116, 121–2, 128, 140, 249, 251–2
   structural funds, 6, 49, 130–6, 253
Exchange Rate Mechanism, 4, 12, 16, 20–2, 25, 26
   devaluations, 4, 15, 26, 47, 62, 255, 256
   single currency, 21
exports, 18, 20, 24, 26

Family Income Supplement (FIS), 208, 209, 235–6, 237, 241–3, 247, 258
fiscal policy, 6, 15–16, 17, 26–9, 105, 140–1, 210
foreign investment, 4–5, 12, 13, 22, 48, 106, 107, 251–2

government policy, 1, 14, 16, 54–6, 255–6, 259; see also budgets; fiscal policy; tax
Gross Domestic Product (GDP), 2, 6, 18, 24, 26, 28, 29–32, 141, 146, 255–6
Gross National Product (GNP), 13–14, 24, 25, 26, 30, 117, 144–5, 146, 148, 151, 253, 255

human capital, 50, 97–105, 137, 250, 253; see also education; productivity; training
human resources development, xx–xxi, 129, 130–3
hysteresis, 84, 86

immigration, 34–5, 68–9, 70

income,
   national, 24, 30–1, 168–70
   real disposable, 7, 17, 172–4, 197–213
   see also Gross Domestic Product; Gross National Product; living standards; pay levels; tax, income; tax wedge
income replacement ratios (IRRs), 54, 230–38, 240, 243
   basic, 230–5
   including secondary benefits, 235–8
   see also unemployment traps
industrial disputes, 155–6
industry, 36, 37
inflation, 13, 17, 19–20, 62, 138, 143, 153–5, 173–4, 179, 199, 211, 254–5
interest rates, 24–5, 26
internal rate of return, 112–13, 114; see also education
International Labour Office (ILO), 3, 36–7, 56–7, 81; see also labour force; unemployment, measuring
investment, 24–5, 26, 46, 50, 98, 106, 107, 251–2

"jobless growth", 2, 28, 42, 43, 46, 78

labour force, 2, 51, 52, 61
   composition of, 2–3, 33–4, 40–2, 66–7, 75–6, 81
   flexibility, 100, 106–7
   growth of, 3–4, 51, 64–6, 73, 249

Index

measuring, 35–6, 71–2
participation rates, 66, 71–6, 256
quality of, 97–136
see also employment; population; unemployment
Labour Force Surveys, 28, 35–6, 40, 90–95, 162, 169; *see also* unemployment, measuring
labour market, *xix*, *xxi*, 1, 49, 61, 63, 72, 76, 80, 87, 107–8, 109, 127, 134, 136, 137, 139, 215–26, 228, 247, 256, 257–9
   demand, 63, 77, 80–1, 87–9, 107, 135, 215, 256
   supply, 63, 64–80, 89, 107, 135, 256
   see also employment; tax wedge; unemployment traps
Live Register, 91–4; *see also* Labour Force Surveys; unemployment, measuring
living standards, 1, 8, 11, 28, 138, 153, 172–4, 199–213, 249
   comparisons, 210–13
   of average earners, 199–203, 210–12
   of high earners, 203–6, 210–12
   of low earners, 206–9, 210–12
   see also income; pay levels

Maastricht criteria, 28, 140–1, 149
medical card, 8, 227, 243
"money illusion", 186; *see also* income, real disposable

National Agreements, 146–7, 149, 154, 156–60, 171, 255
Partnership 2000, 147, 156–8
Programme for Competitiveness and Work (PCW), 156, 158
Programme for Economic and Social Progress (PESP), 147, 156, 158, 210
Programme for National Recovery (PNR), 15, 17, 146, 147, 156–8, 166, 175, 210

Okun's Law, 79
Organisation for Economic Co-operation and Development (OECD), 56, 57, 75, 84, 94, 102, 104, 114, 116

Pay As You Earn (PAYE), *see* tax, income
pay levels, 7, 138, 153–74
   comparisons, 170–4
   executive, 166–8, 170, 171
   manufacturing industry, 7, 160–3, 170, 180
   national income data, 168–70, 171
   public sector, 160, 163–6, 170
   public service, 163, 165–6, 170, 171, 173–4, 255
   see also tax, income
Pay Related Social Insurance (PRSI), *xx*, 8, 149, 150, 152, 176, 178, 181, 238, 241
   employees', 190–2, 198, 208
   employers', 193–5, 198, 216, 217, 218, 221–2, 223, 225
   see also tax wedge

population, 1, 11, 14, 29, 32, 33, 34, 66–7, 71, 72, 249; *see also* emigration; immigration
poverty, 83, 86, 237
poverty traps, *xx*, 8–9, 228, 239–40, 243
prices, 153–74; *see also* inflation
"Principal Economic Status", 35–6, 51–2, 71–2, 90–5; *see also* Labour Force Surveys; unemployment, measuring
private sector, 2, 38–9, 159, 168, 255; *see also* pay levels
productivity, 48, 100–1, 106, 108
public sector 38–9, 159, 163–6; 168; *see also* pay levels
Public Sector Borrowing Requirement, 27; *see also* fiscal policy
purchasing power, 31–2, 137, 172–4, 204, 208, 210–12; *see also* income, real disposable; inflation; living standards

services, 36, 37
skills, *xx*, 6, 89, 100, 106, 107, 111, 124, 135, 137, 153; *see also* education; training
social welfare, *xix*, *xx*, 8, 55, 89, 227–8, 235–9, 244, 245; *see also* Back to Work Allowance; child benefit; Family Income Supplement (FIS); income replacement ratios; medical card; unemployment assistance
supply-side, 9, 17, 48, 49–50, 127, 249–60; *see also* labour market

tax,
  corporation, 12, 47, 50, 107, 150, 251–2
  indirect, 174
  revenues from, 6, 149–52
tax, income, 7, 113, 137–52, 153, 175–95; 197–213, 215–16, 232, 257–8
  allowances, *xx*, 175, 248, 260
    basic, 178–81, 198
    discretionary, 188–90, 198
  bands, *xx*, 175, 181–7, 198, 202, 260
  burden, 150–2, 182
  determinants of, 140–8
  employment levy, 190, 192–3
  exemption thresholds, 175, 176–8, 206
  health contributions, 190, 192, 198, 207
  impact on economy, 139–40, 148–52
  on average earnings, 197, 199–203
  on high earnings, 197, 203–6
  on low earnings, 197–8, 206–9, 259–60
  on married couples, 176, 184–7, 201, 205–6, 208–12
  on single people, 176, 182–3, 185–7, 204–7, 210–12
  rates, 55, 62, 139–40, 175, 181–7, 198, 260
    average, 198, 200, 201, 203, 204, 205, 206, 207, 209, 212–13
    marginal, 55, 139, 182, 187, 198, 200–1, 202, 204, 206, 207, 209

reductions, 8, 9, 48, 50, 62, 211, 213, 221
temporary income levy, 190, 193, 198
training levy, 190, 192–3, 198, 207
see also income; living standards; pay levels; tax wedge
tax wedge, 8, 48, 54, 55, 62, 215–26
  and average married earners, 219–20
  and average single earners, 218–19
  and better-off married earners, 222–3
  and better-off single earners, 220–2
  and low-paid married earners, 224–6
  and low-paid single earners, 223–4
  calculating, 198–9, 217–18
  see also labour market; tax, income; Pay Related Social Insurance (PRSI)
technology, 100, 105, 120
training, *xx*, 6, 49, 89, 99, 100, 101, 106–8, 109, 113, 121–30, 131, 133, 134, 137, 139, 259
  management, 124
  markets, 125–7
  problems, 127–30
  see also education; skills

unemployment, *xx*, 3, 51–95, 217, 226, 240–8, 254, 256–7
  and labour supply, 64–80
  and marginalisation, 84, 86, 133
  assistance/benefits, 63, 95, 227, 229–35, 241
  causes of, 53–6, 63
    labour market, 64–70
  definitions, 57
  demography, 59–60, 66, 68–73
  long-term, *xix*, 4, 60–2, 80–7, 108, 120, 226, 229, 238–9, 243, 245, 246, 248, 257
    causes, 85–7
  measuring, 57, 90–5
  rates, 56–8, 109
  structural, 80–7, 107, 257
  traps, *xx*, 8, 9, 85, 89, 228–39, 243, 258–9; *see also* income replacement ratios; poverty traps; tax wedge
  trends in, 4, 29, 57–8, 61, 65
  see also employment; labour market; labour force; Live Register

vacancies, 87–9

women's participation in labour force, 3, 66, 71, 73, 75–6, 256
work incentives, *xx*, 63, 87–90, 232, 240–8; *see also* Back to Work Allowance
"workers, discouraged", 62, 63, 81